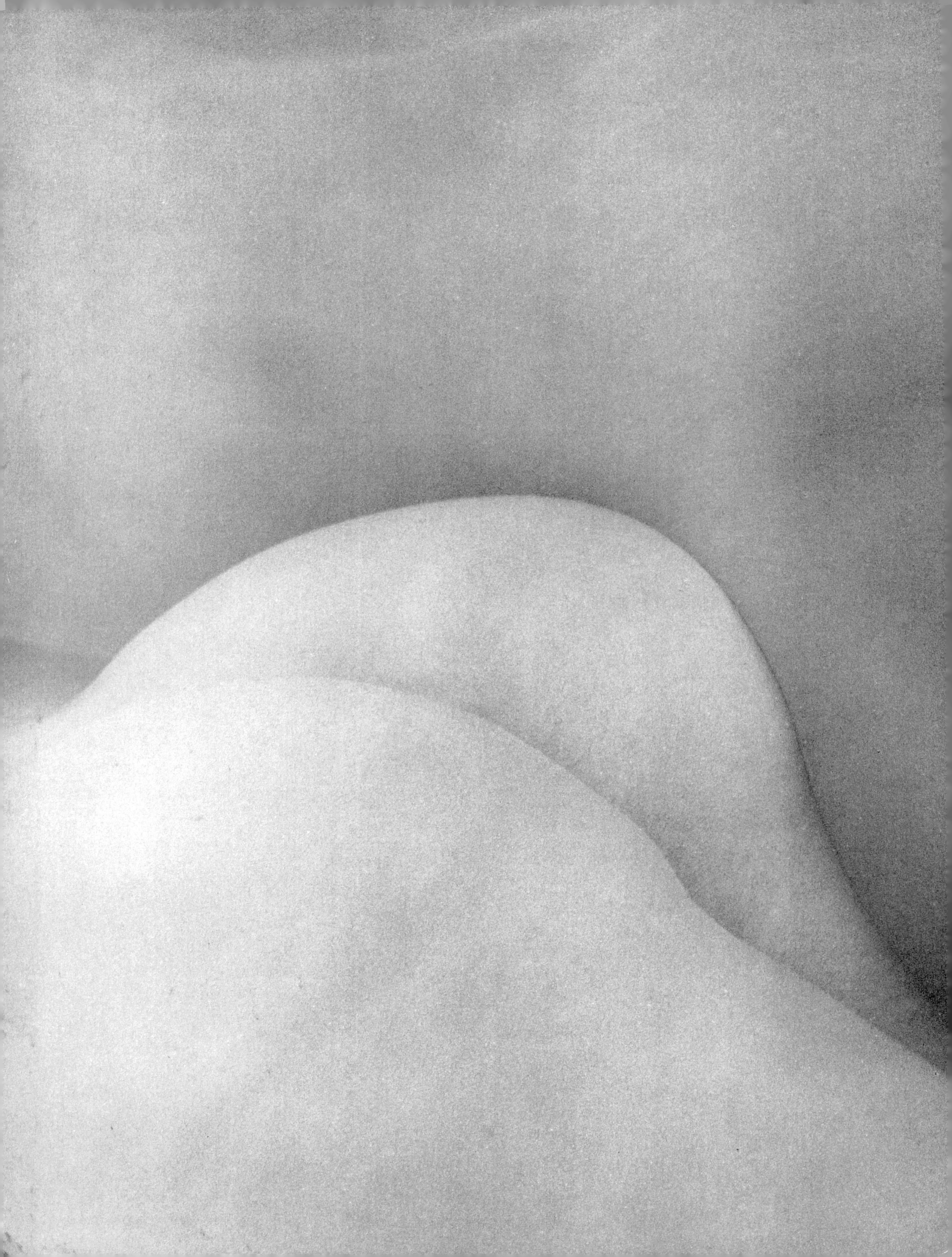

lders

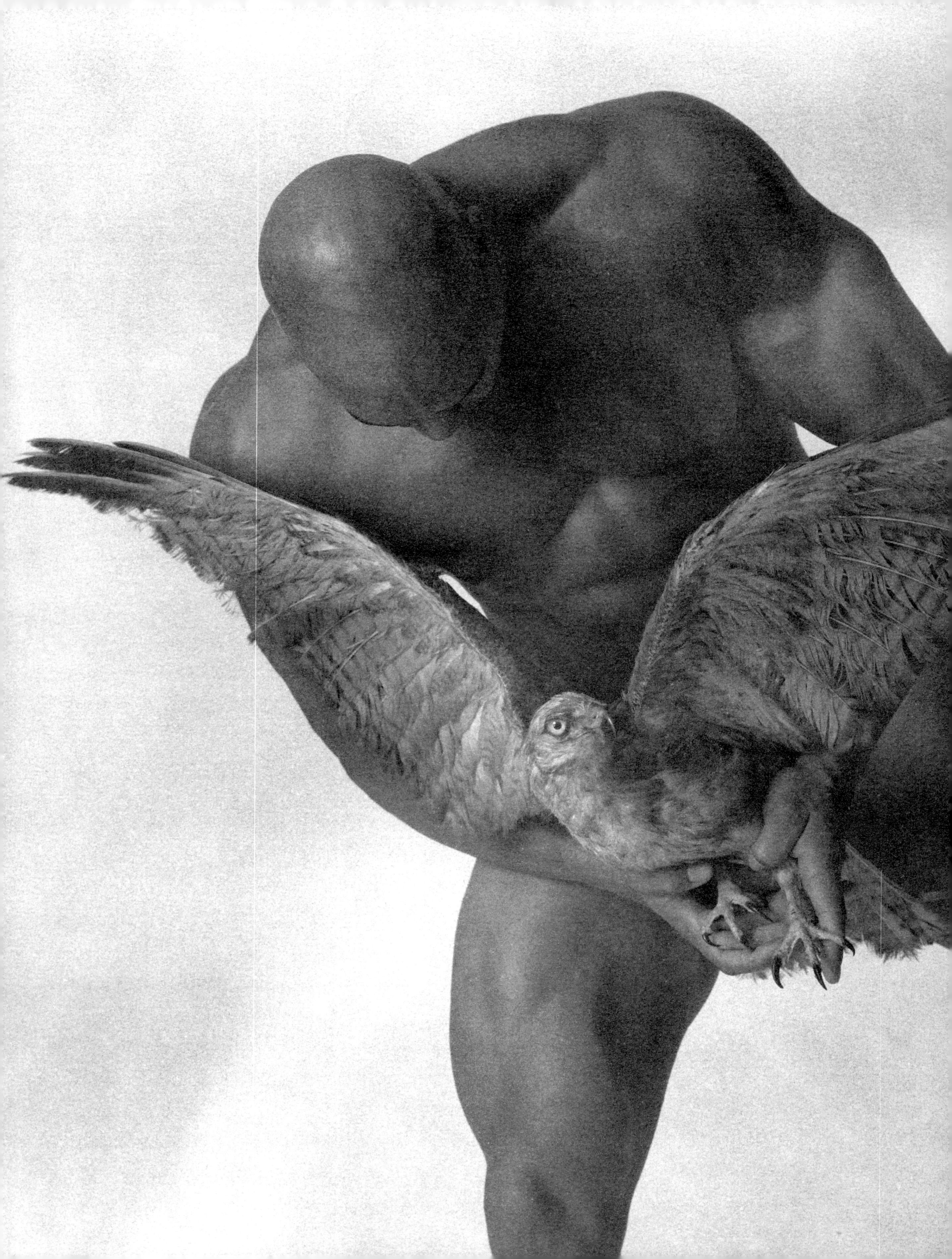

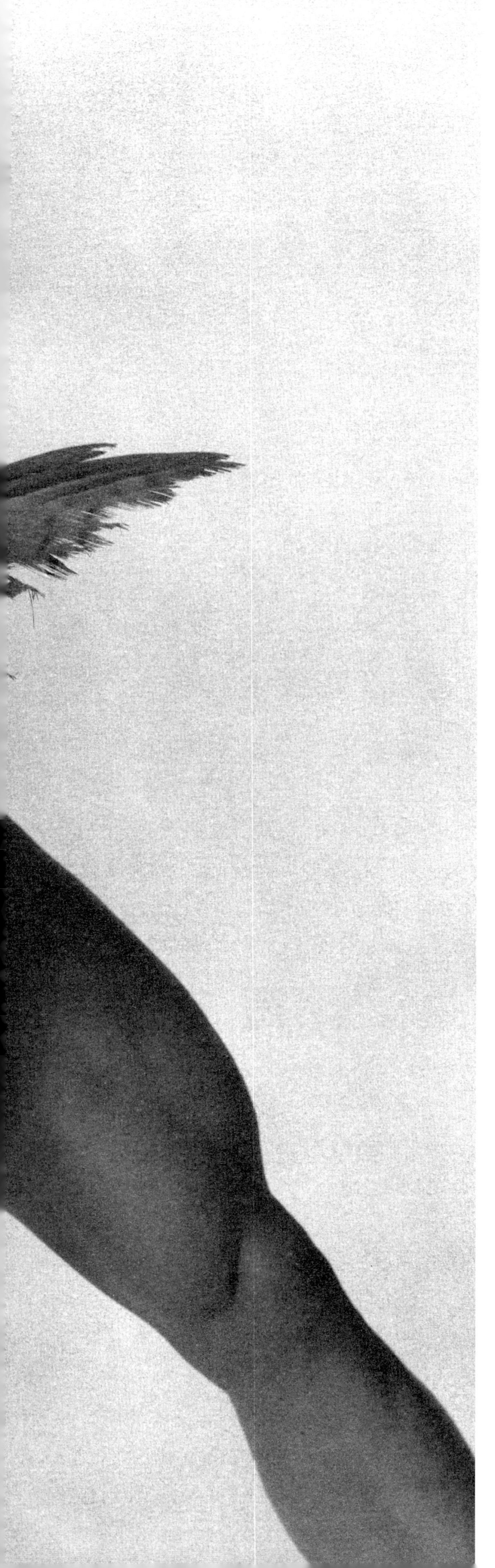

Dedicated to

John Schlesinger
Joe Santoro

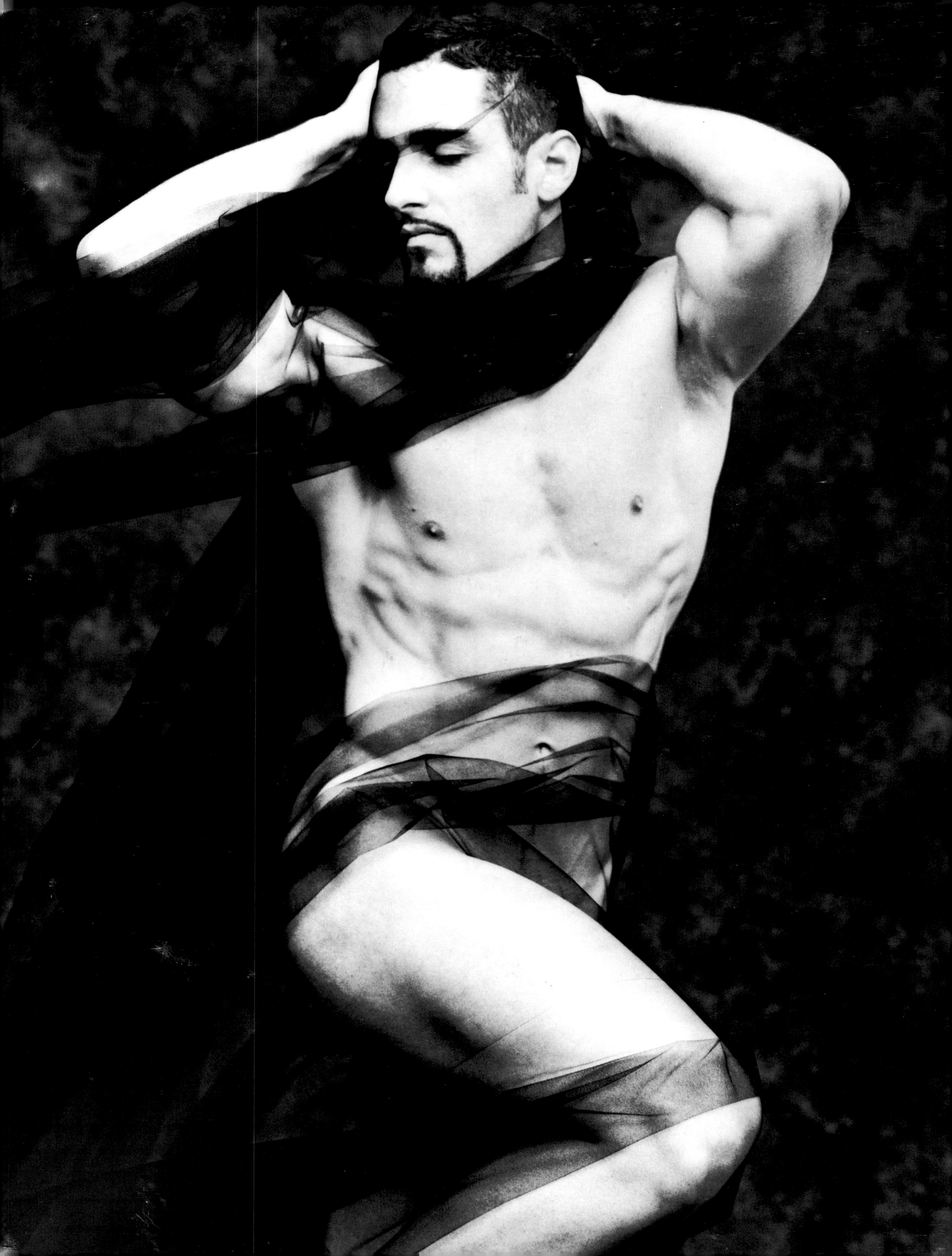

Hollywood
Voyeur

JANSSEN

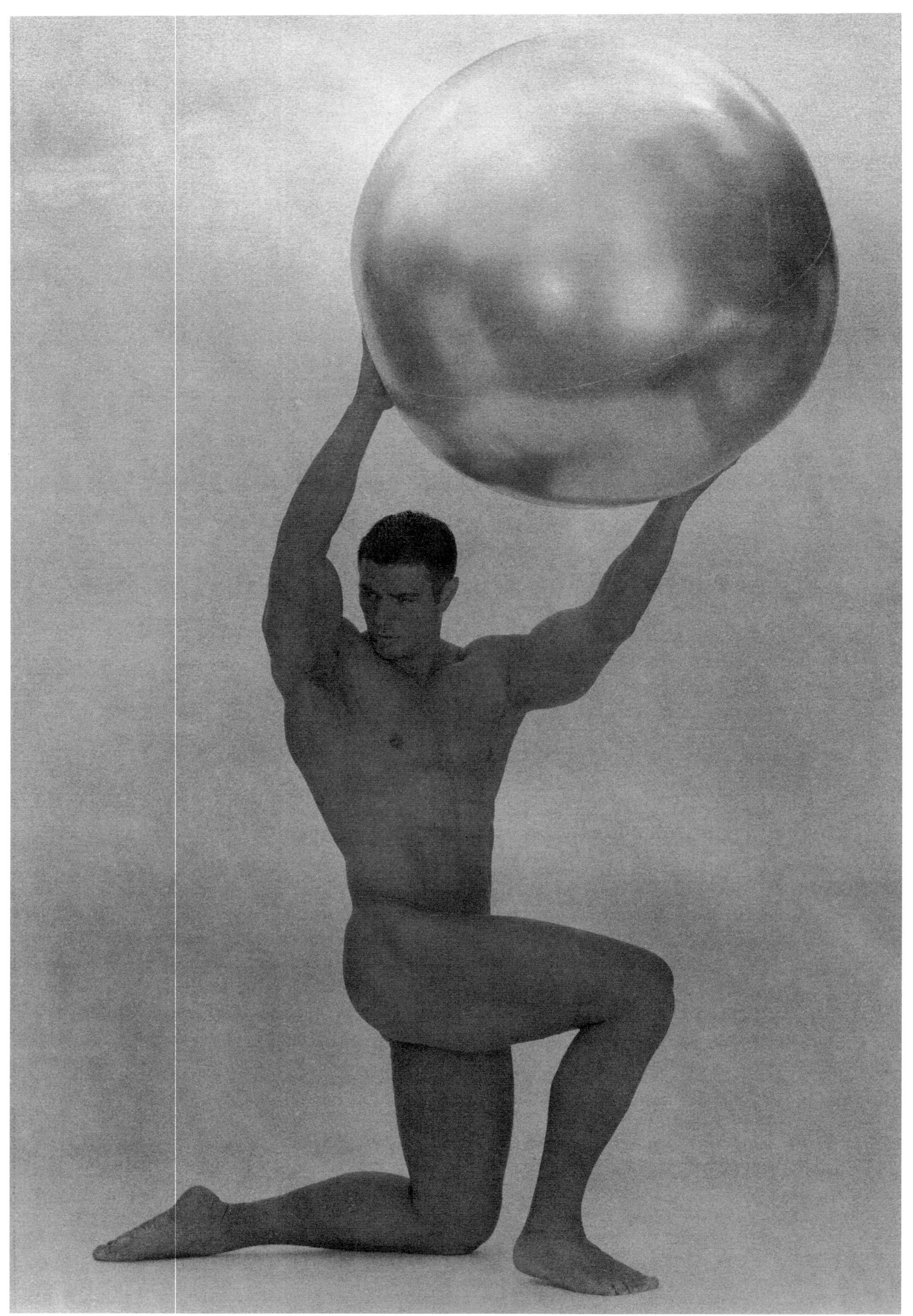

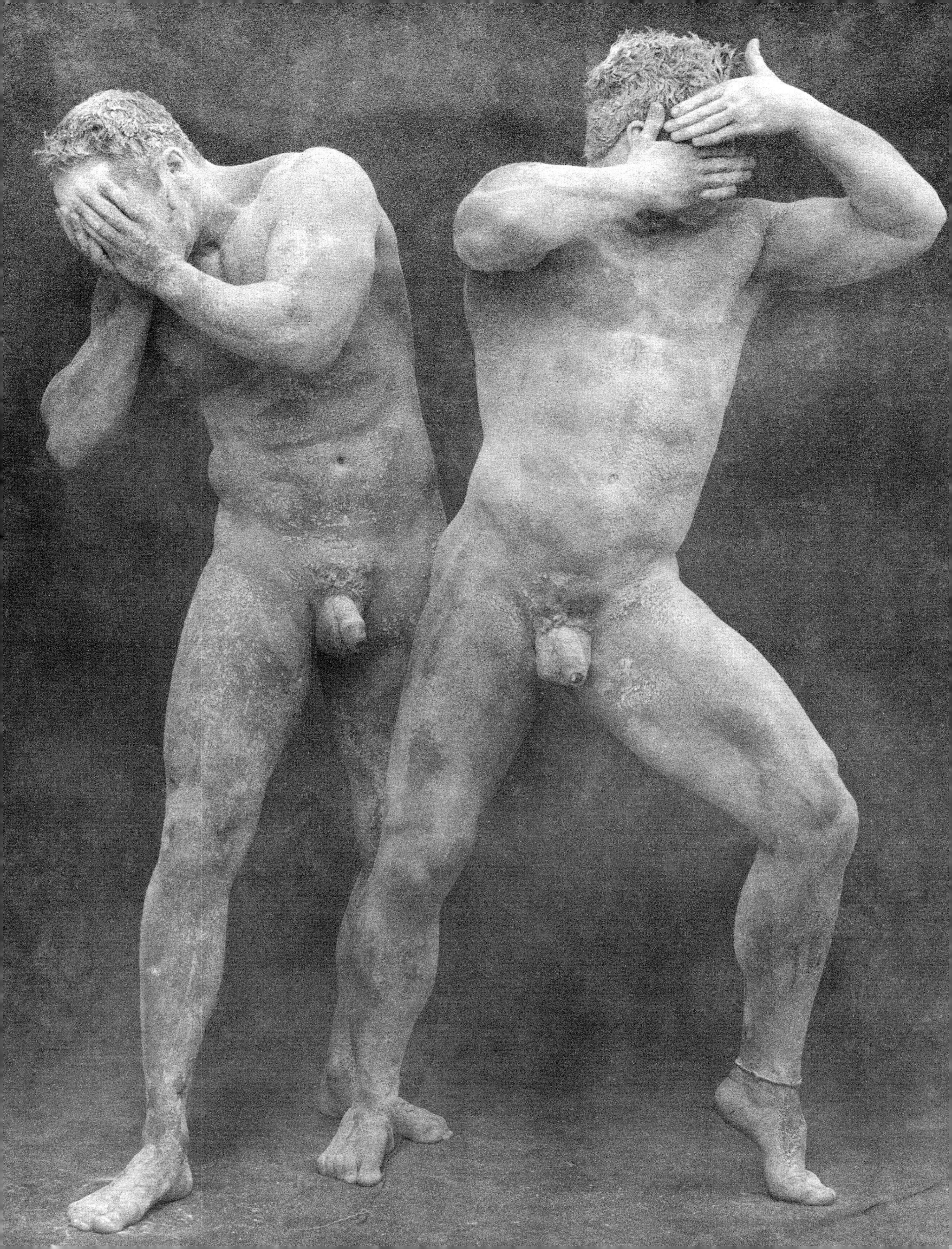

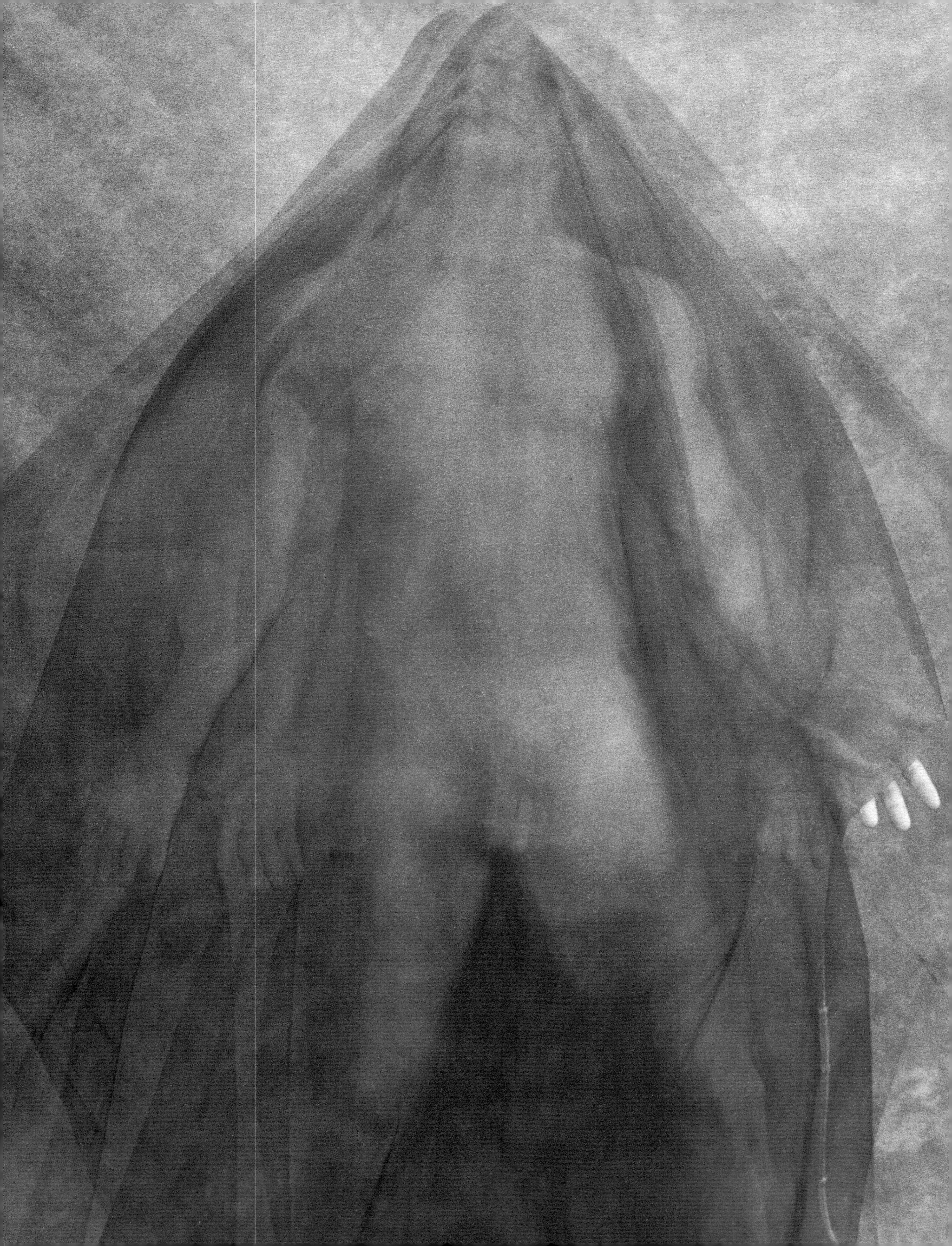

Preface

"Photography is something which everybody can 'do' now", British photographer Angus McBean once remarked. "So because photography has become such an instantaneous art-form and because everybody can 'do' it, people want a bit more."

Also providing more than a bit more, the two sides of Michael Childers reflect his imaginative response to the world of theatre and movies, and a homoerotic surrealism. As well creating memorable images of John Travolta, Warren Beatty, Al Pacino, Anjelica Huston and Natalie Wood, of many productions at the National Theatre in London, and of many famous ballet companies for the cover of <u>Dance</u> magazine, Childers has become one of the foremost erotic artists of the camera, with a style that's been described as "Helmut Newton dressed as Oscar Wilde."

This style is on view in **<u>Hollywood Voyeur.</u>** "You *are* beautiful," McBean used to tell all his actresses, "but *feel* it." Childers' beautiful male models not only feel it but enjoy making us feel it too. Deliberately unrealistic lighting gives their bodies a high romantic gloss, and the camera places them in sexually charged yet mysterious theatrical settings or situations. A pair of young blondes, languorously nude and bronzed, stand with their eyes closed, each clasping a pair of phallic, Art Nouveau-ish imitation cactus leaves. A white nude wearing a black blindfold duels with a black nude wearing a white blindfold. A cobra, twined around the bodies of two young men standing knee to knee, is presumably an exotic fetish to stimulate foreplay, since they're kissing its neck, not (yet) each other.

Although snakes and other reptiles, tigers, Tom-of-Finland bikers, black leather, bandaged hands, ropes and chains appear in other photographs, not even the chains are Mapplethorpe-sinister, but decorative or playfully enigmatic props. Whatever goes on in this world of love games, Childers seems to celebrate it. His shadows are purely visual.

The showbiz photographer is also on view here, in two glamorous images of Joe Dallesandro from <u>Midnight Cowboy</u>, in a portrait of Jimmy James' uncanny impersonation of a sad-eyed Marilyn Monroe, and a wonderfully absurd tableau featuring Hollywood porn director-drag queen Chi Chi LaRue. A cunning use of light and shadow allows only Chi Chi's face and left foot to be clearly visible. The spotlit face radiates a smile as triumphant as the shoulder-length blond wig; Childers merges the rest into a black background. Outlined against a strip of white, a bronzed and gleaming male nude advances on Chi Chi with a clapper board that announces TAKE 9. Its hinged stick culminates in an ostrich plume, thrust flirtatiously at the star. Meanwhile, on the floor, two actors rehearse making love.

Like most of Childers' models, they're dream people in a dream world, where nothing leads anywhere. Like the cigarettes that remain unlit, beautiful lovers are always on the verge of consummation, beautiful narcissists on the verge of arousing themselves. Surrealistically caught in their fixed poses and rituals, they tease the imagination by performing an endless Act One.

Gavin Lambert

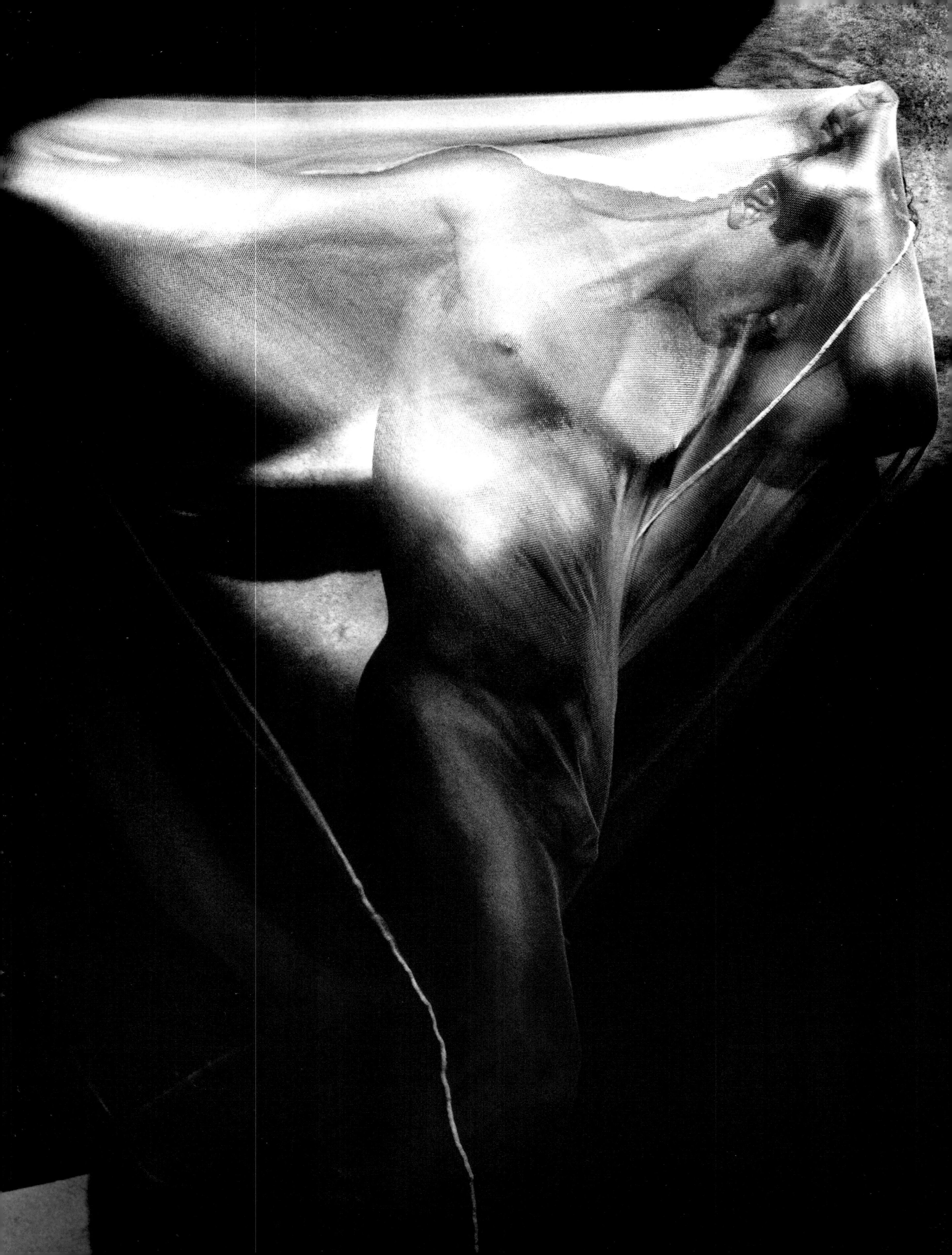

Introduction

Hollywood must be full of voyeurs who get paid highly for it. They are not shy.

The pleasure of looking is celebrated in here, and methods to tell others about are explored fully with all that the latest technology can offer. Michael Childers has been involved in this for thirty-five years.

Here are his choices. They are not snaps, but set ups like they always do in Hollywood, and no one really knows how much reality is here; one can decide for oneself.

Photography for me is all subject matter, its forms seem fixed. 'Exploit it,' he says, and does it with all the gloss and shine the California sun and Hollywood lights have to offer.

David Hockney

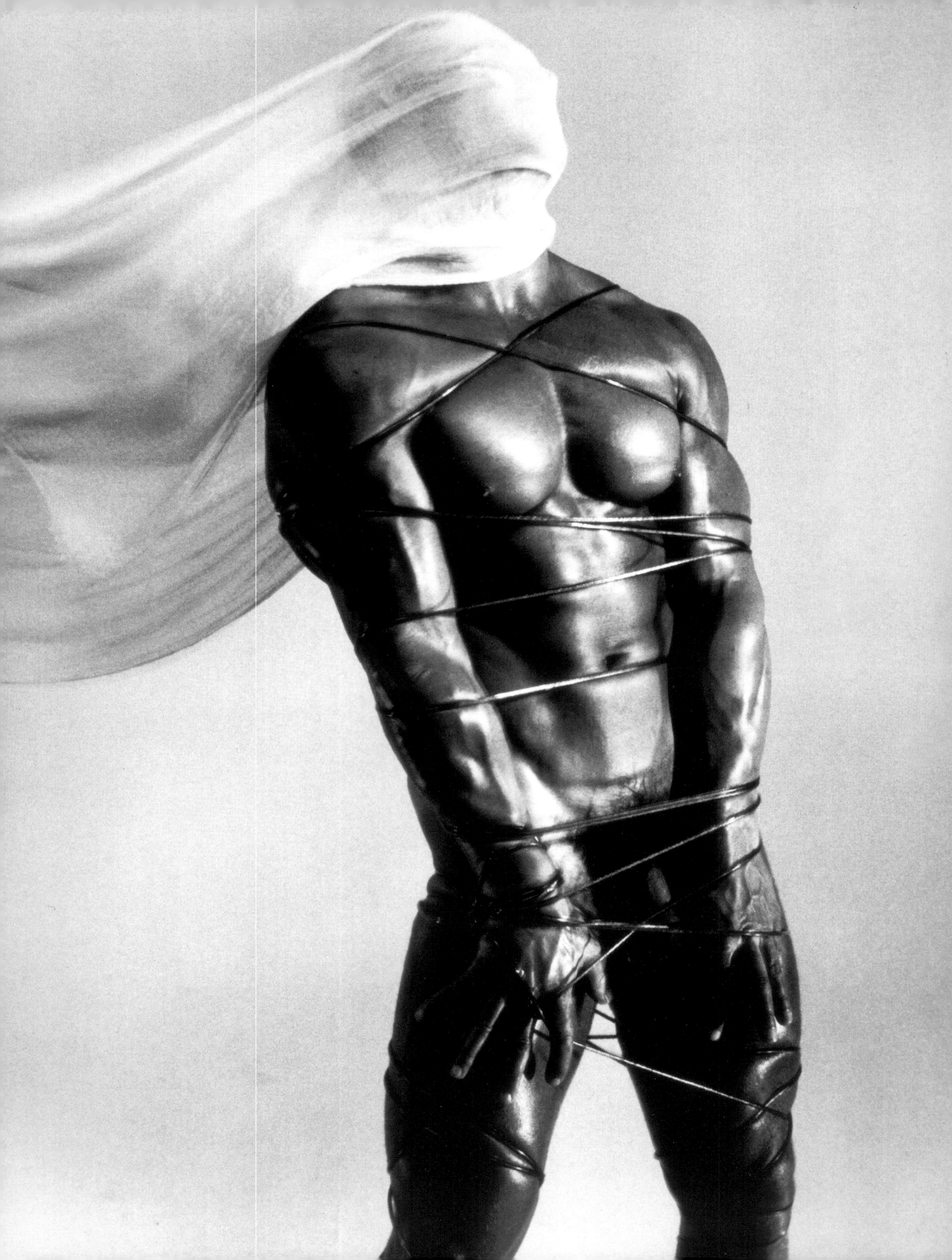

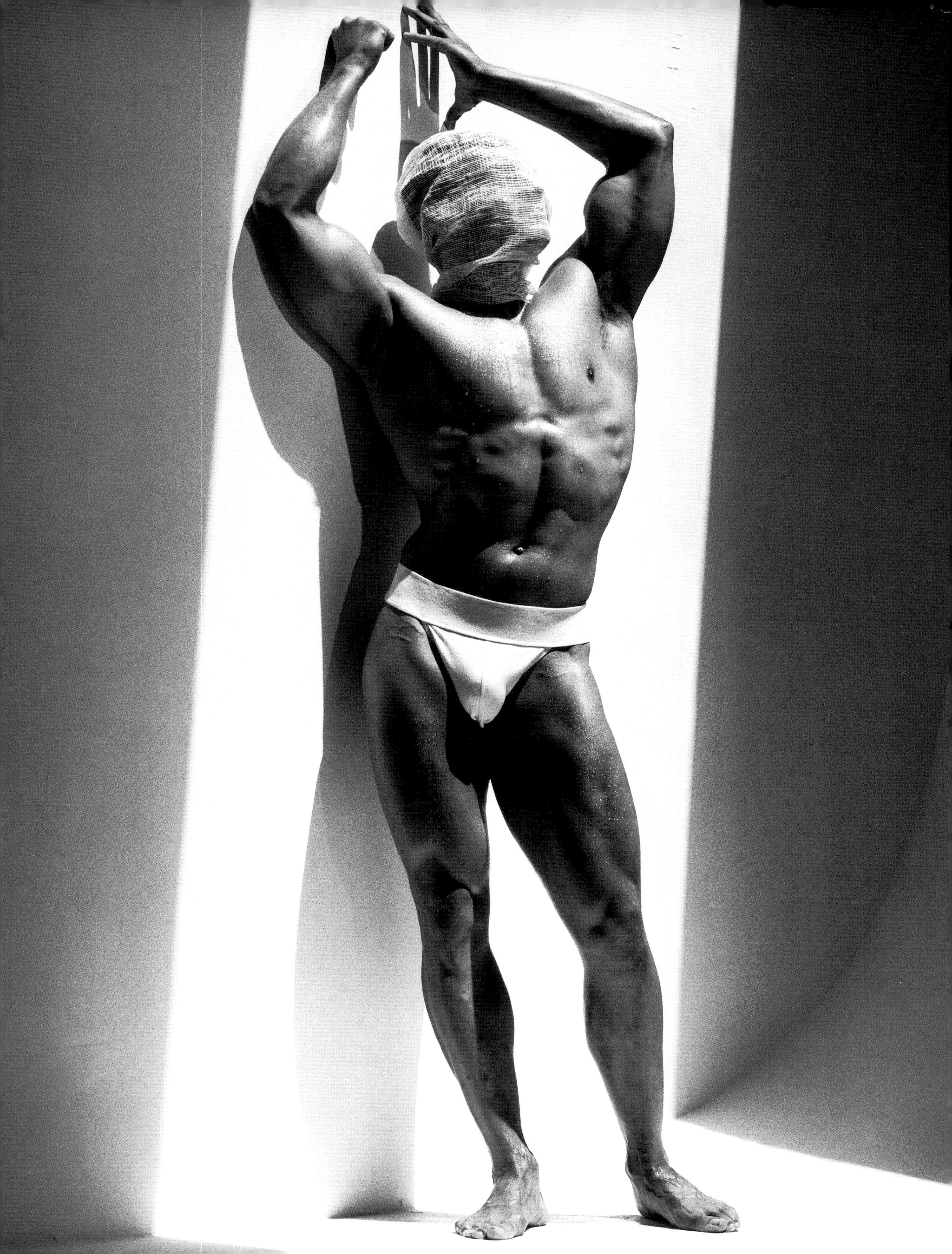

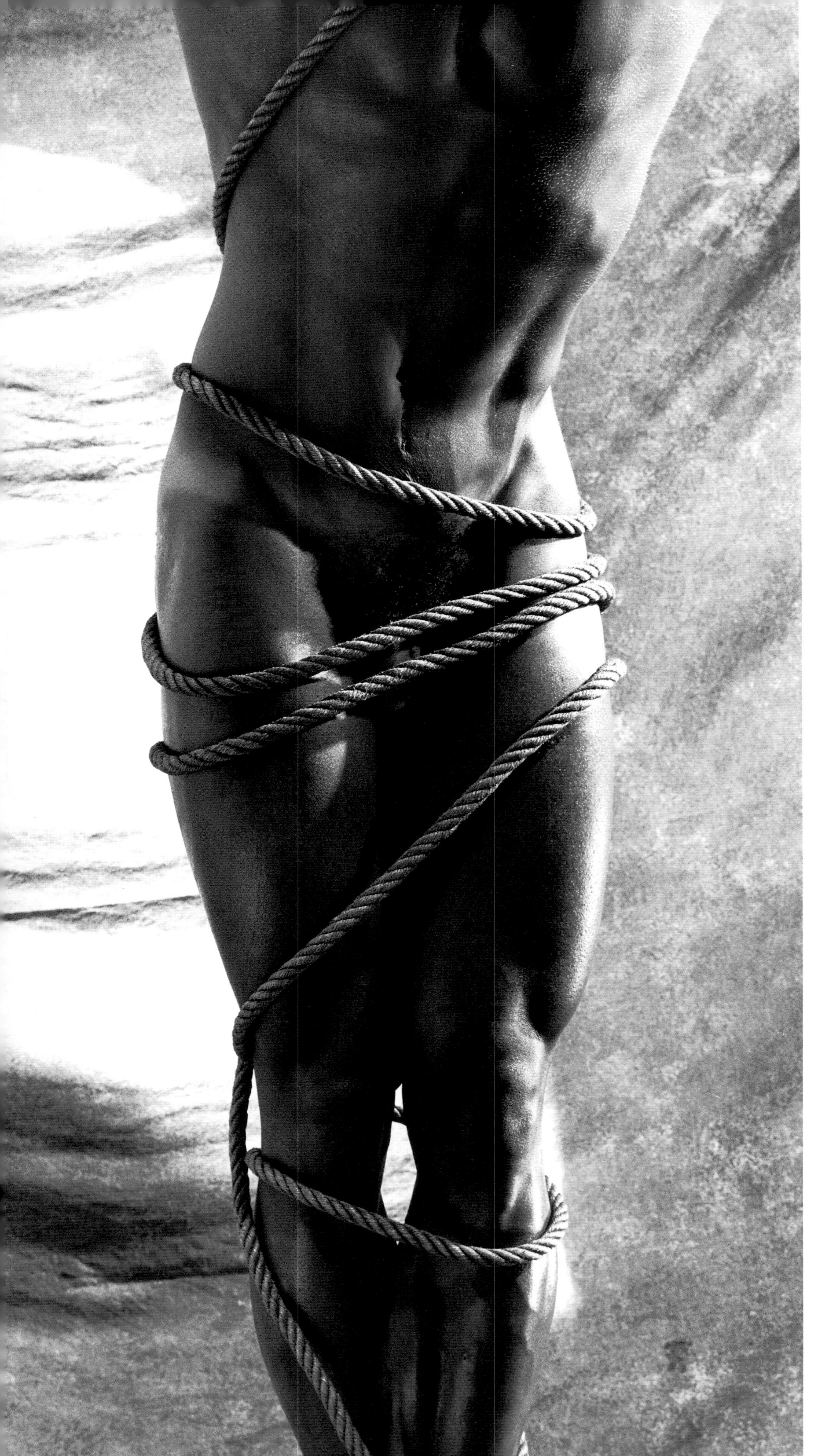

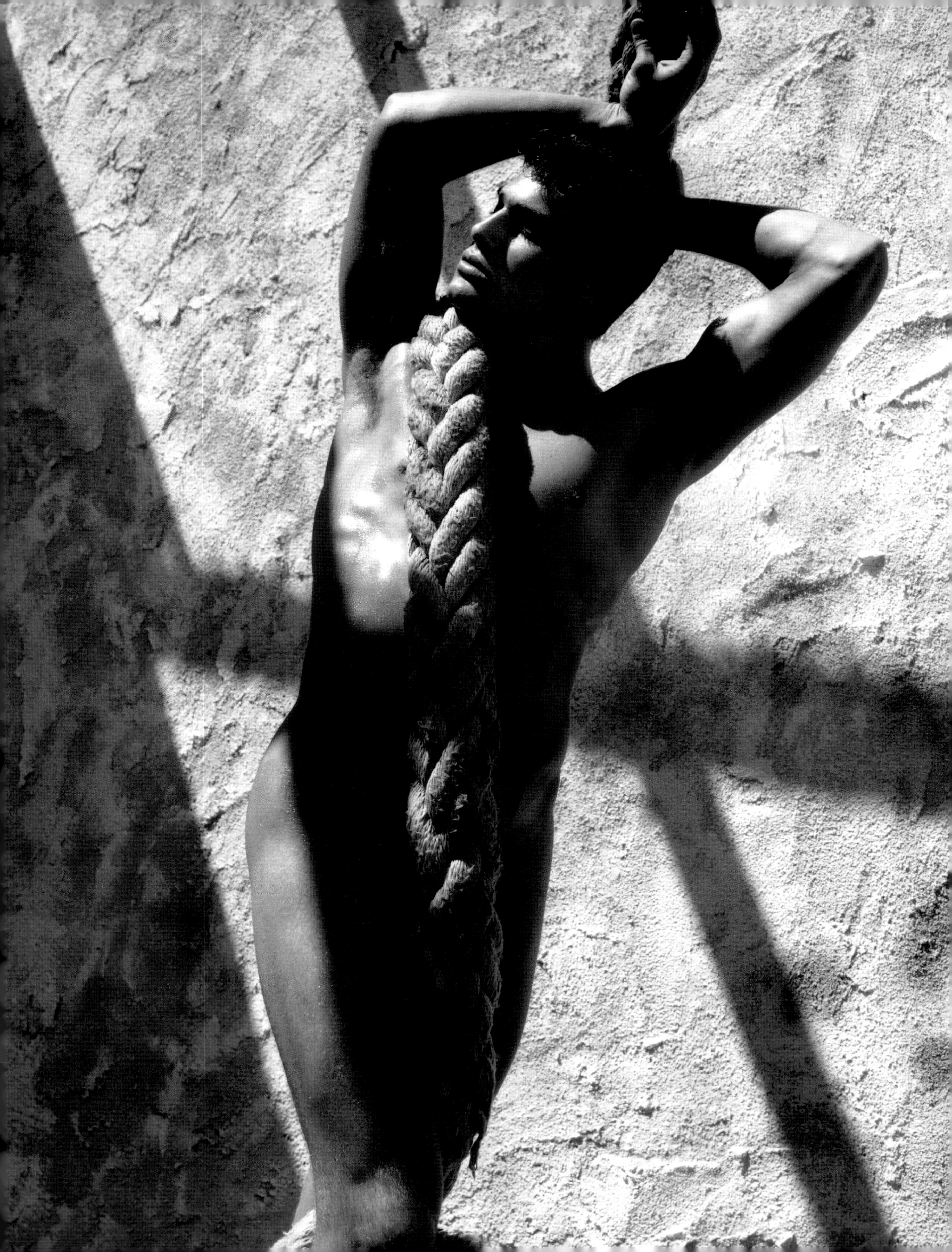

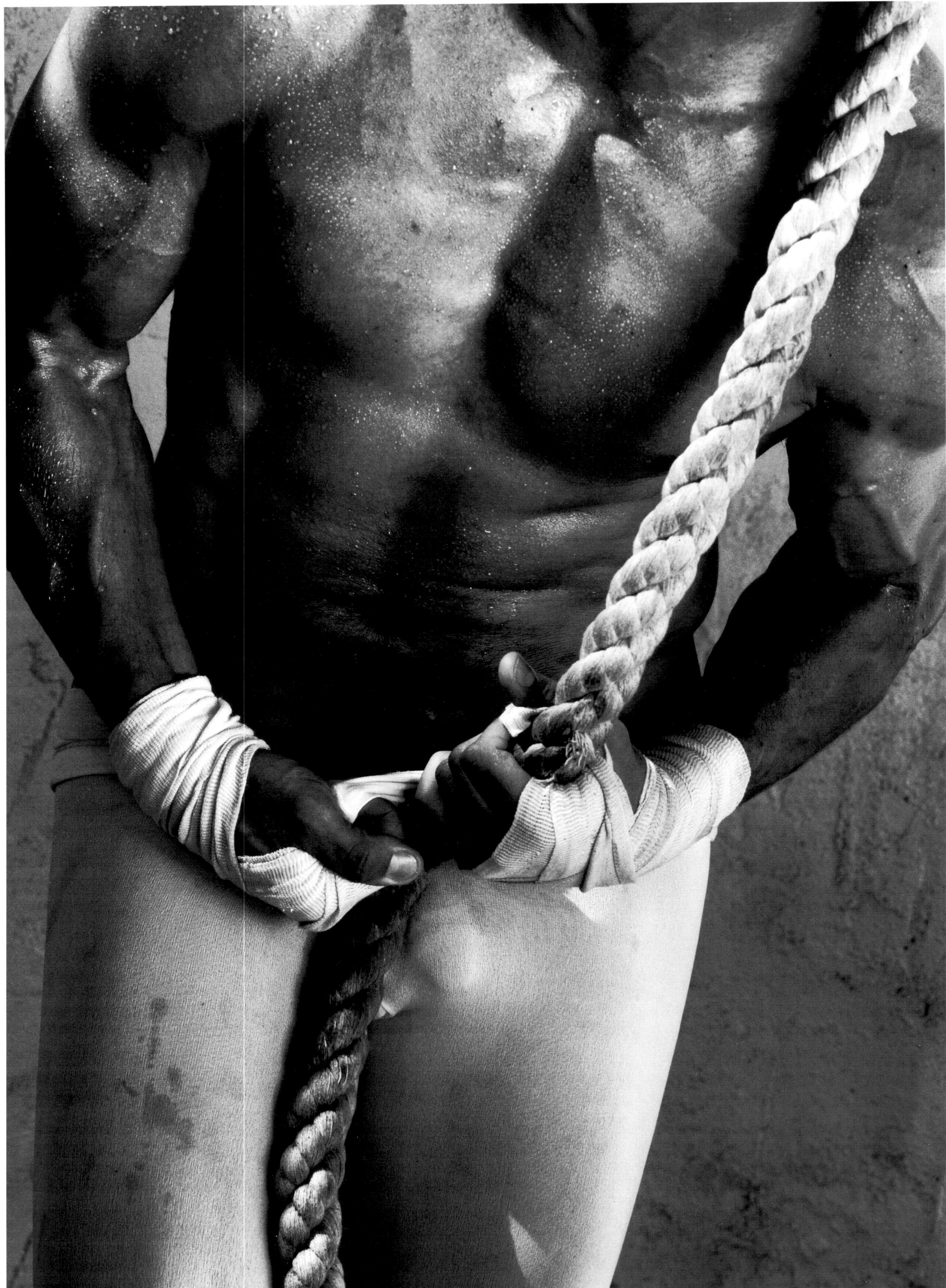

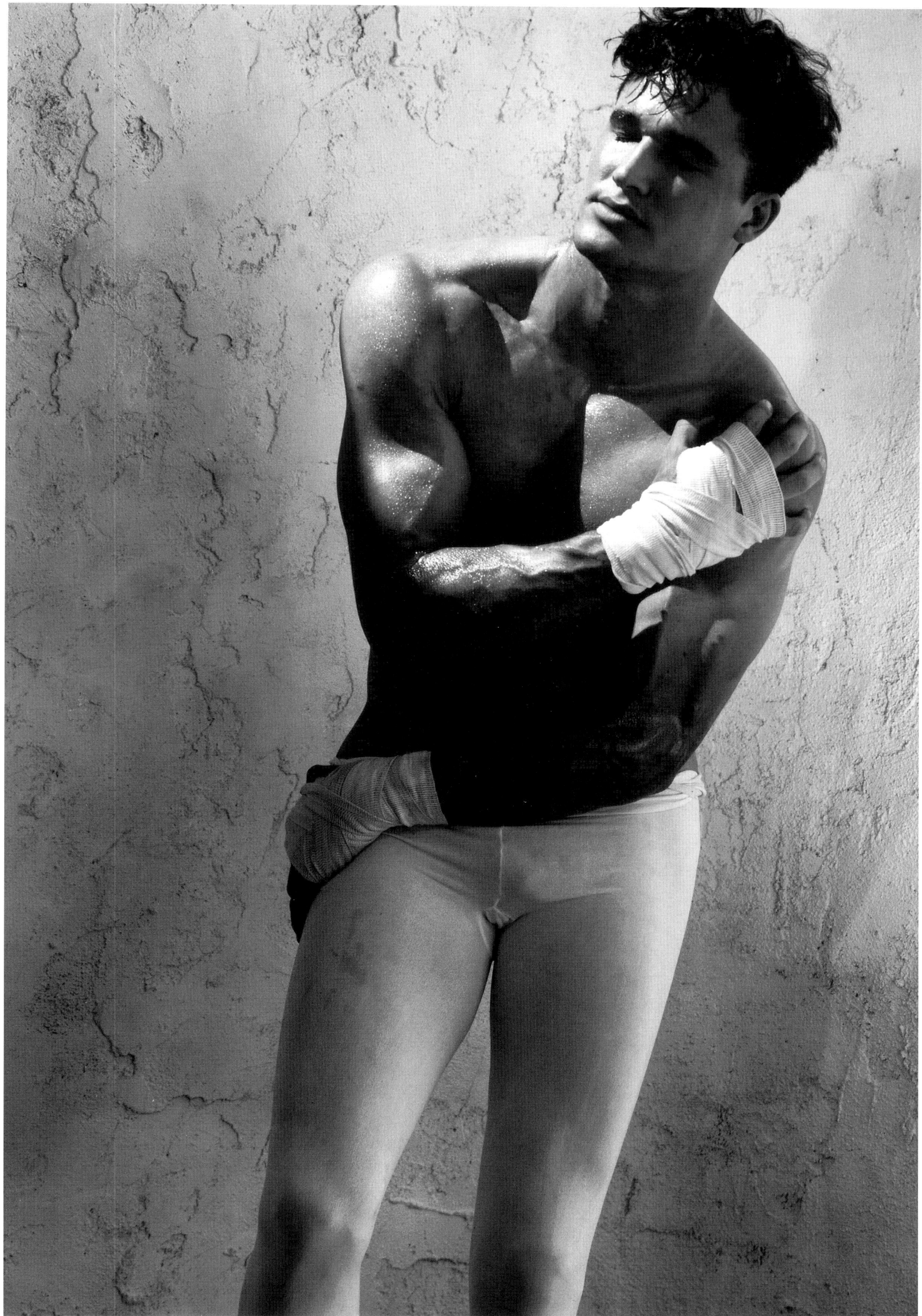

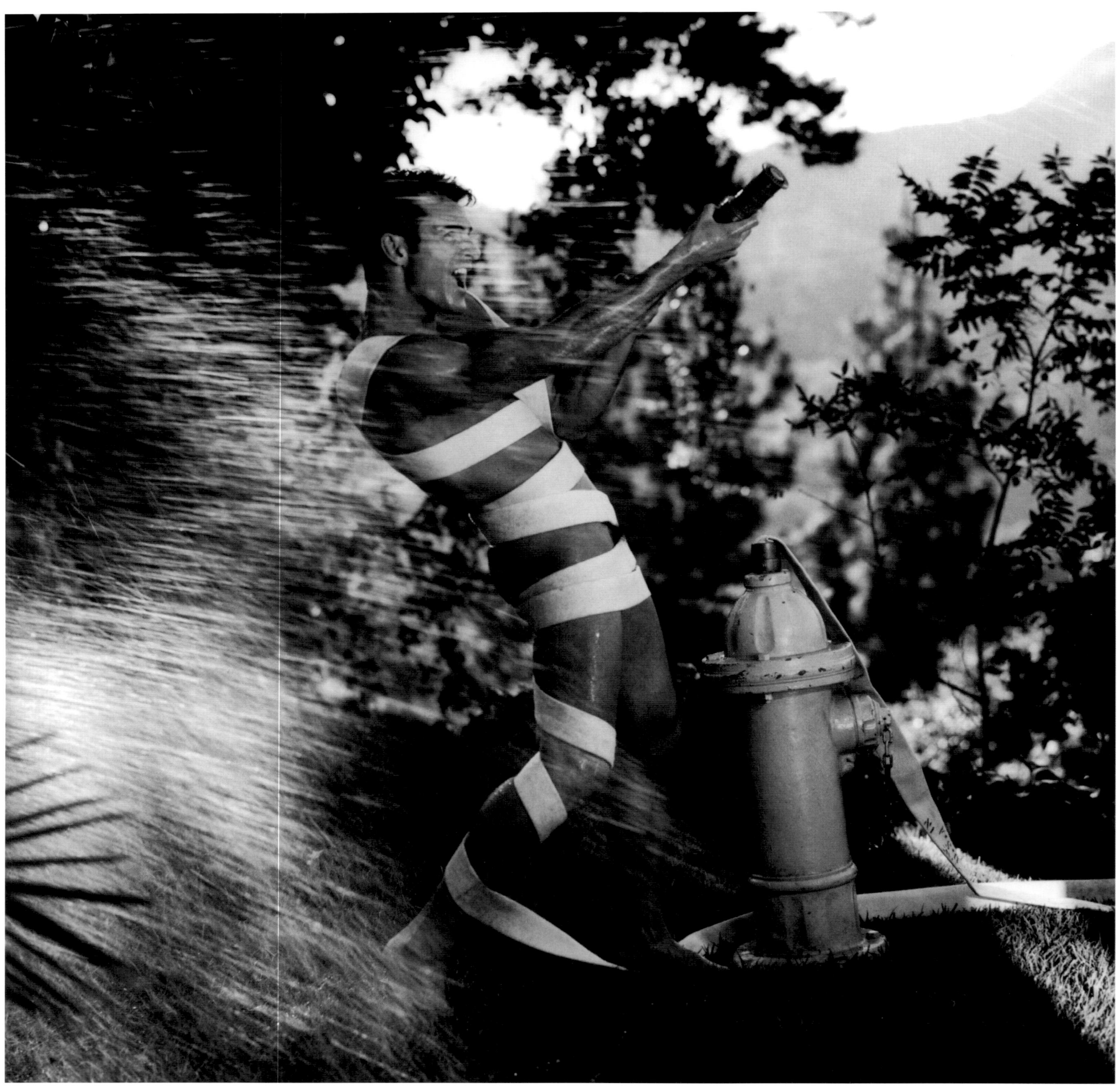

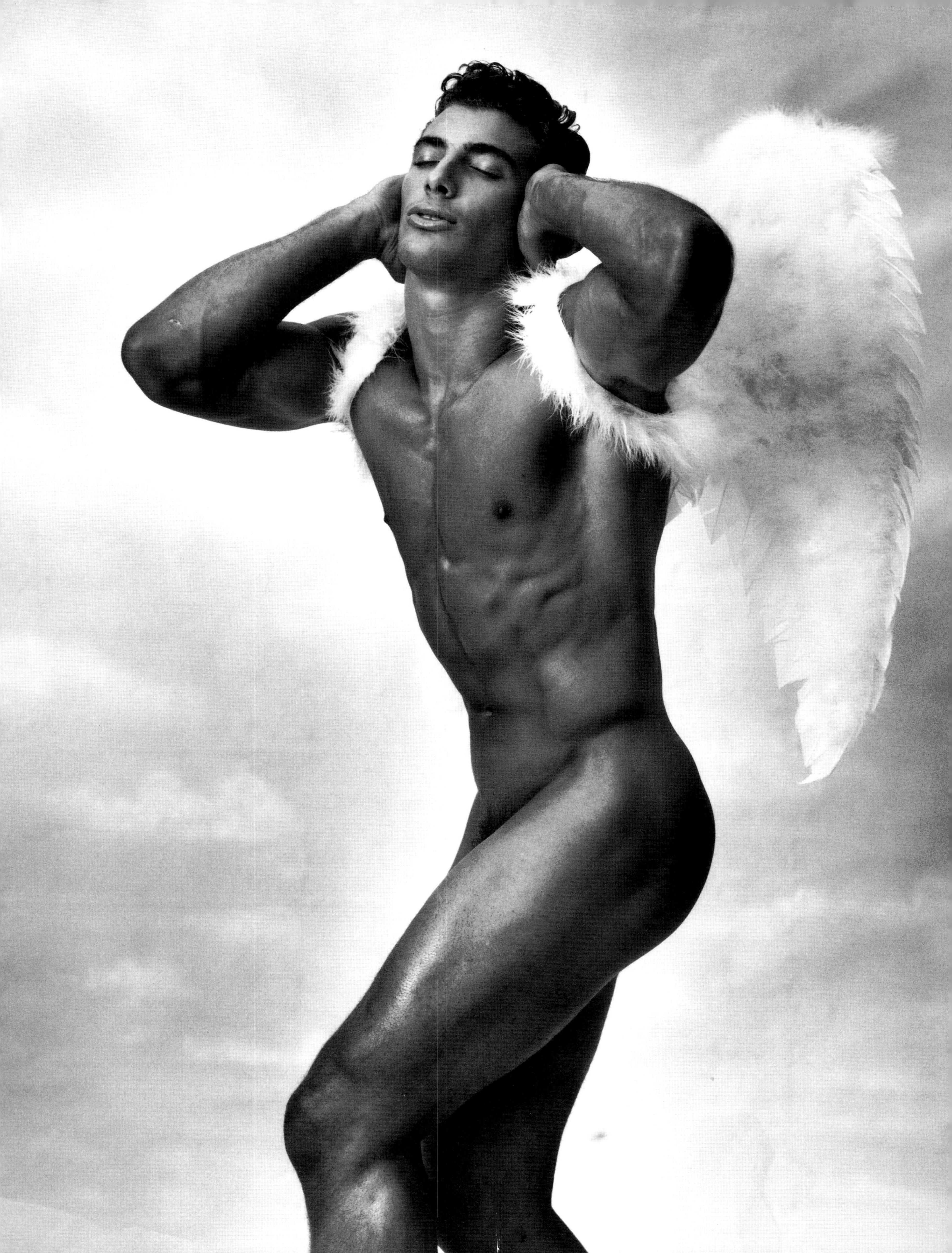

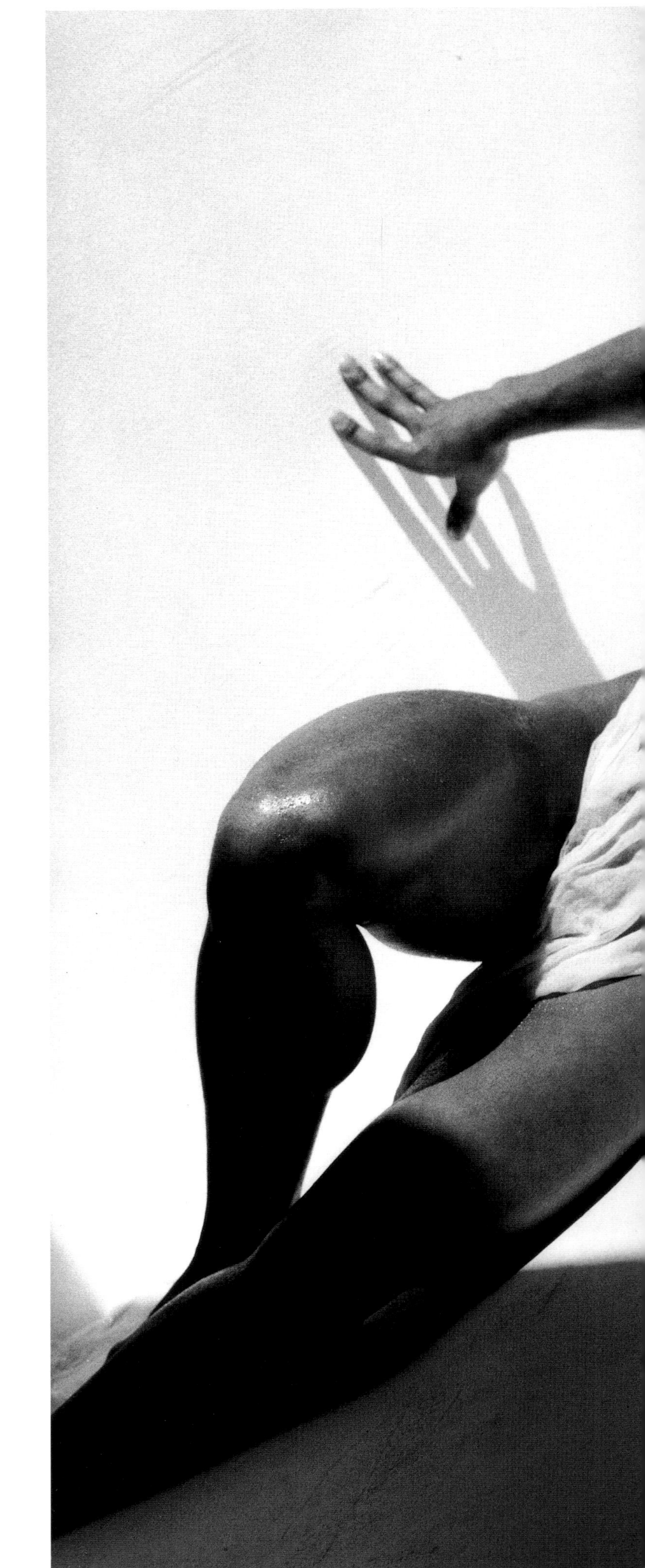

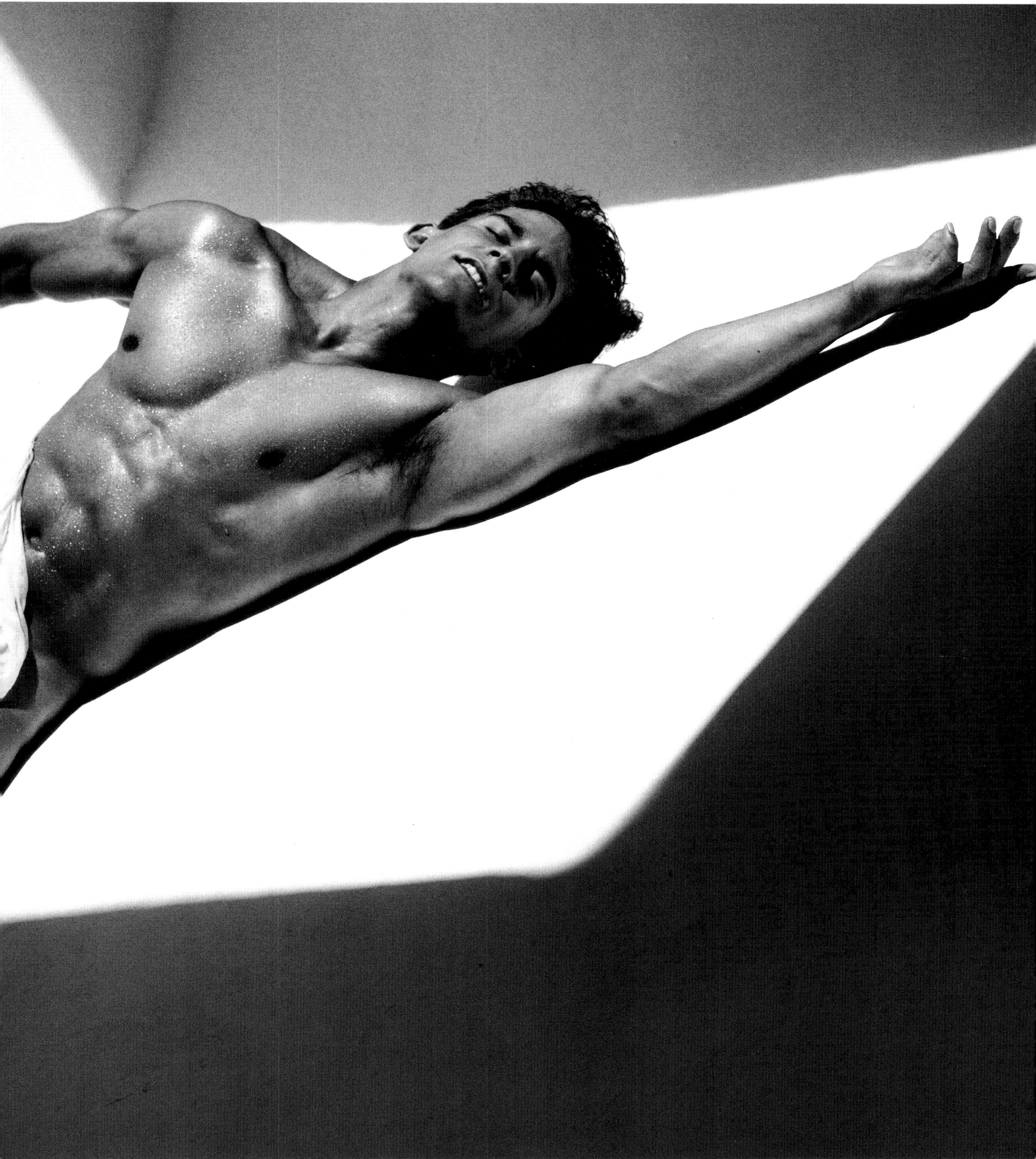

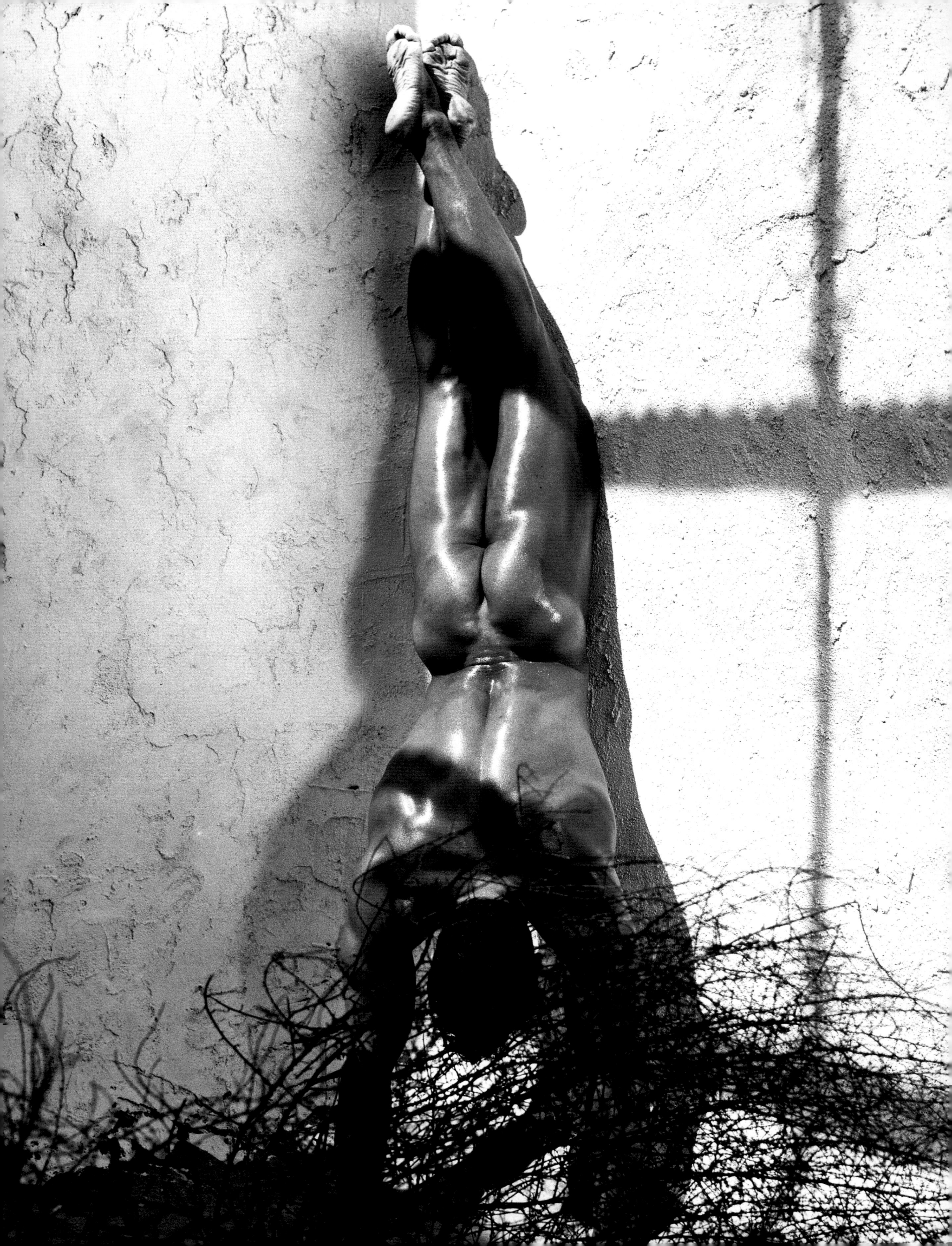

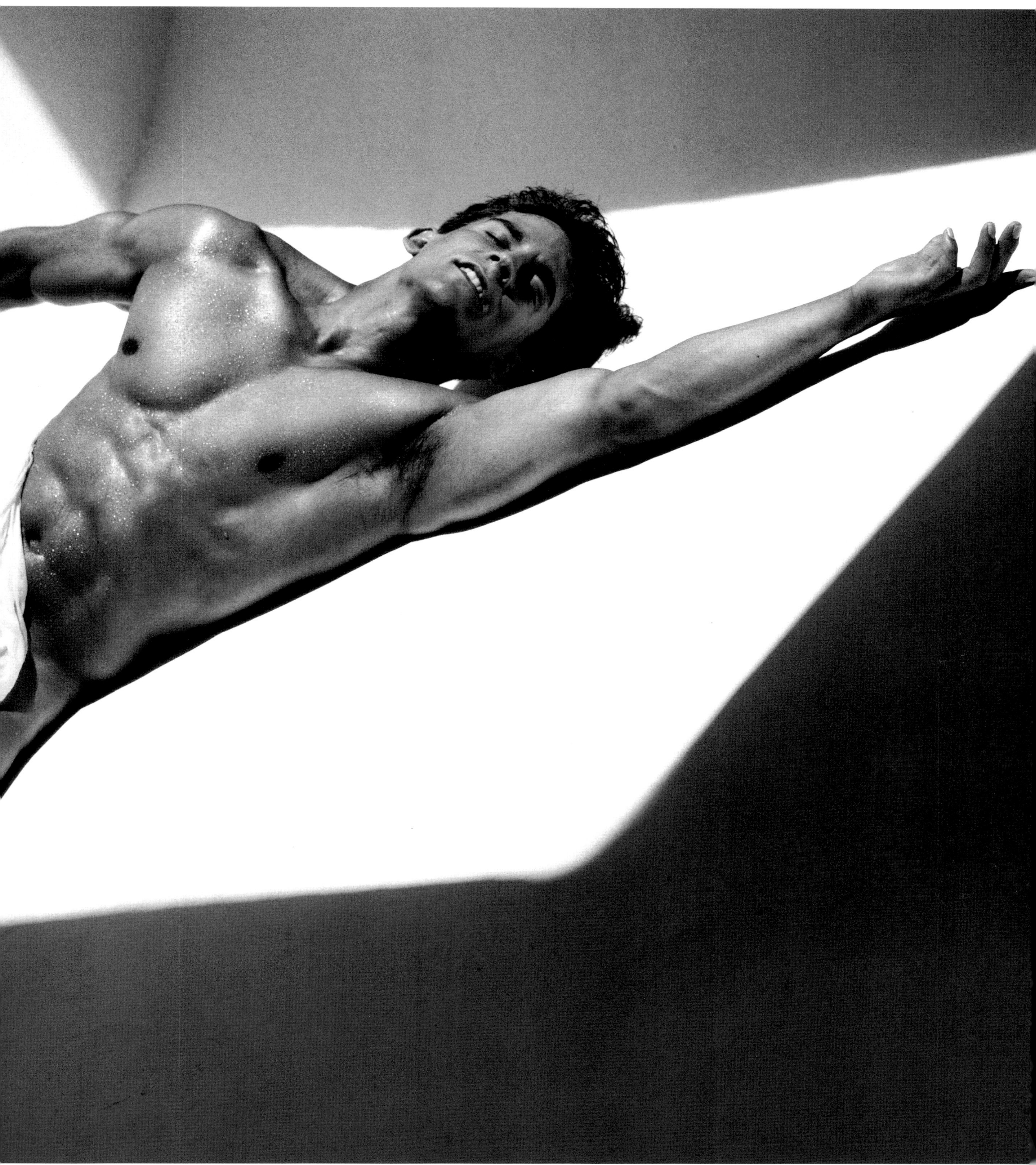

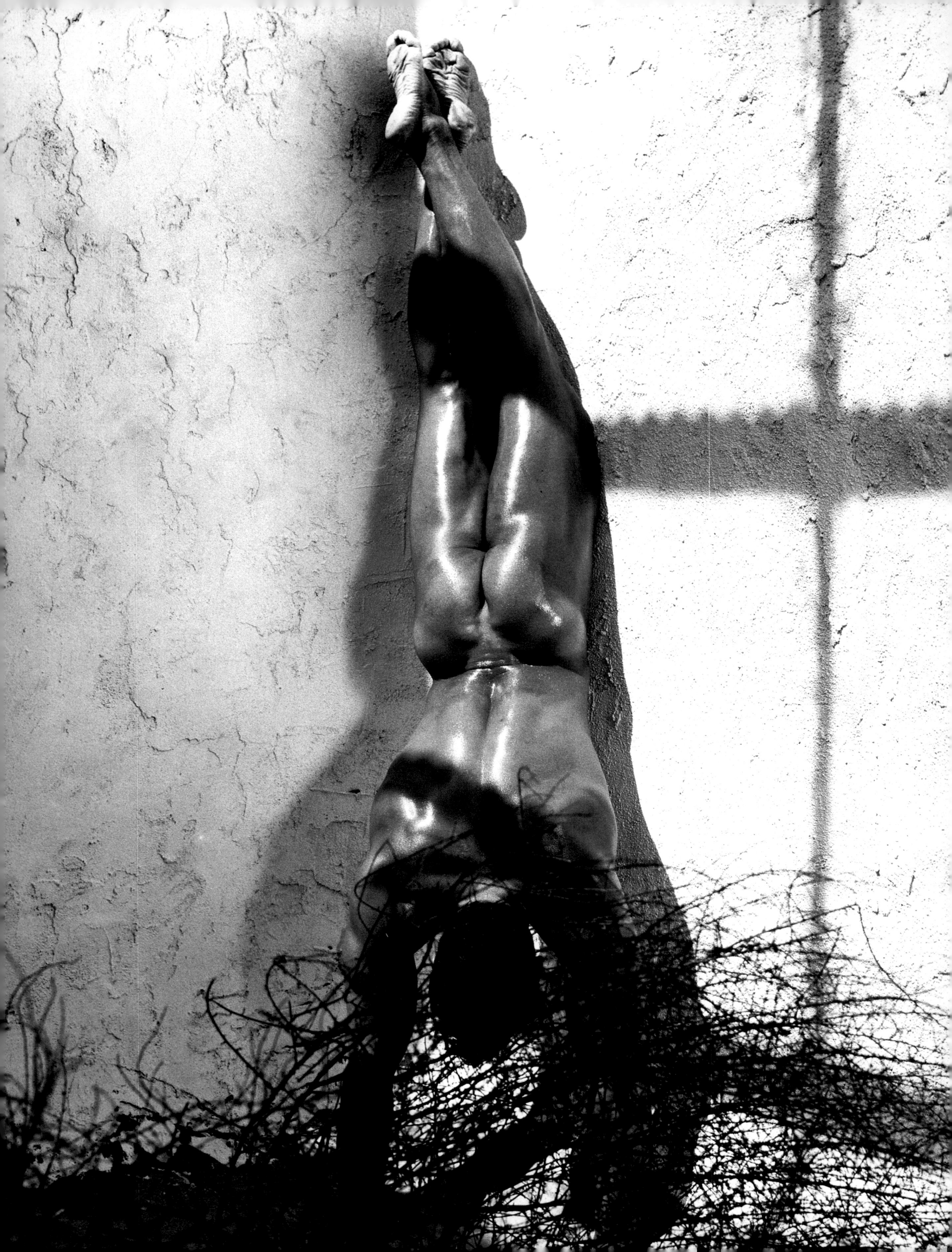

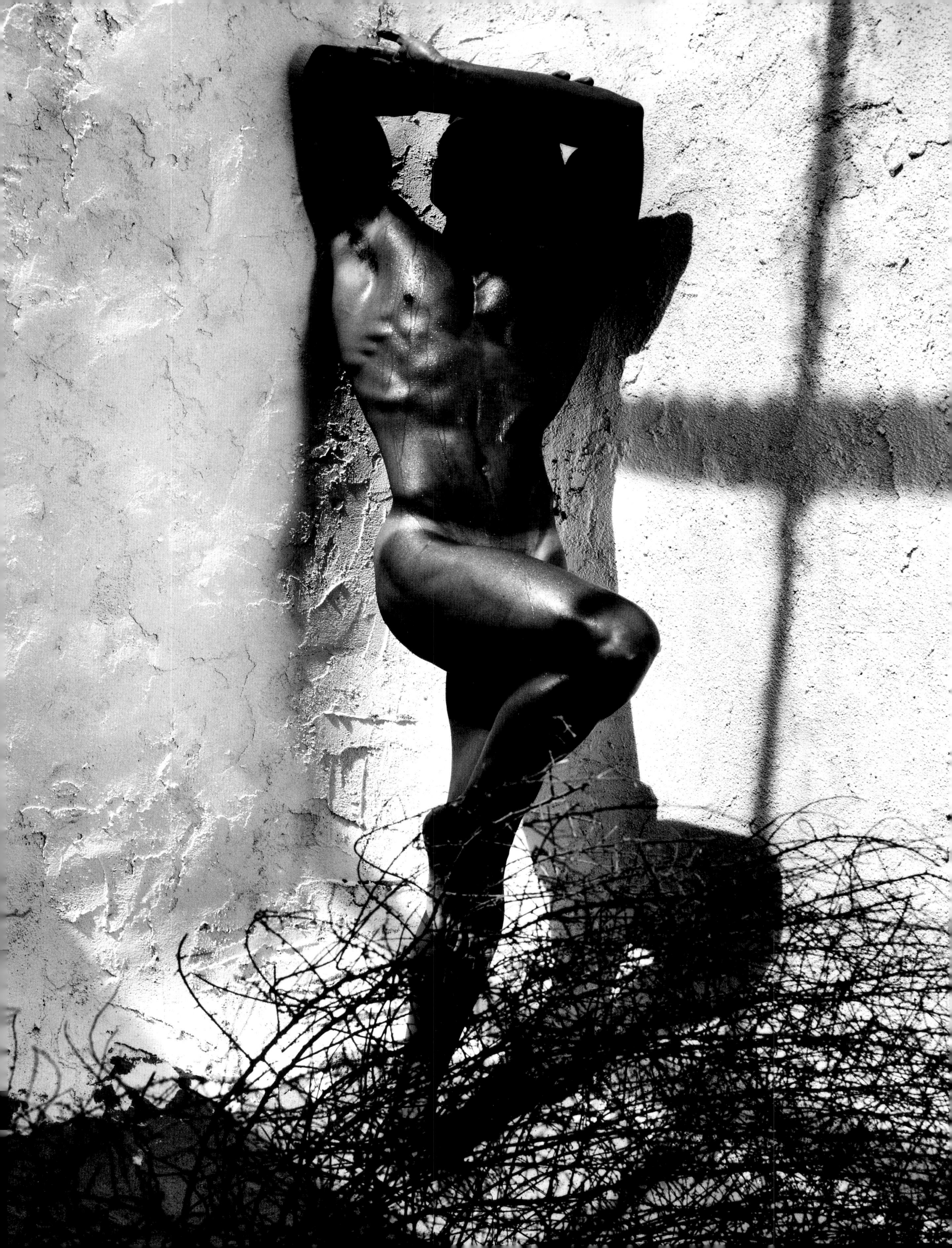

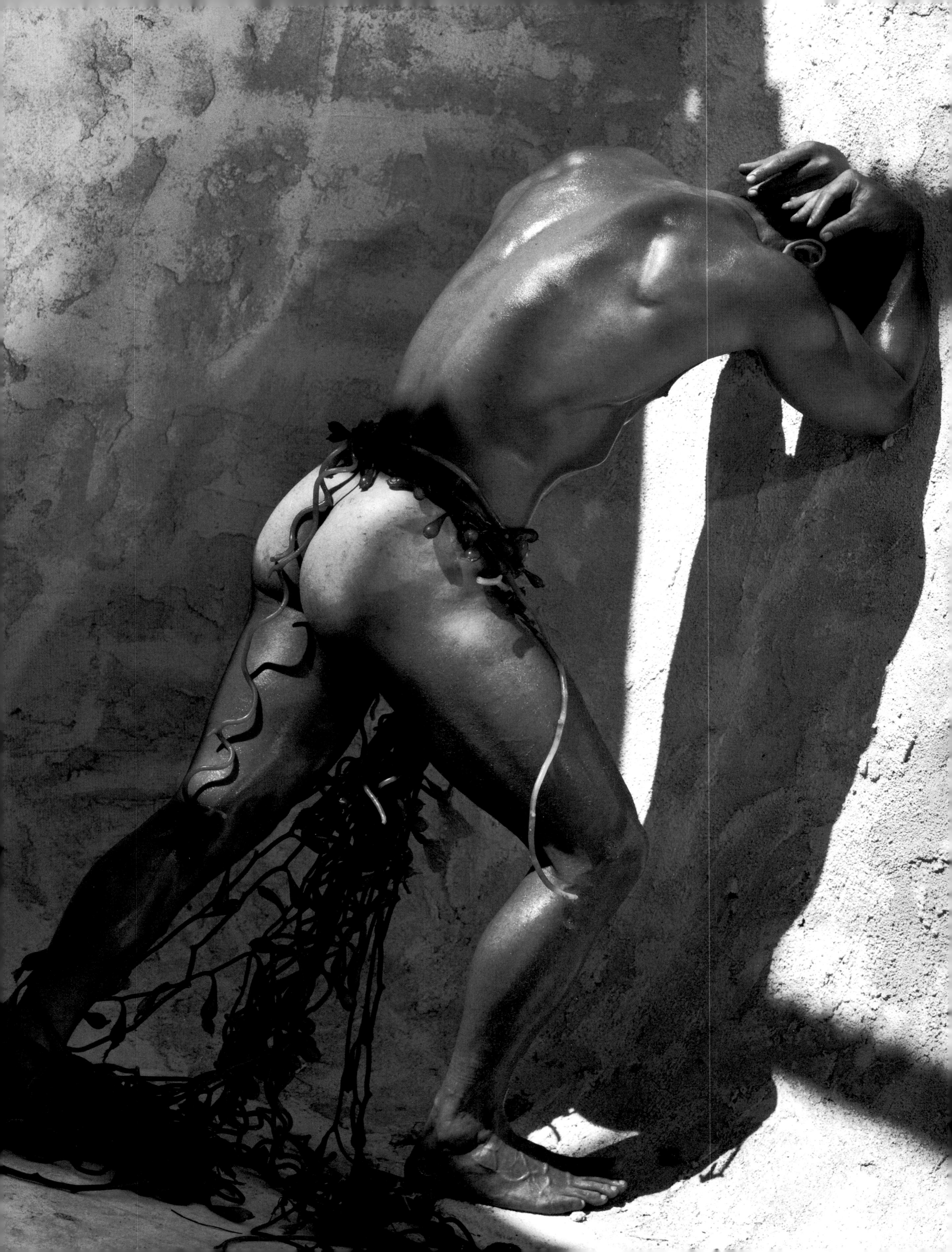

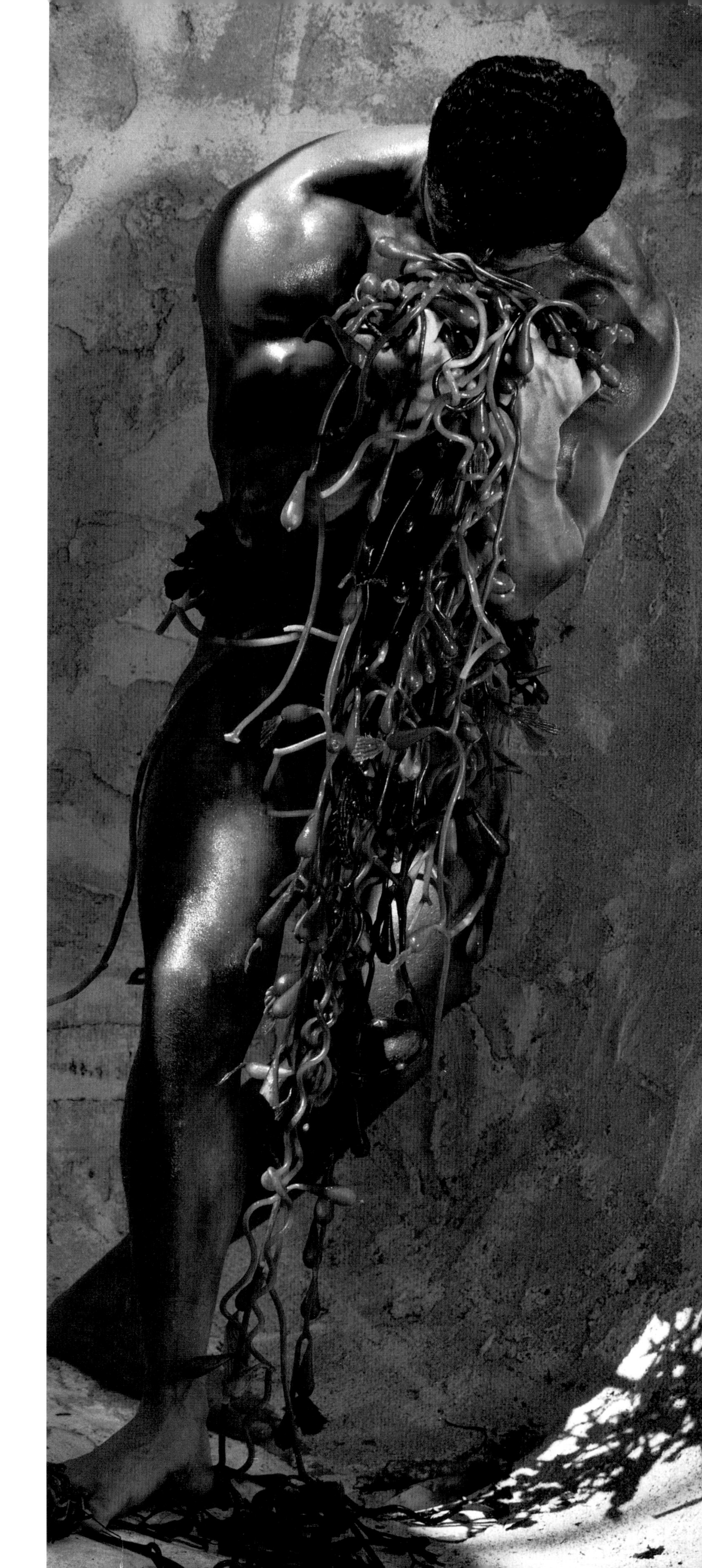

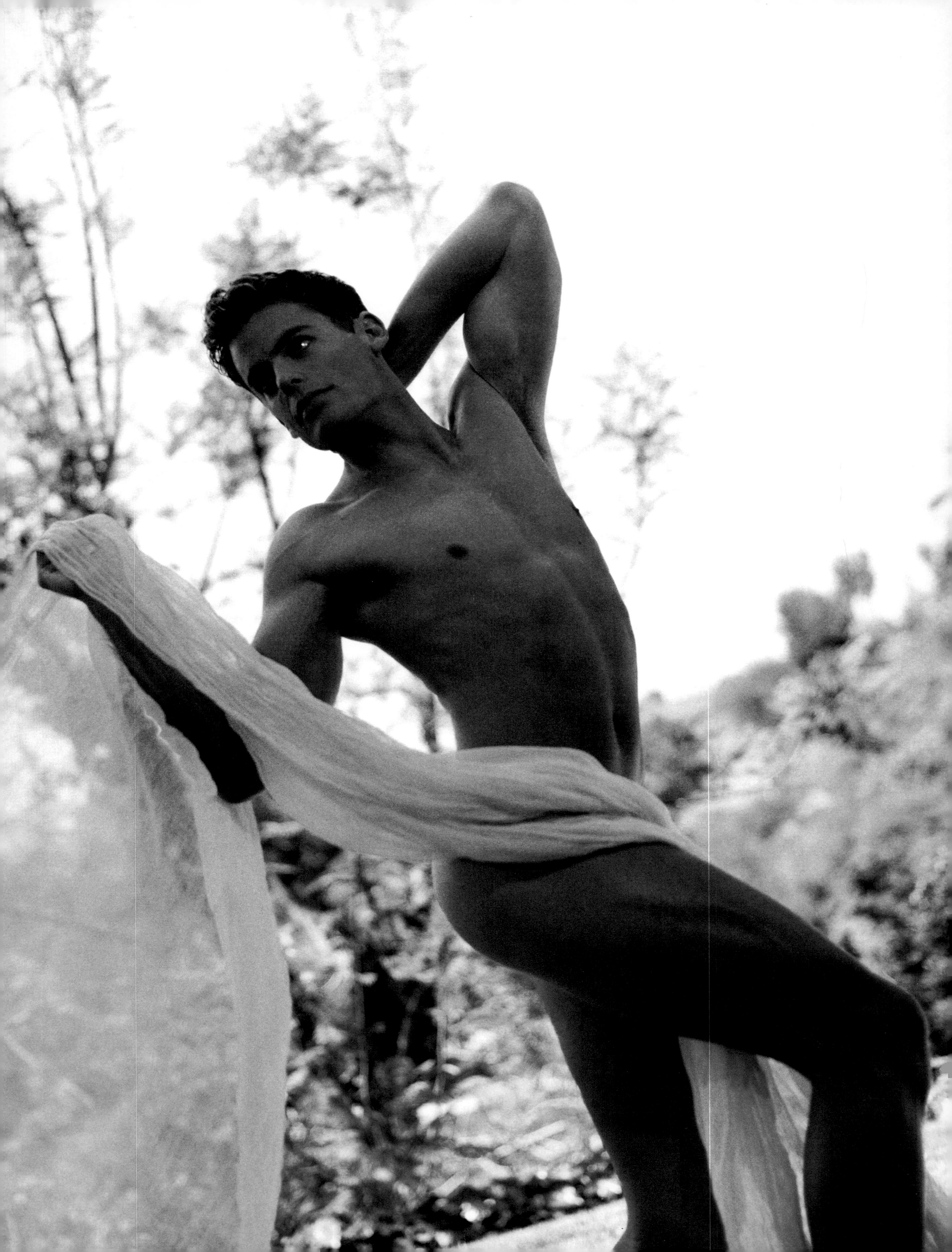

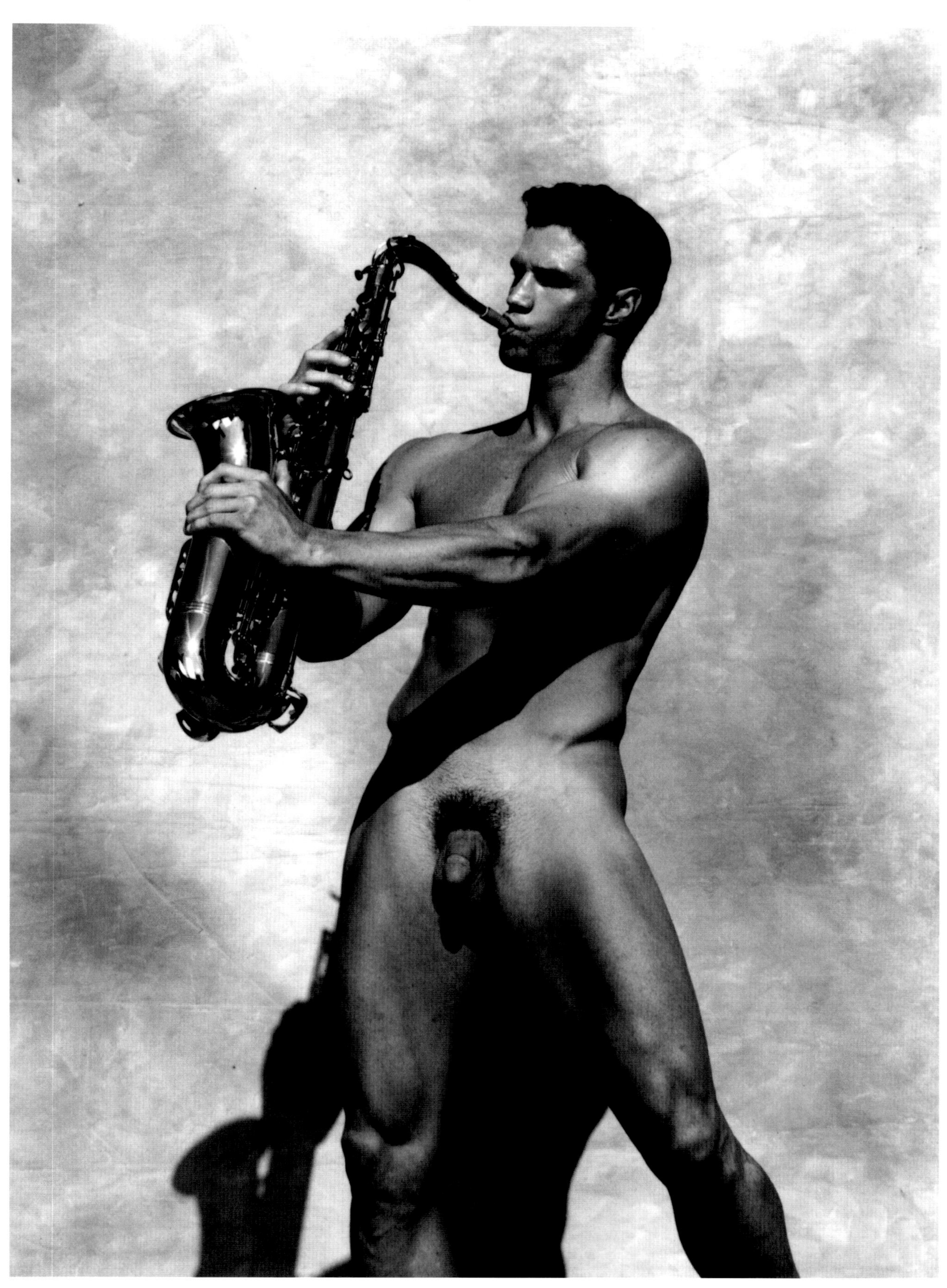

Vaginal Davis

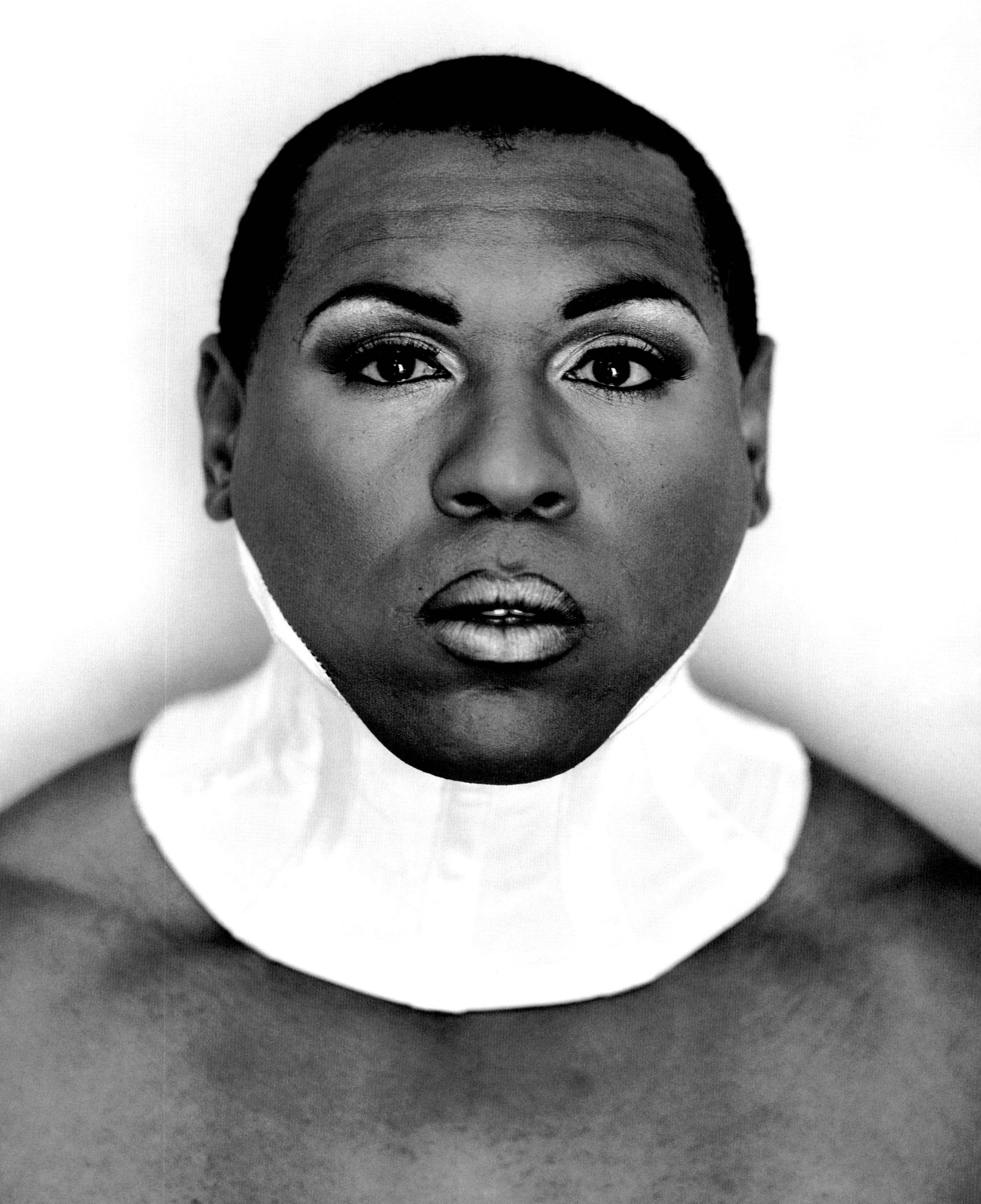

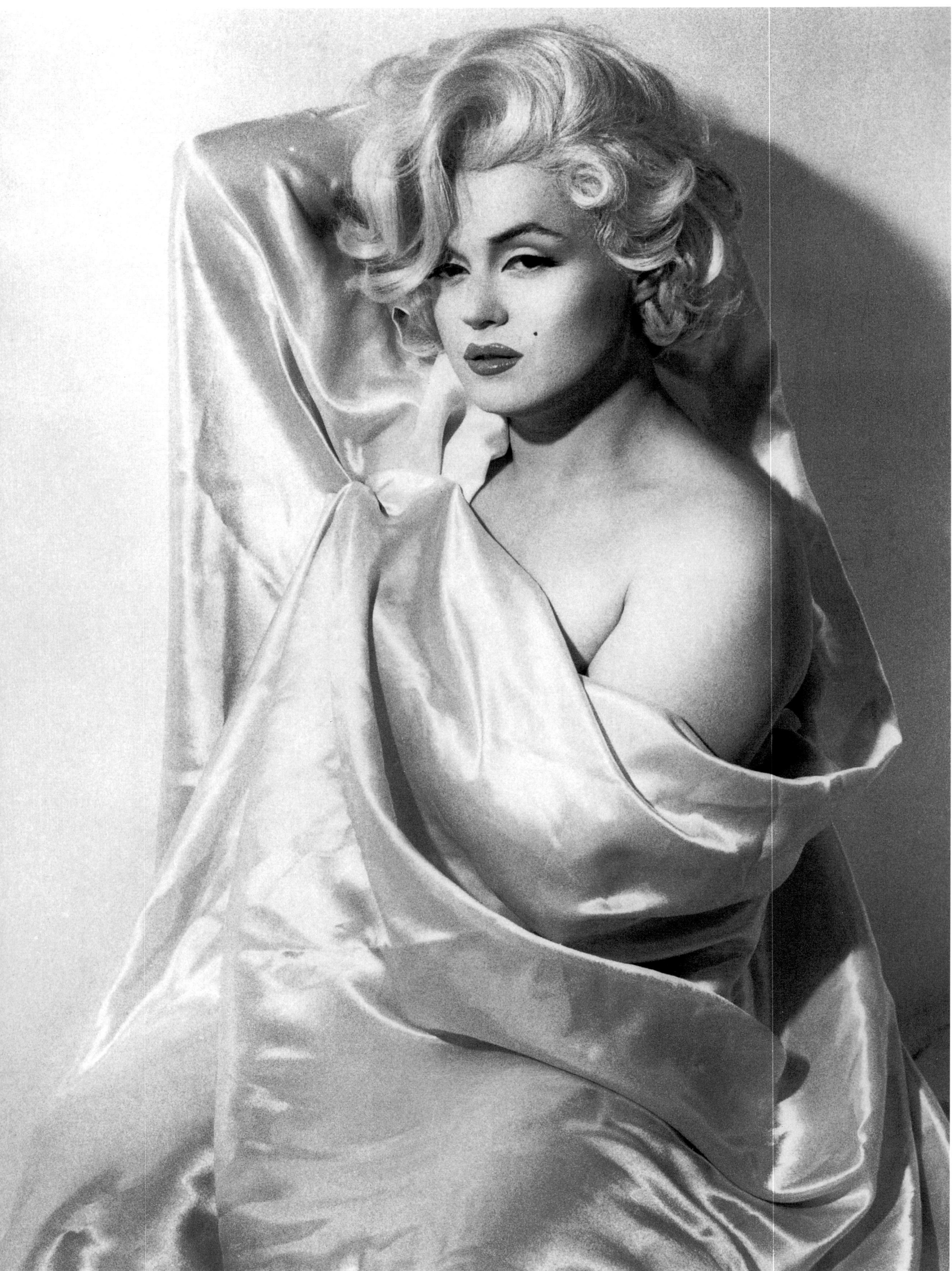

Jimmy James Vocal Impressionist

Chanel Twins >

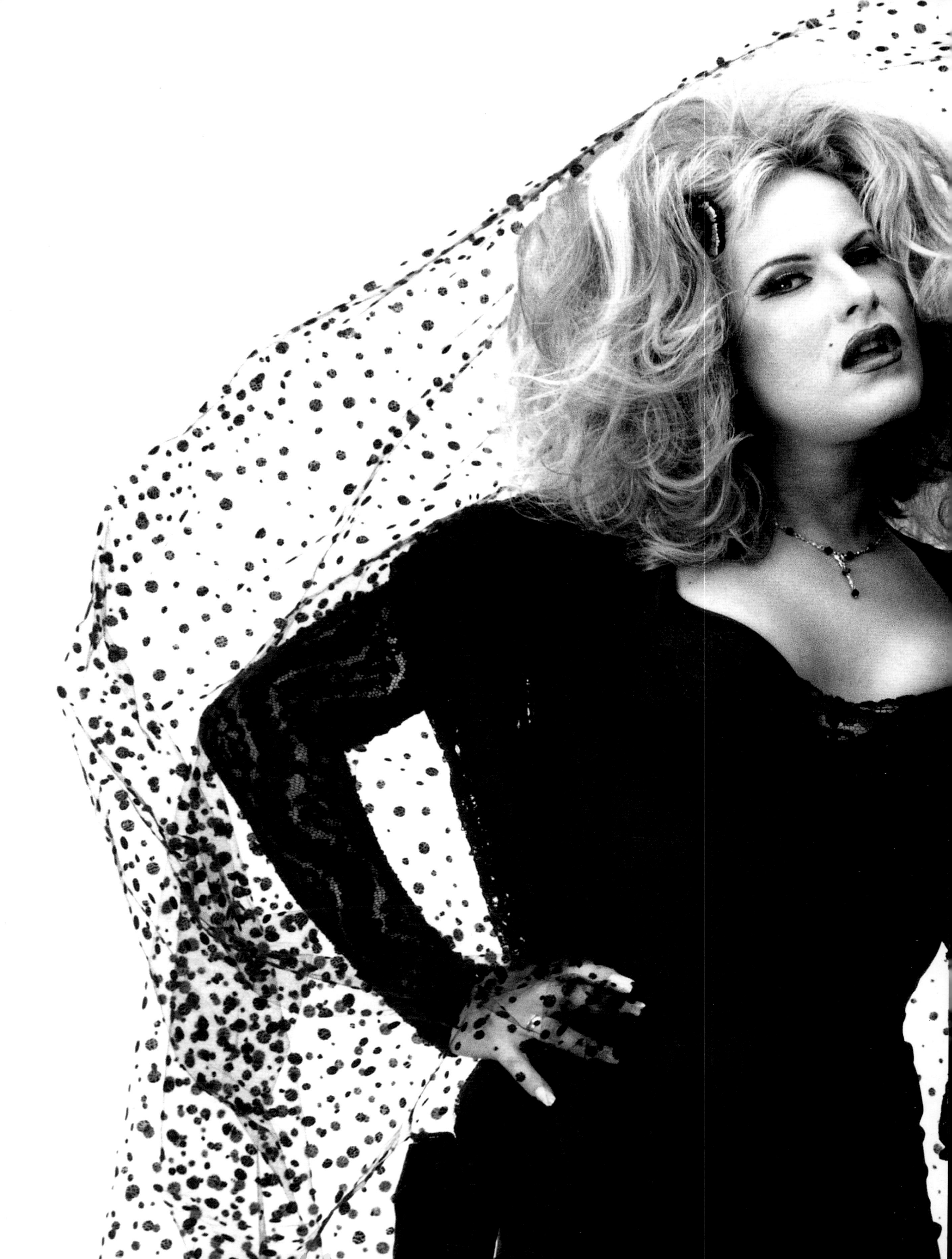

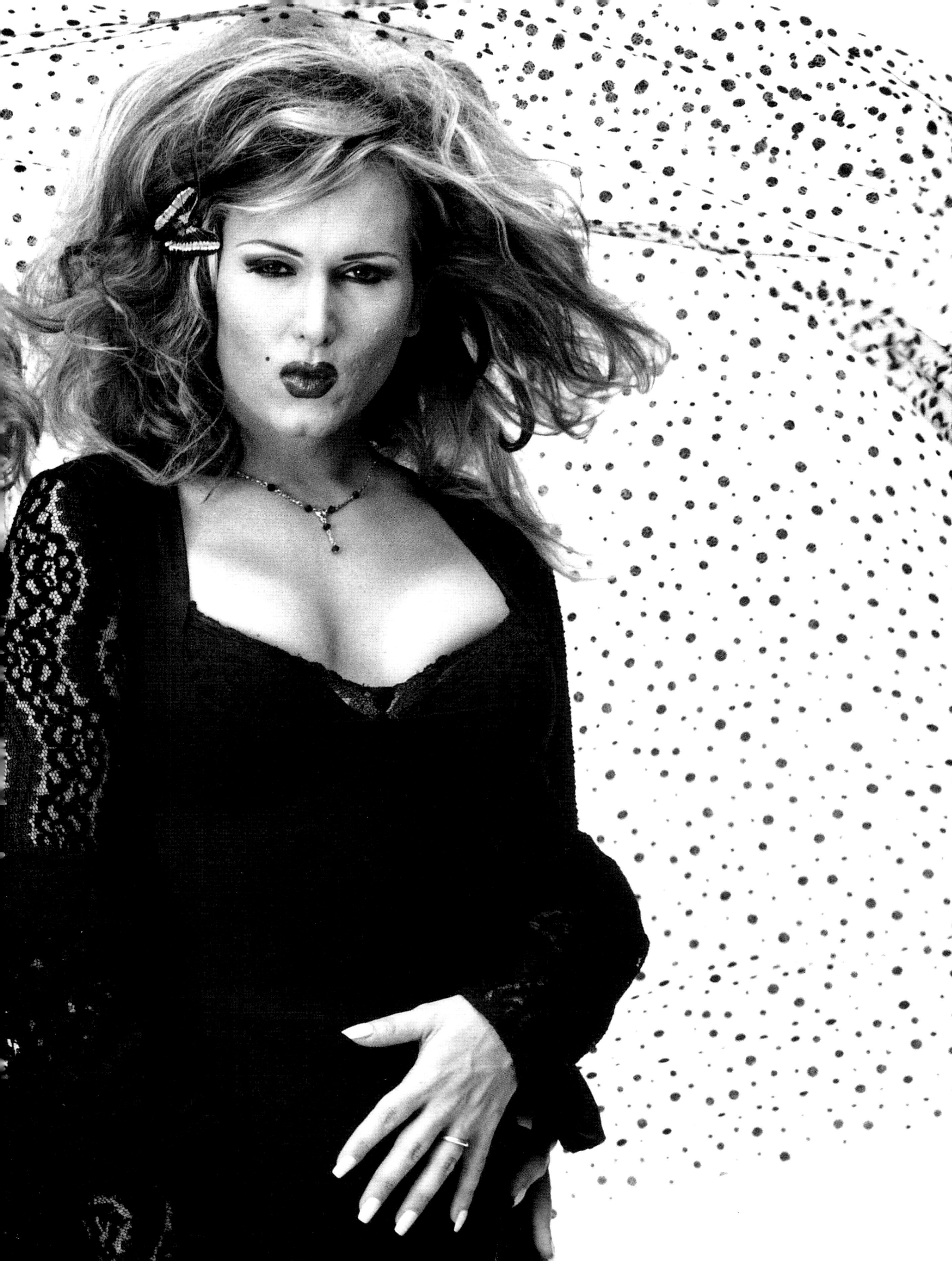

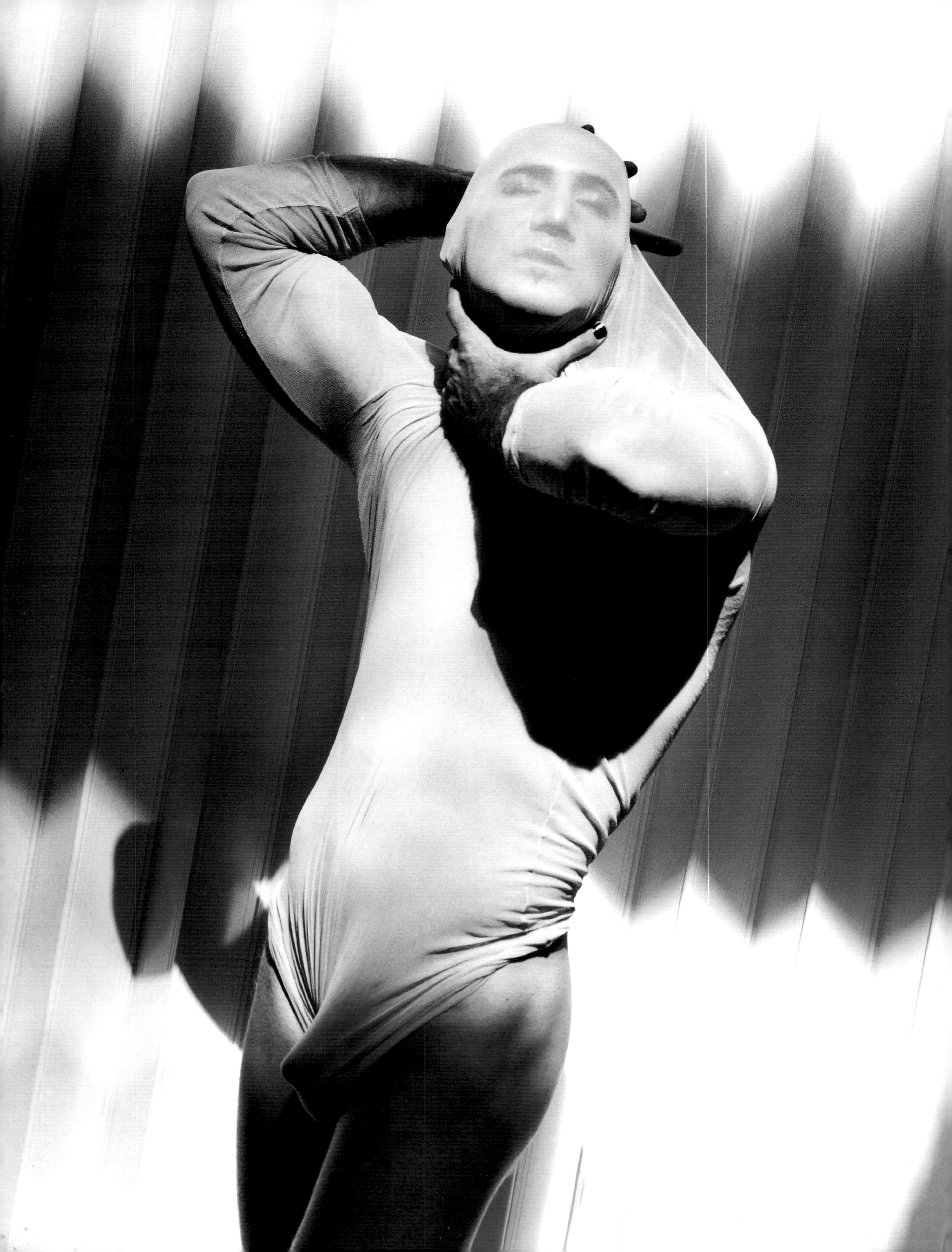

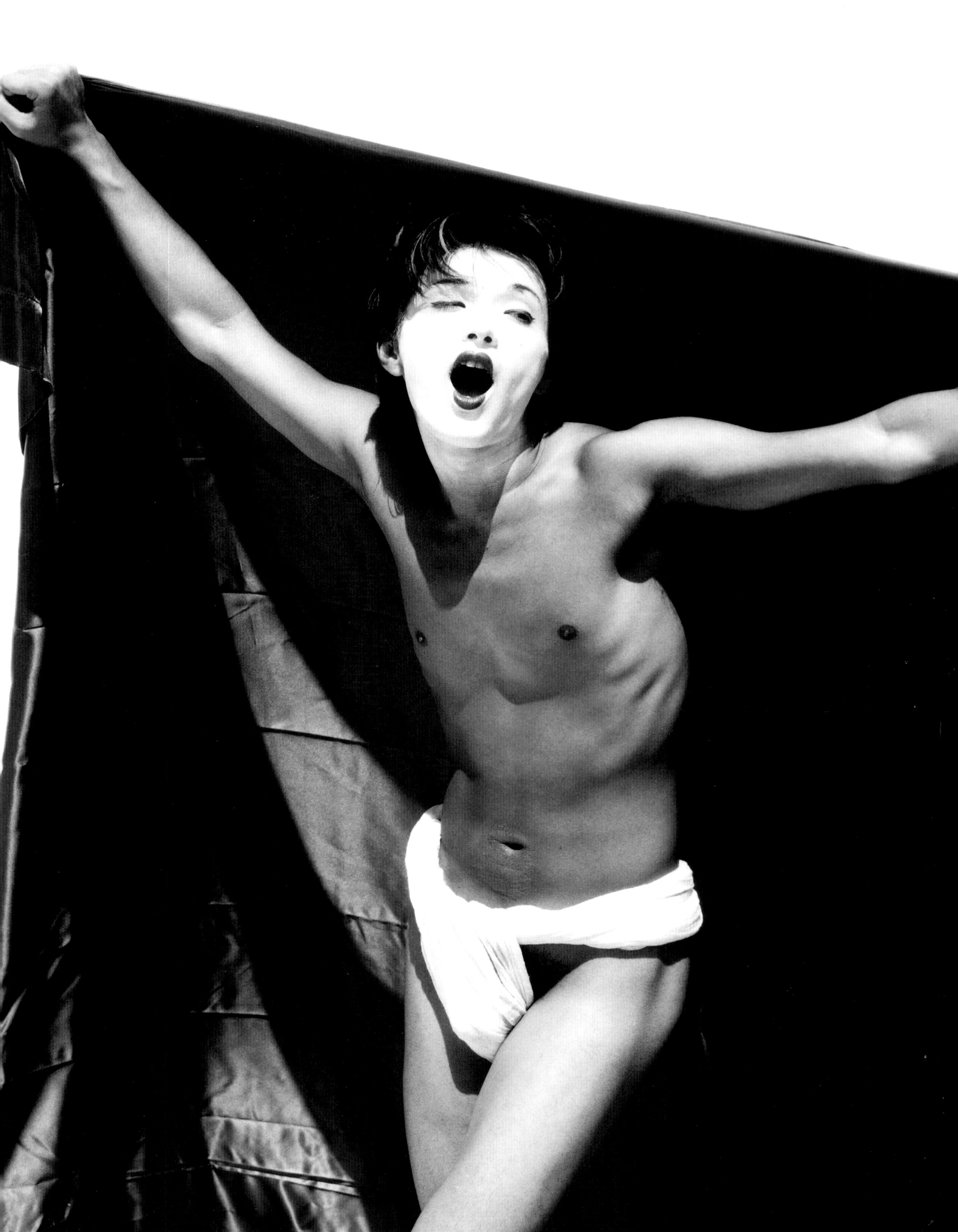

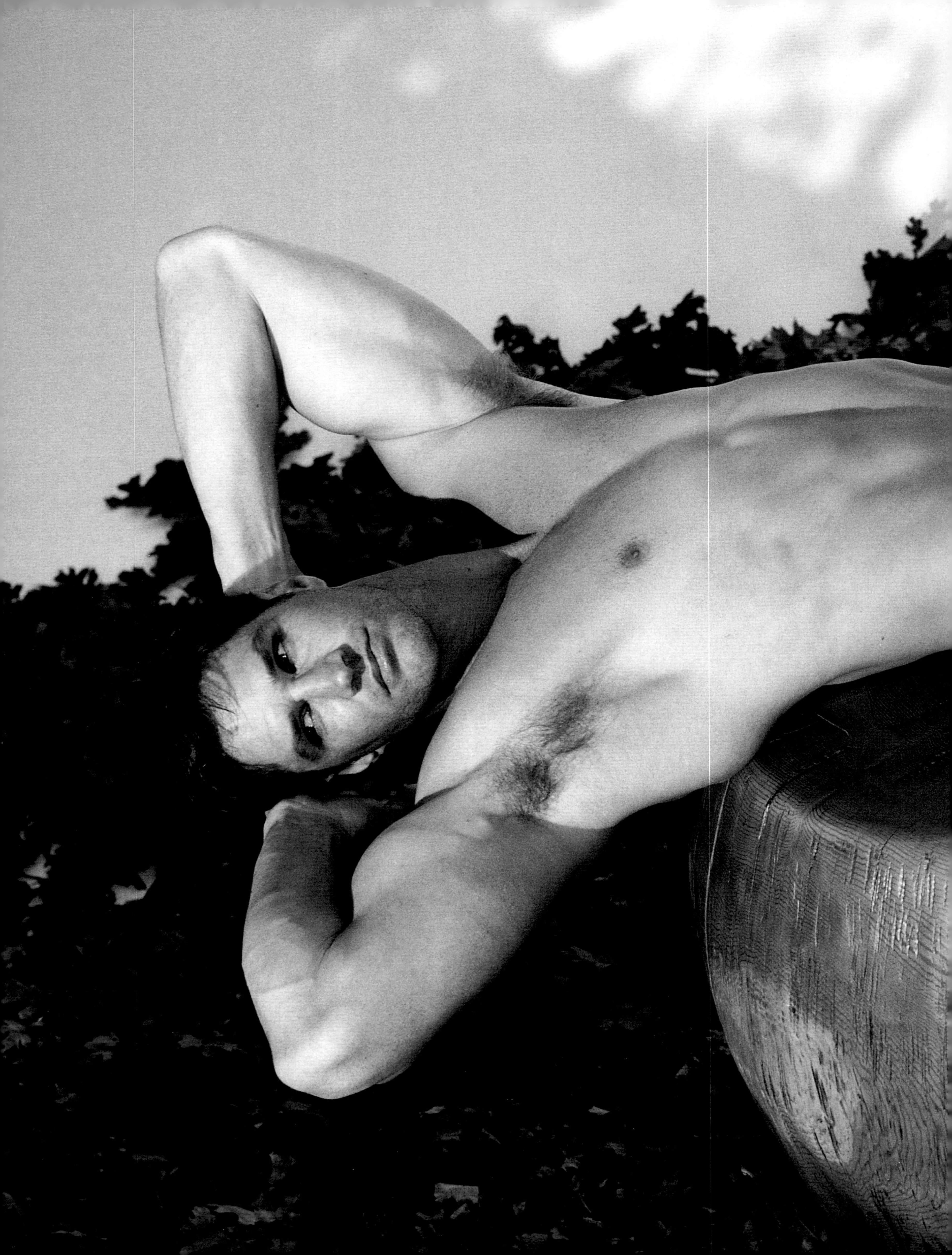

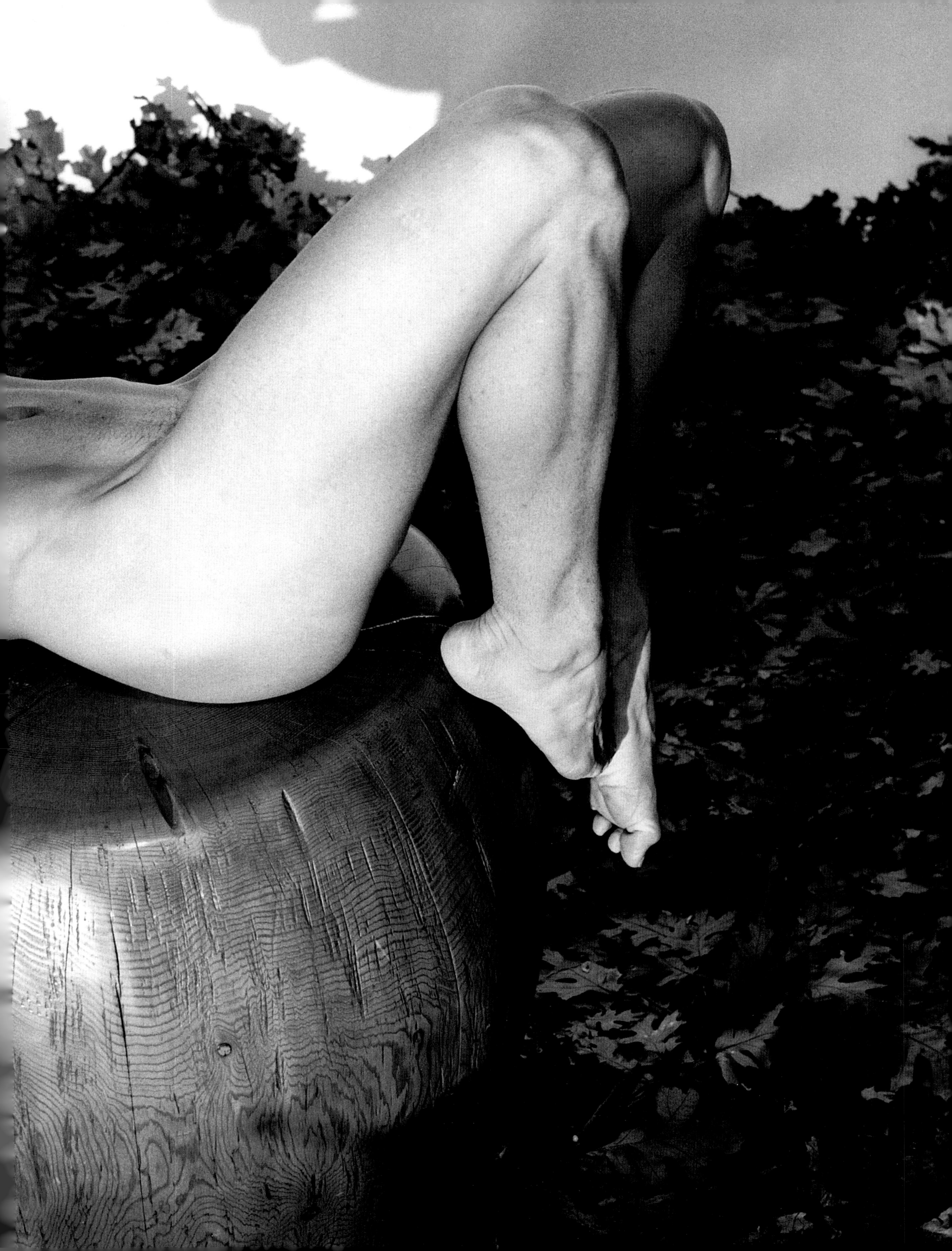

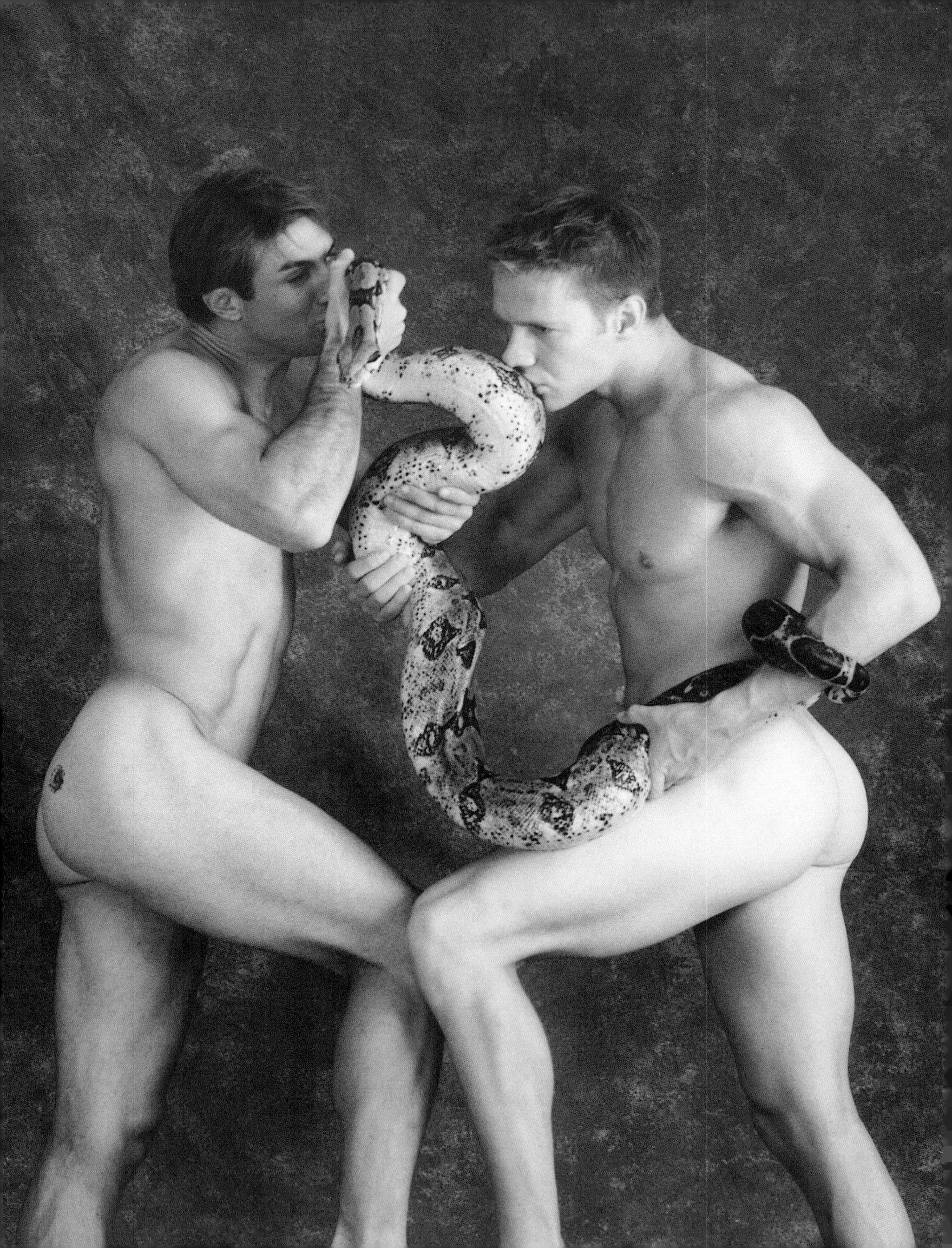

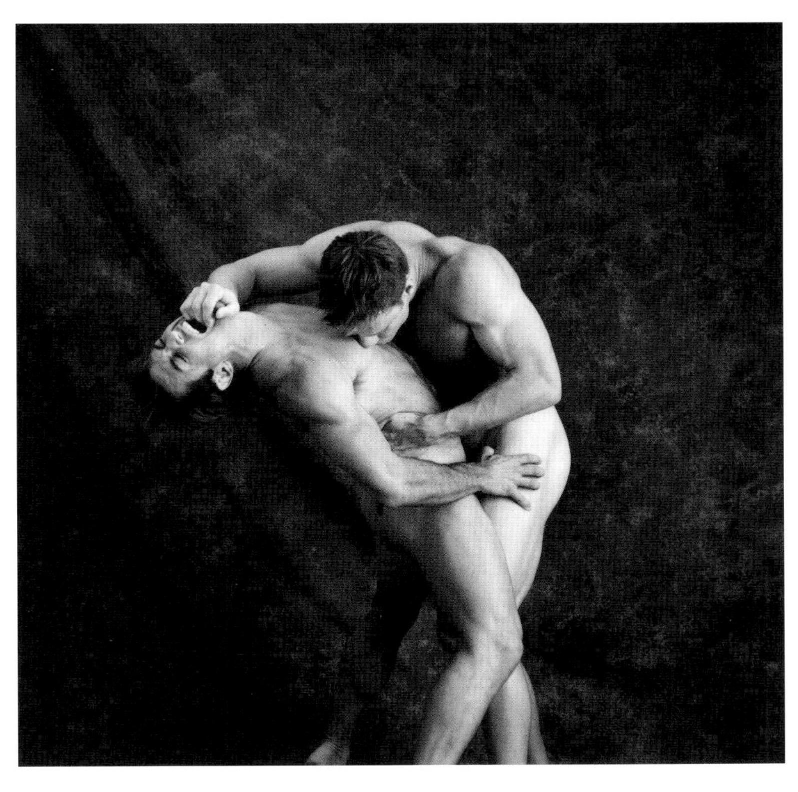

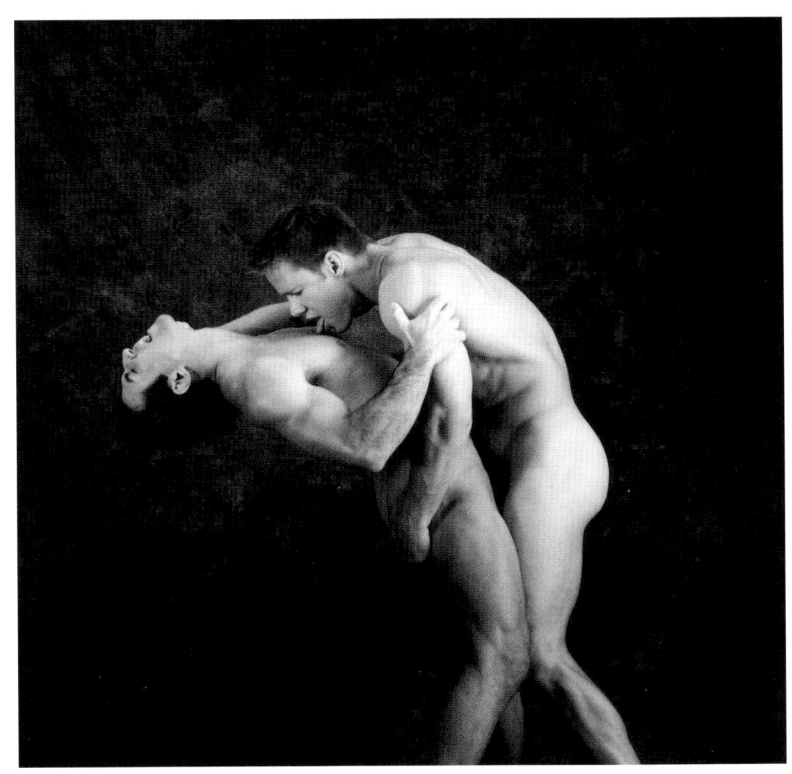

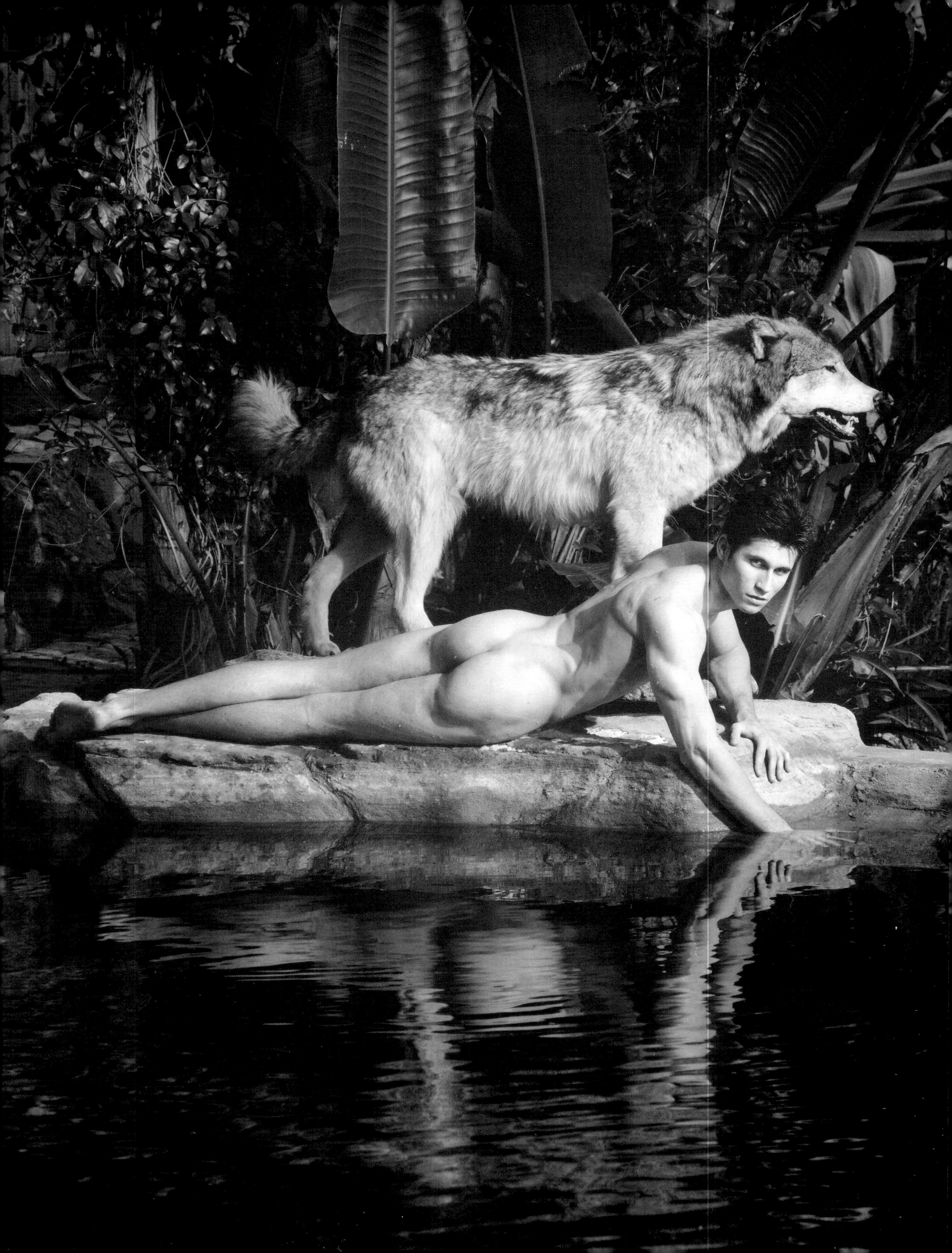

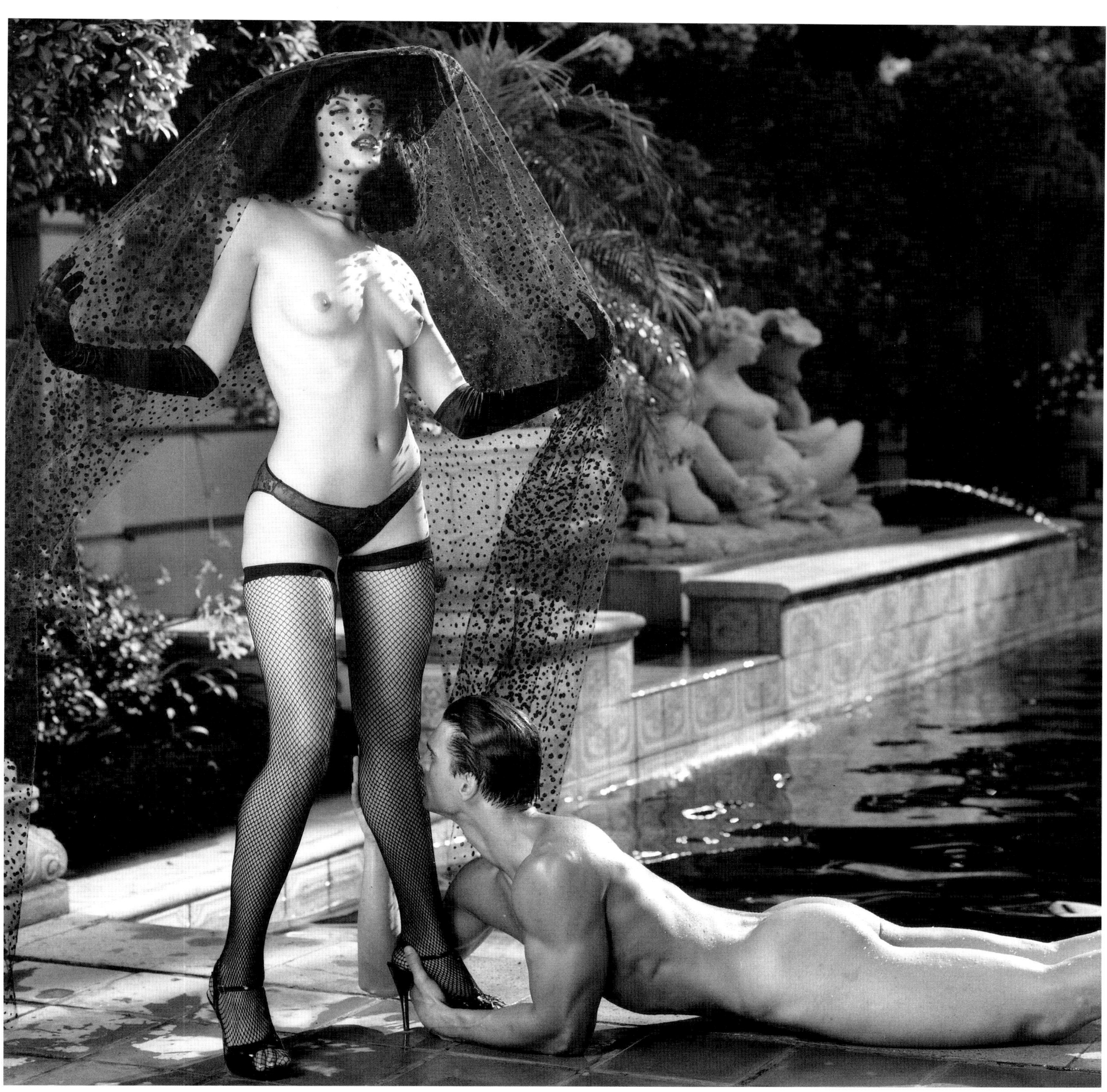

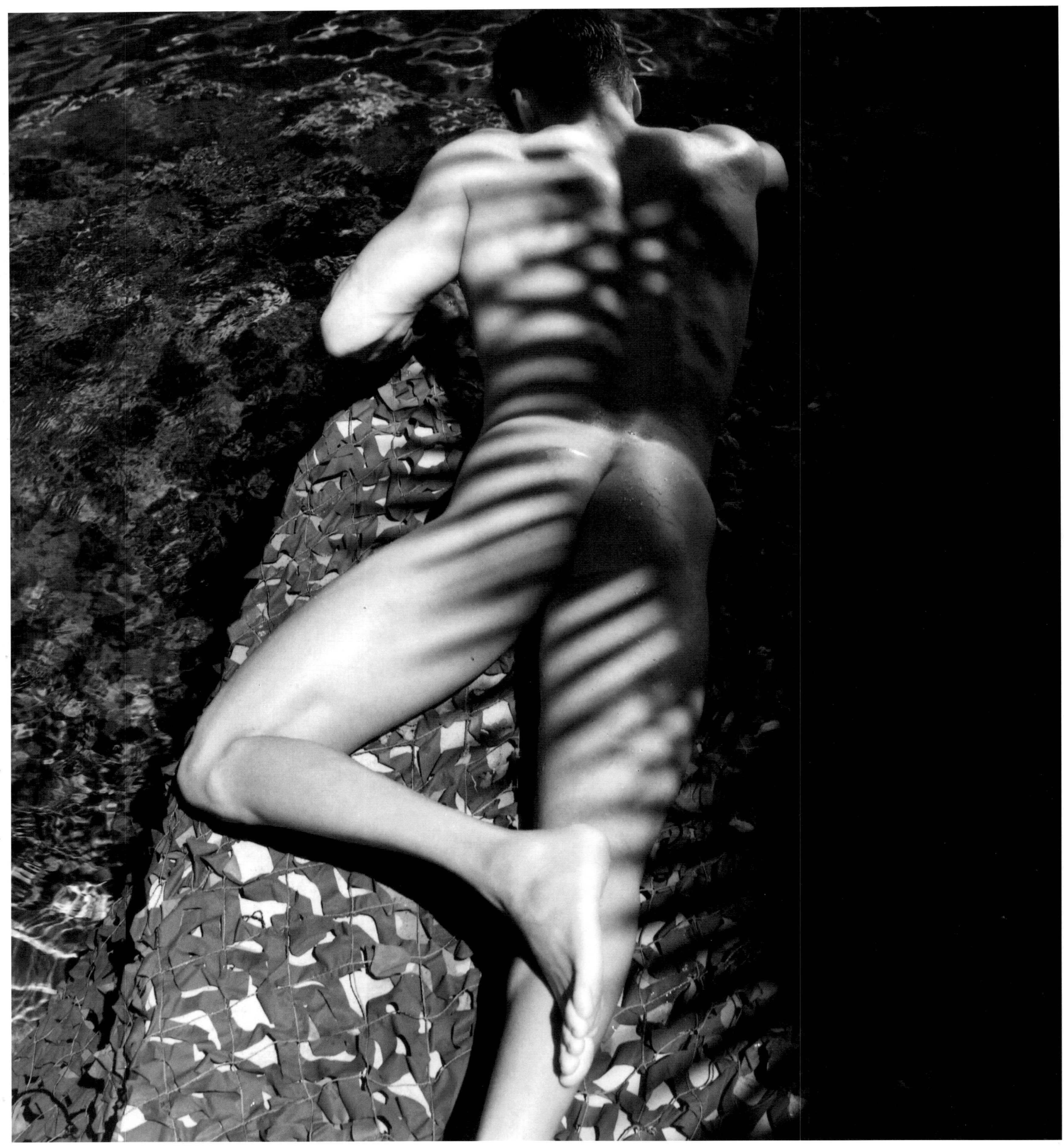

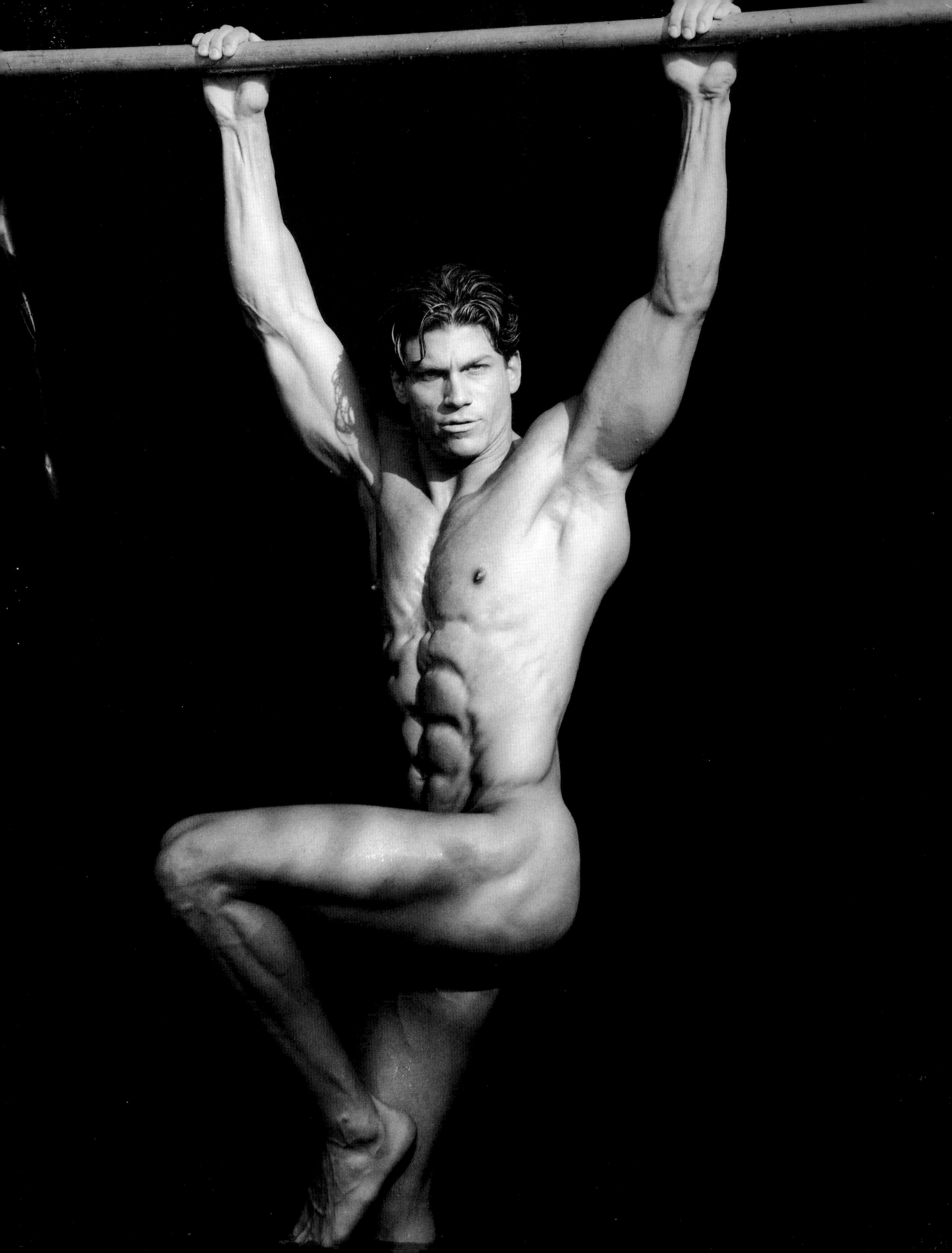

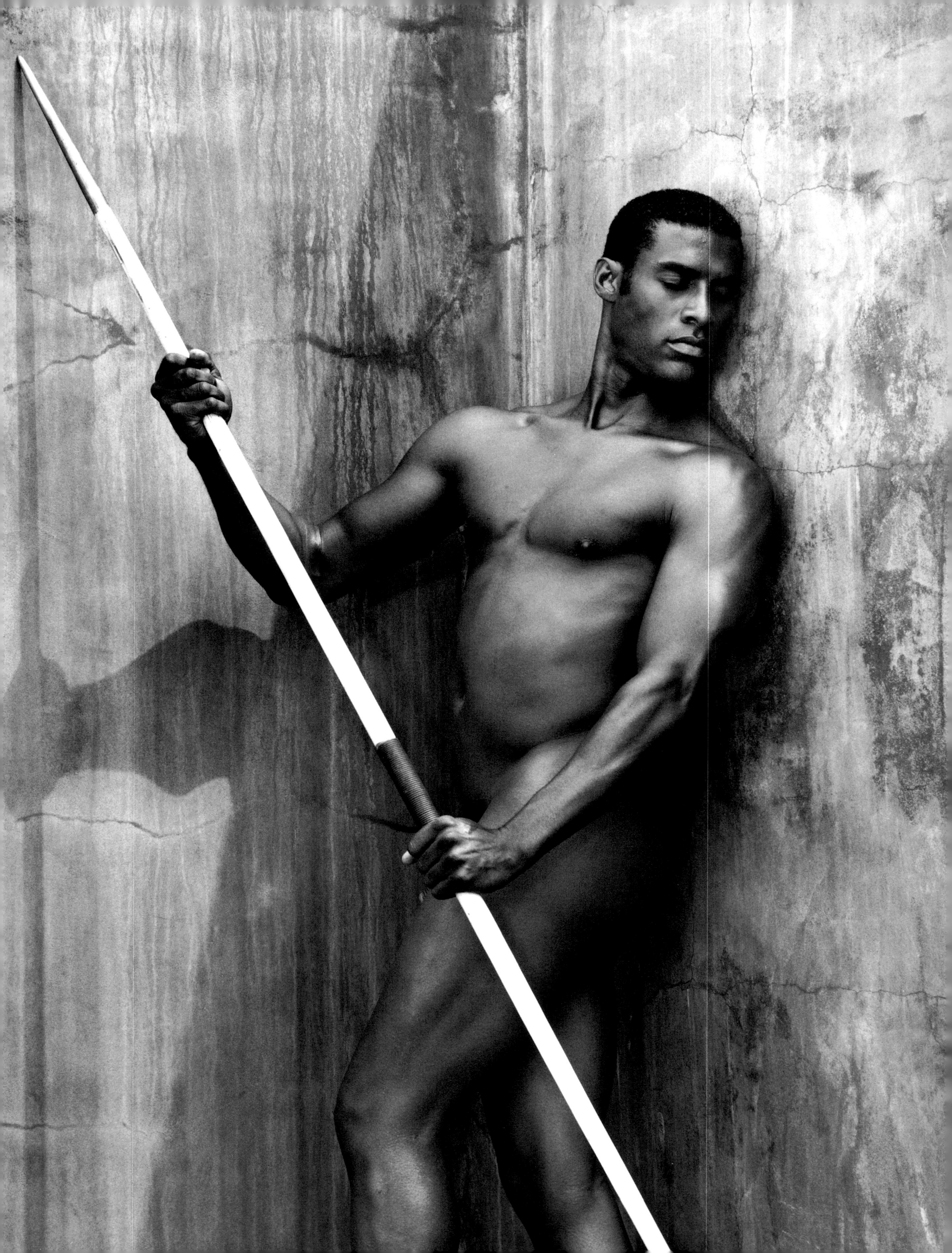

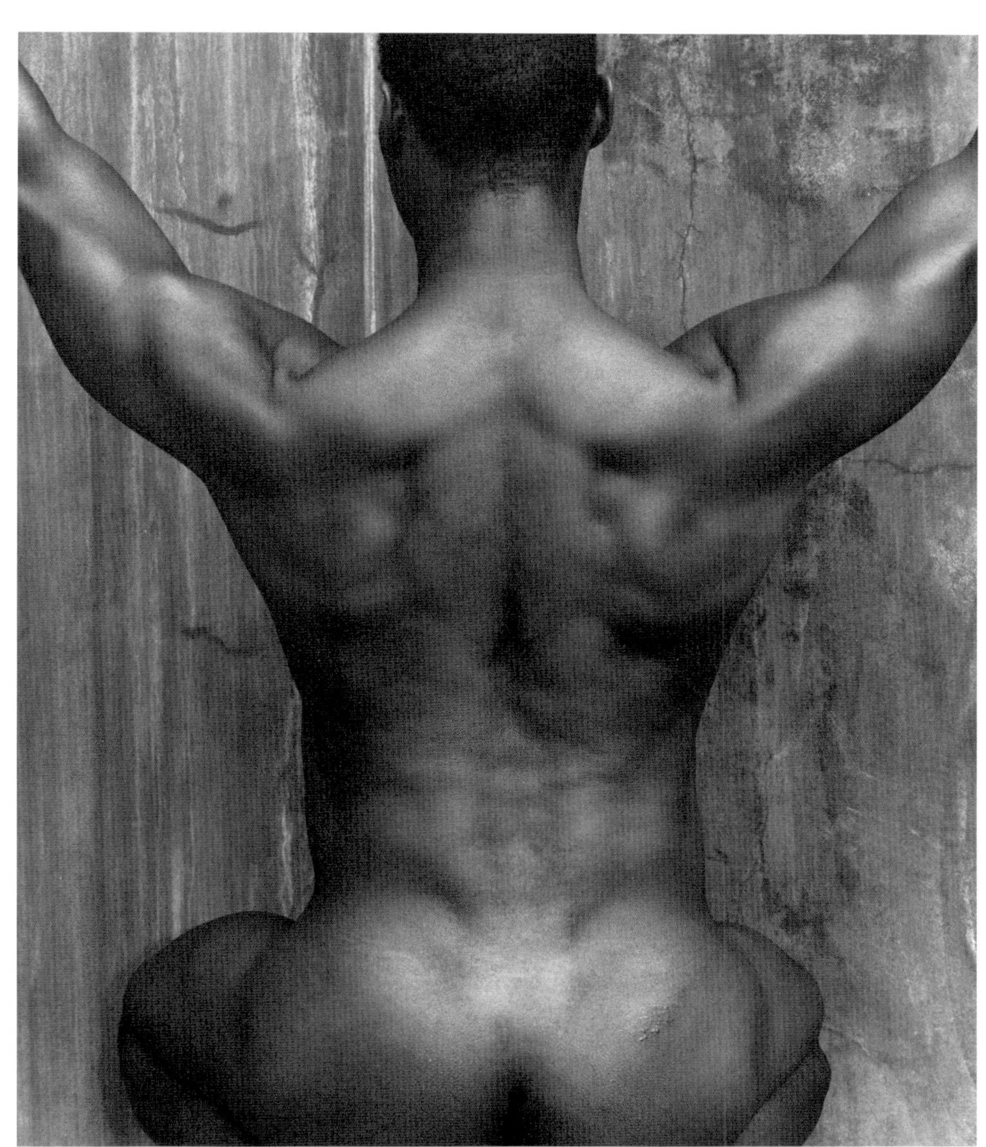

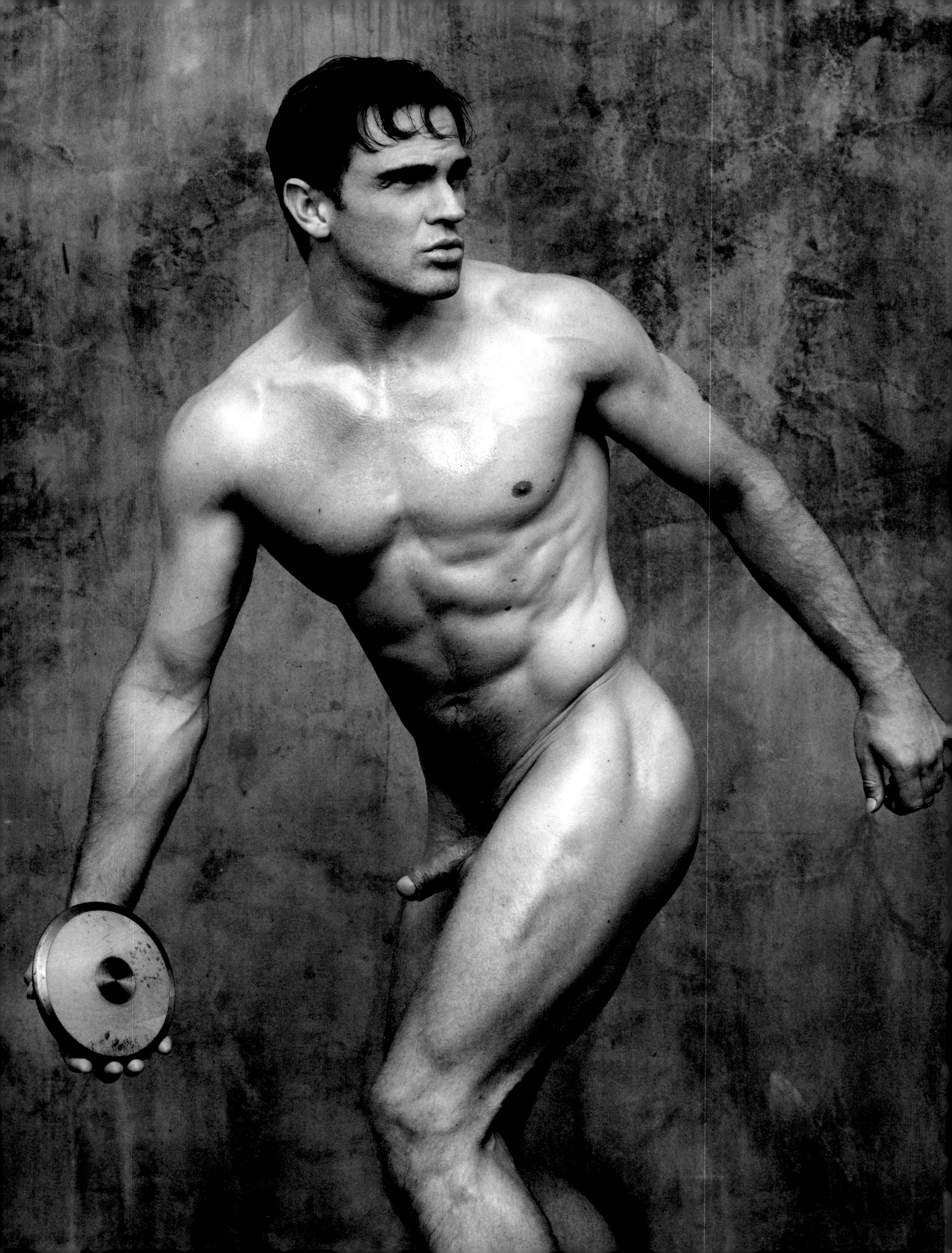

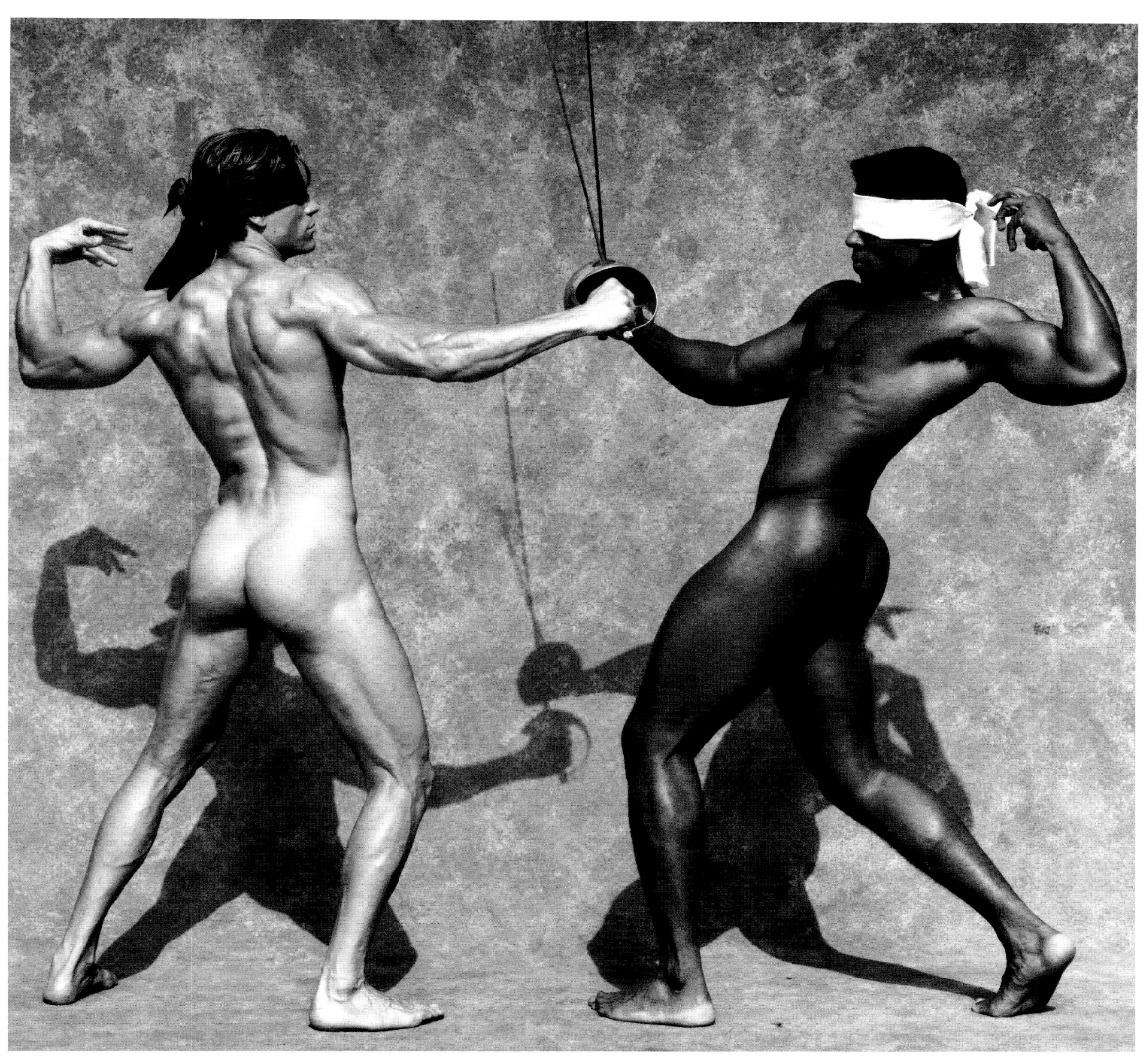

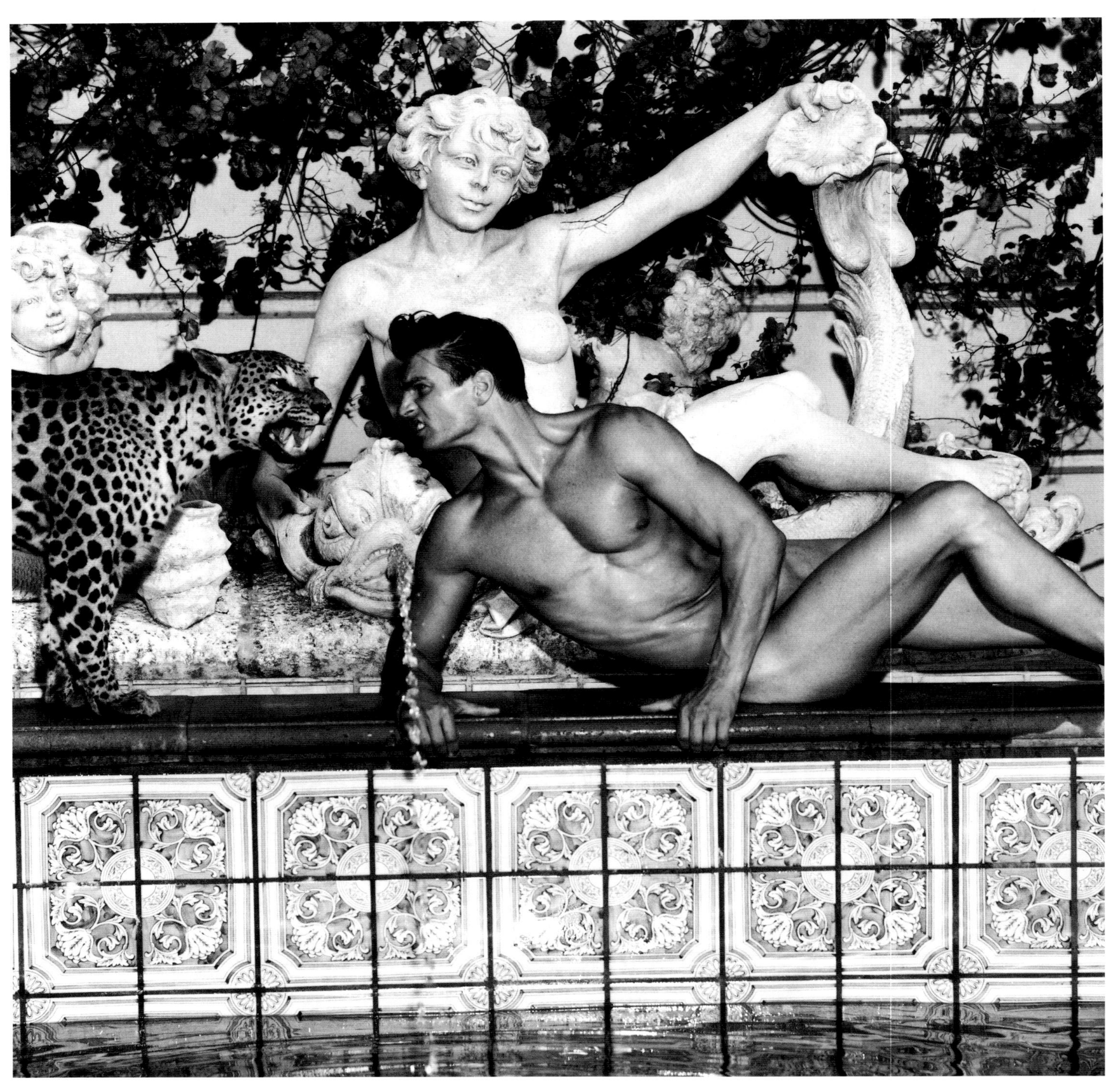

Tom Bianchi Hollywood Photographer

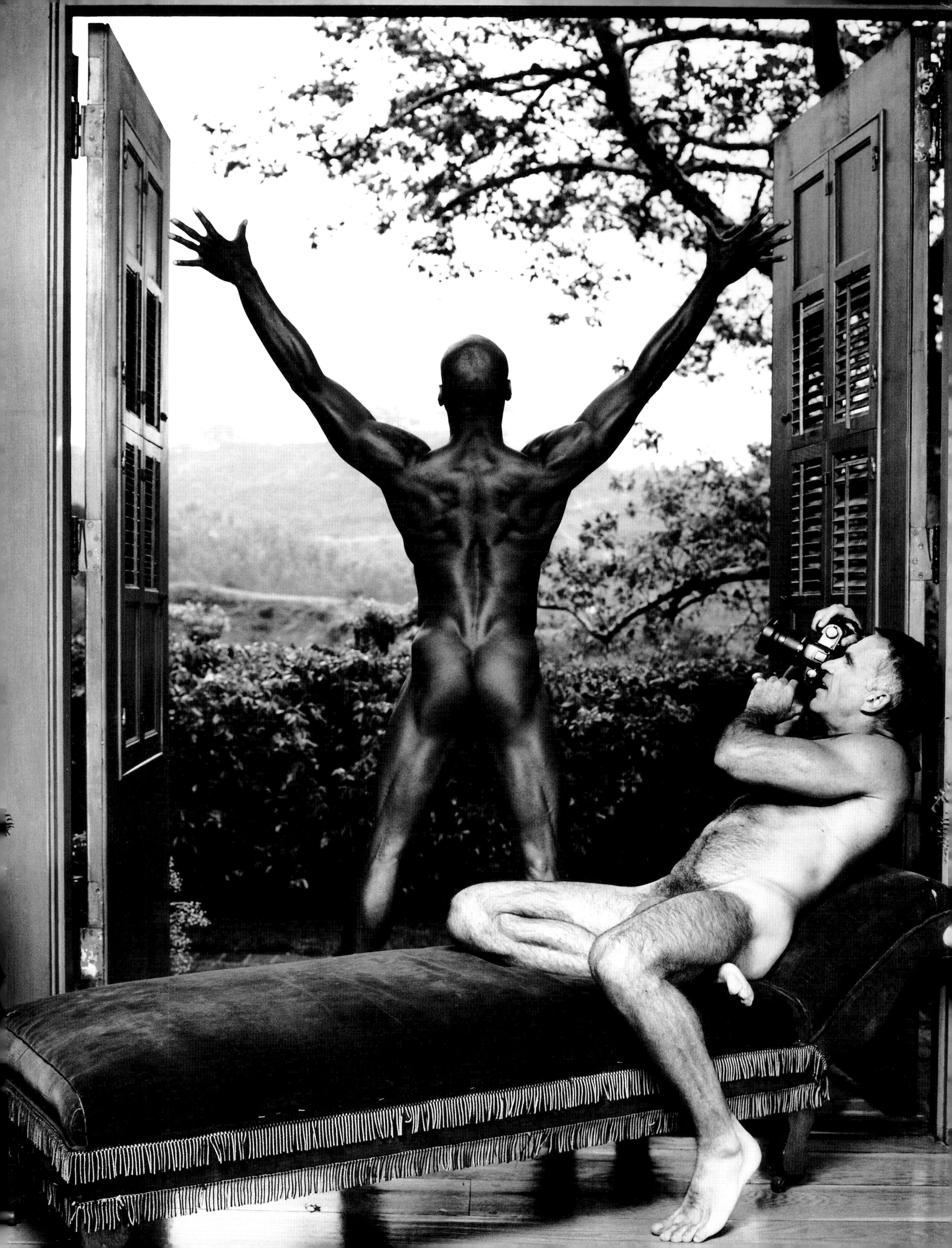

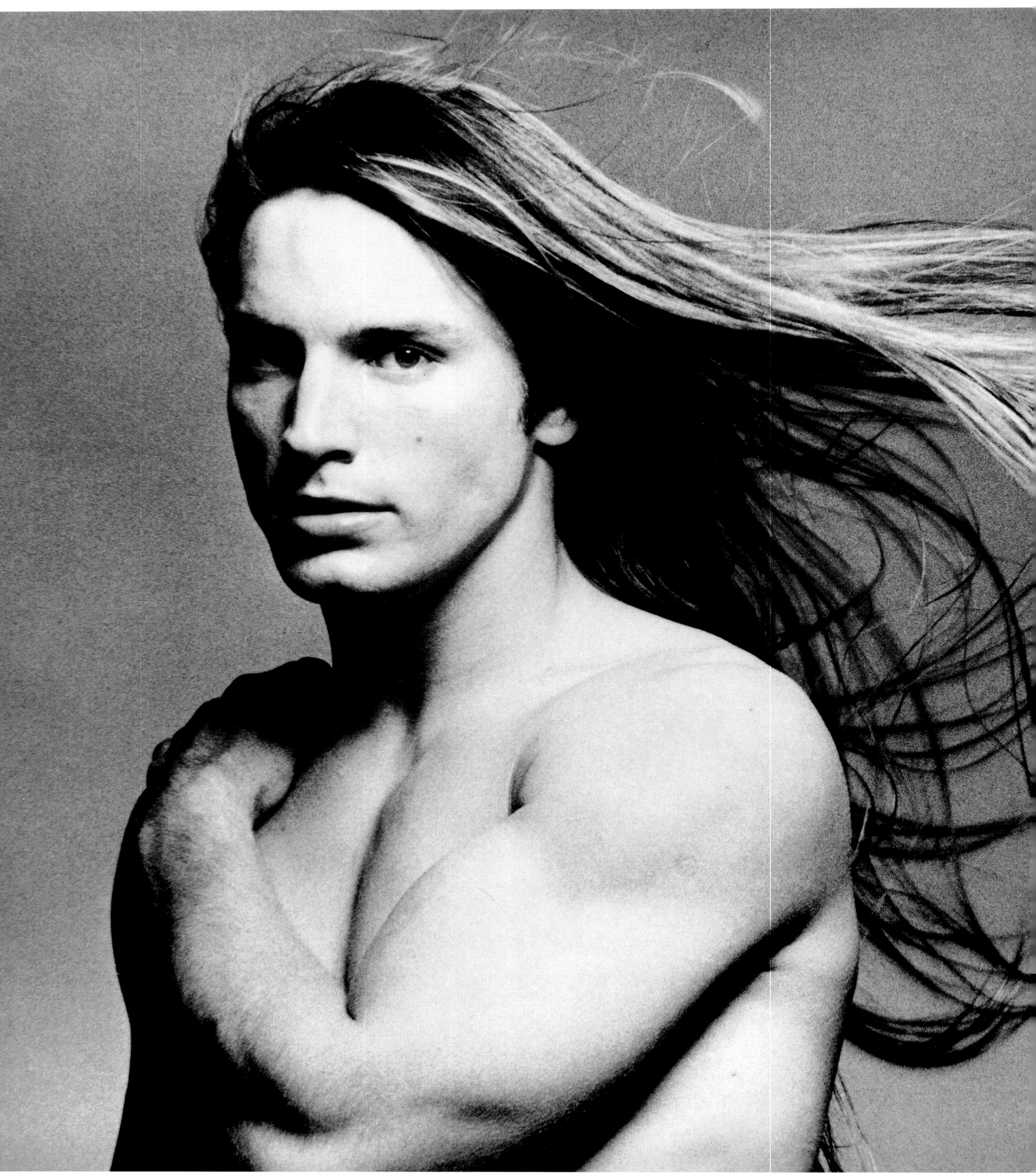

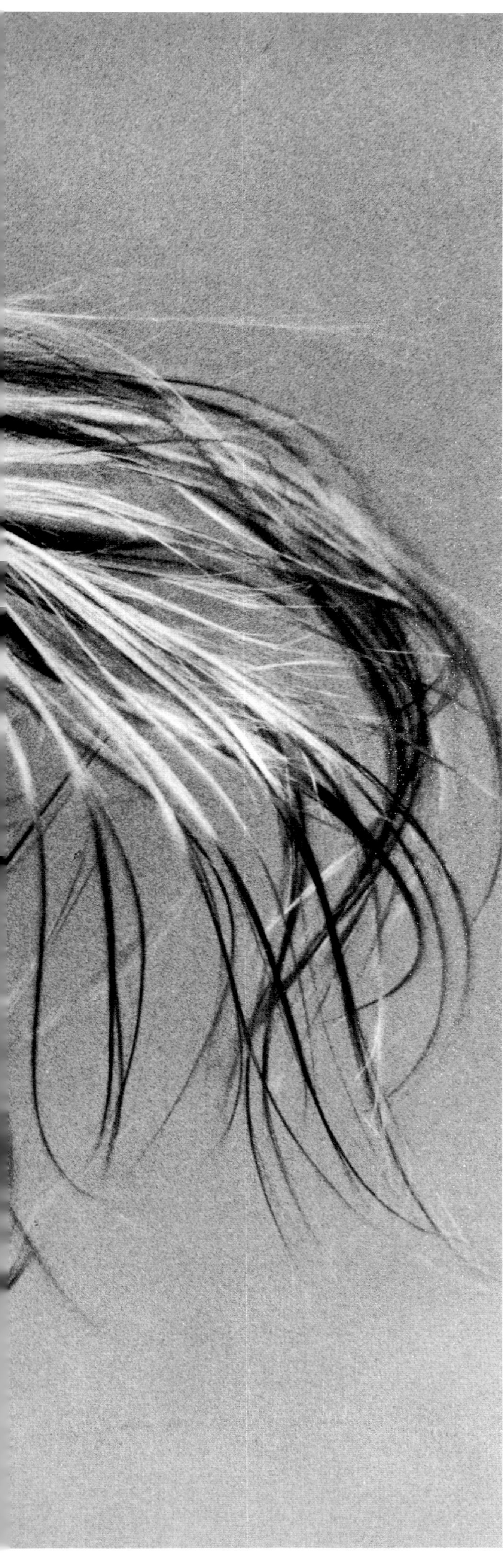

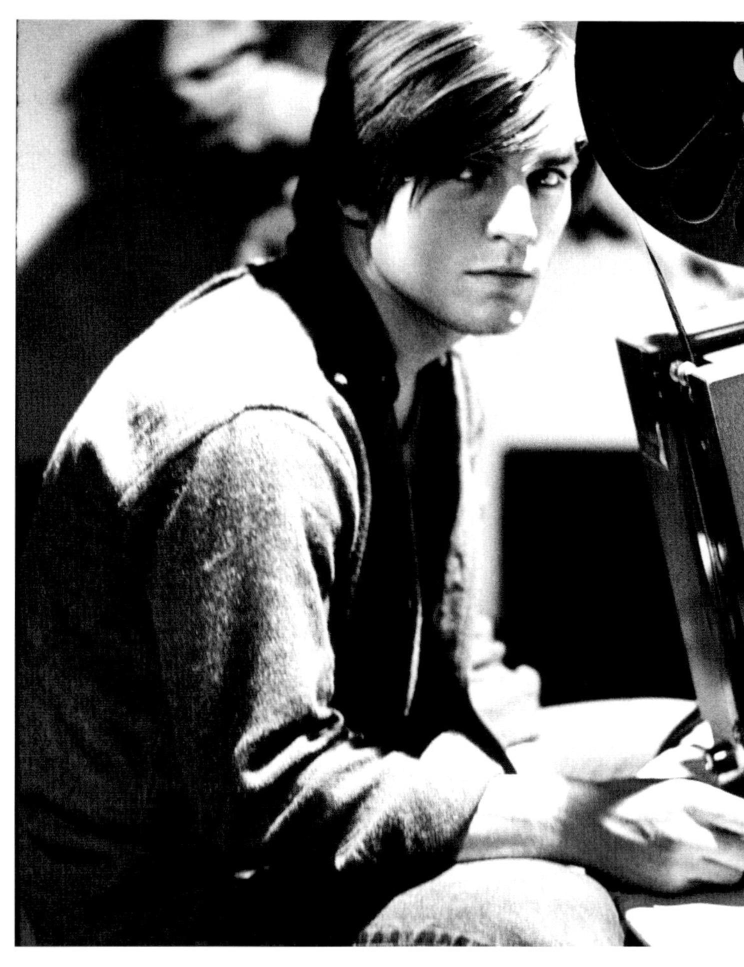

Joe Dallesandro in Midnight Cowboy

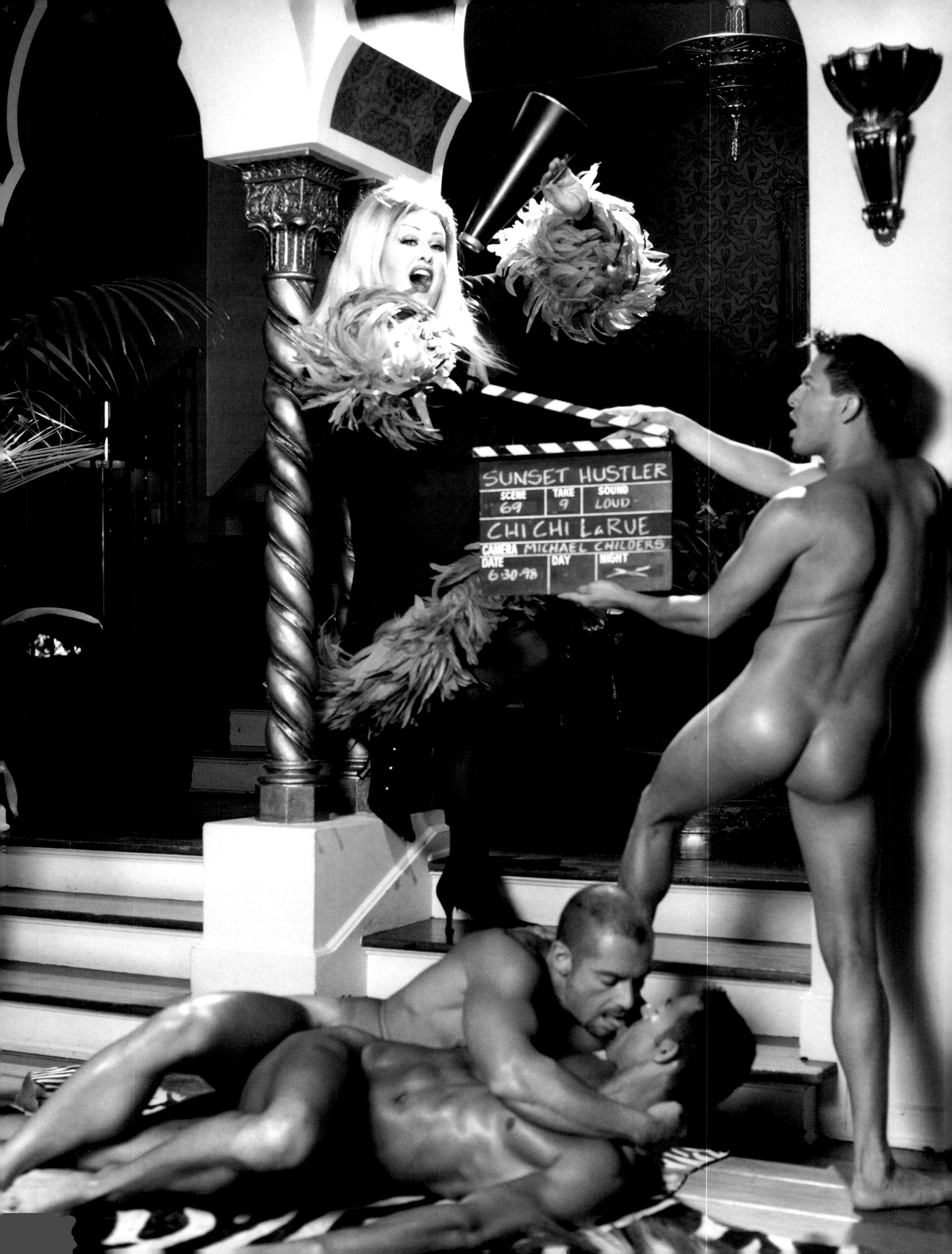

SUNSET HUSTLER
SCENE 69
TAKE 9
SOUND LOUD
CHI CHI LaRUE
CAMERA MICHAEL CHILDERS
DATE 6-30-98
DAY
NIGHT

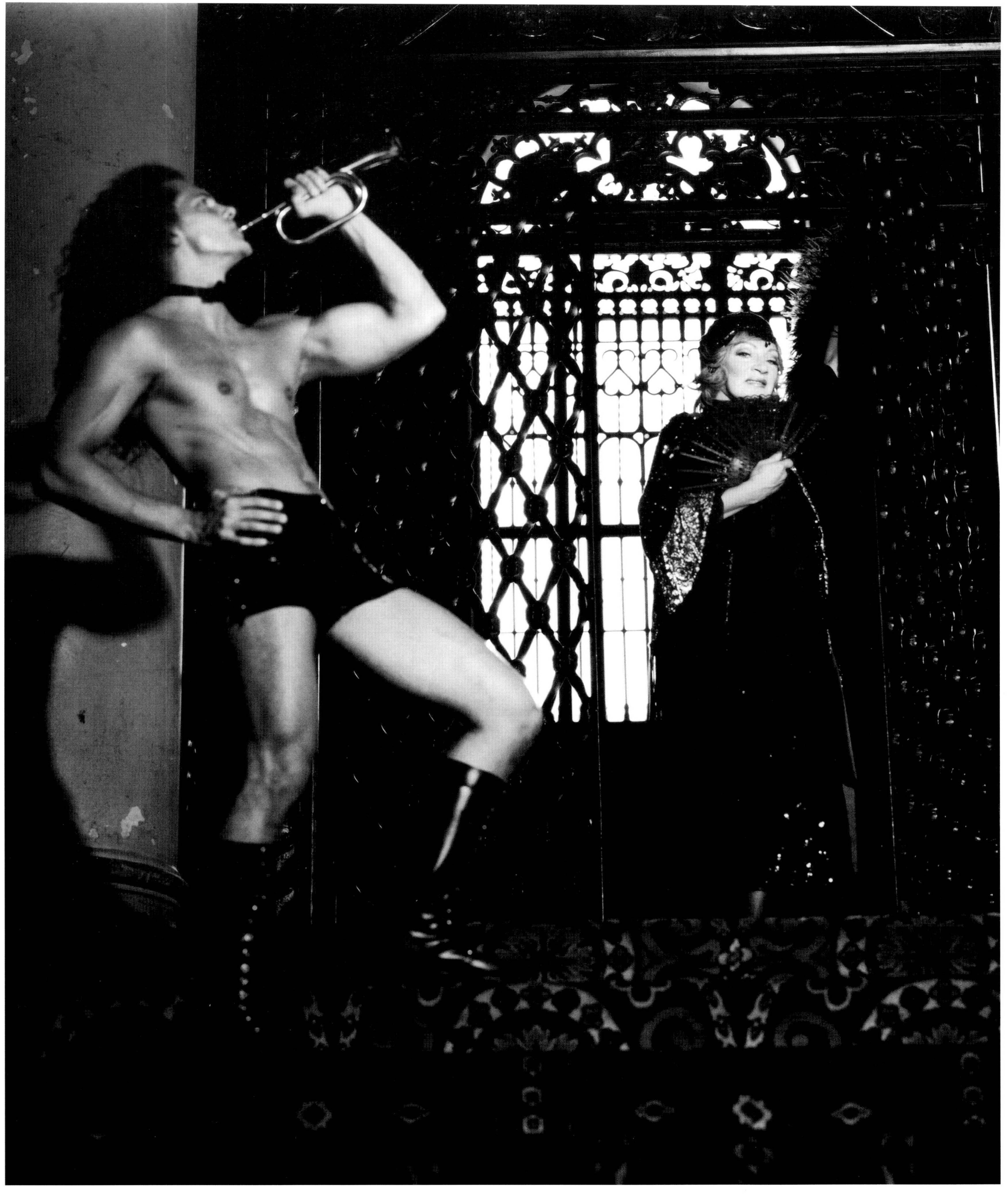

<Chi Chi LaRue Hollywood Porn Director   Holly Woodlawn as Norma Desmond

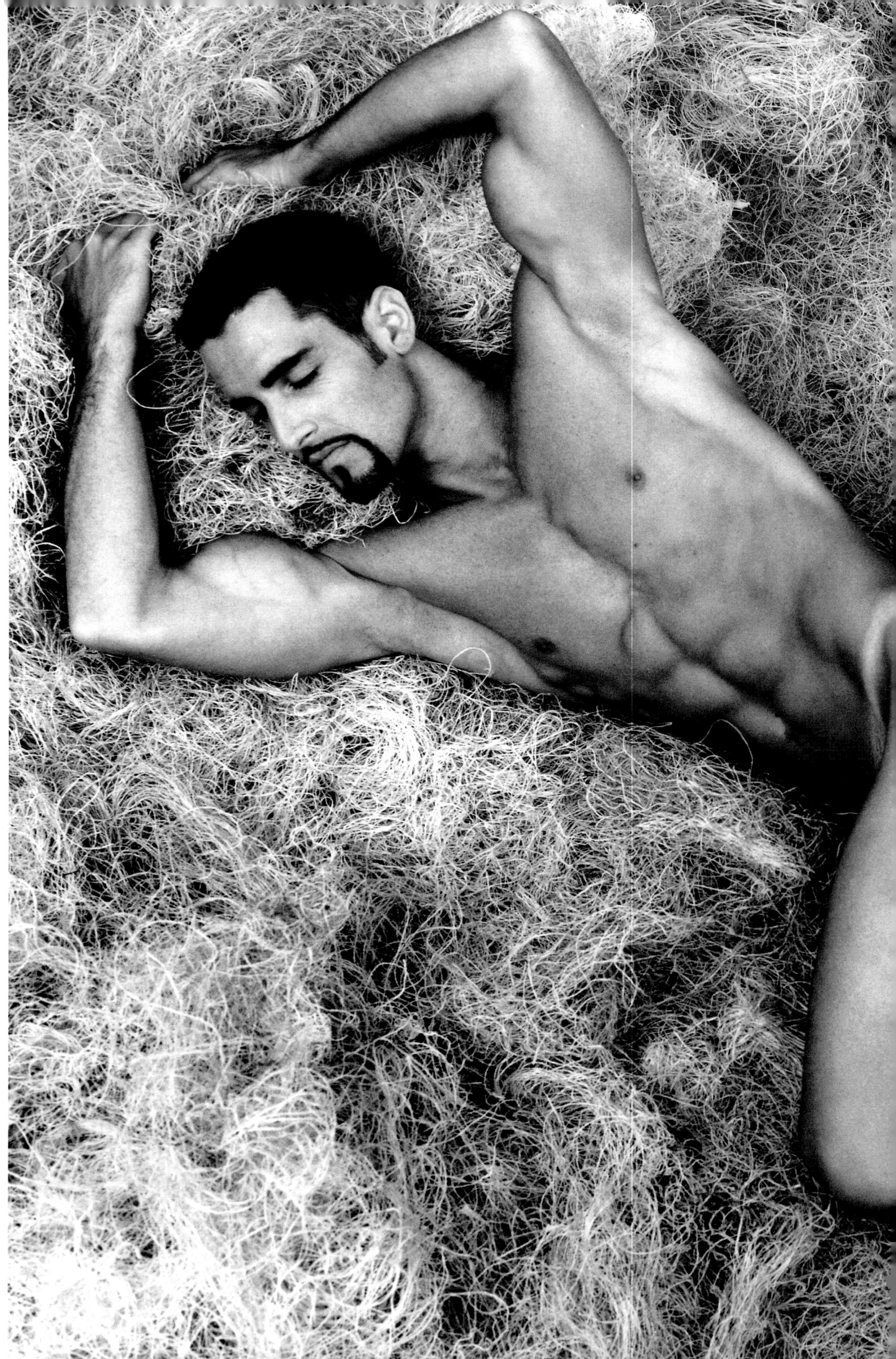

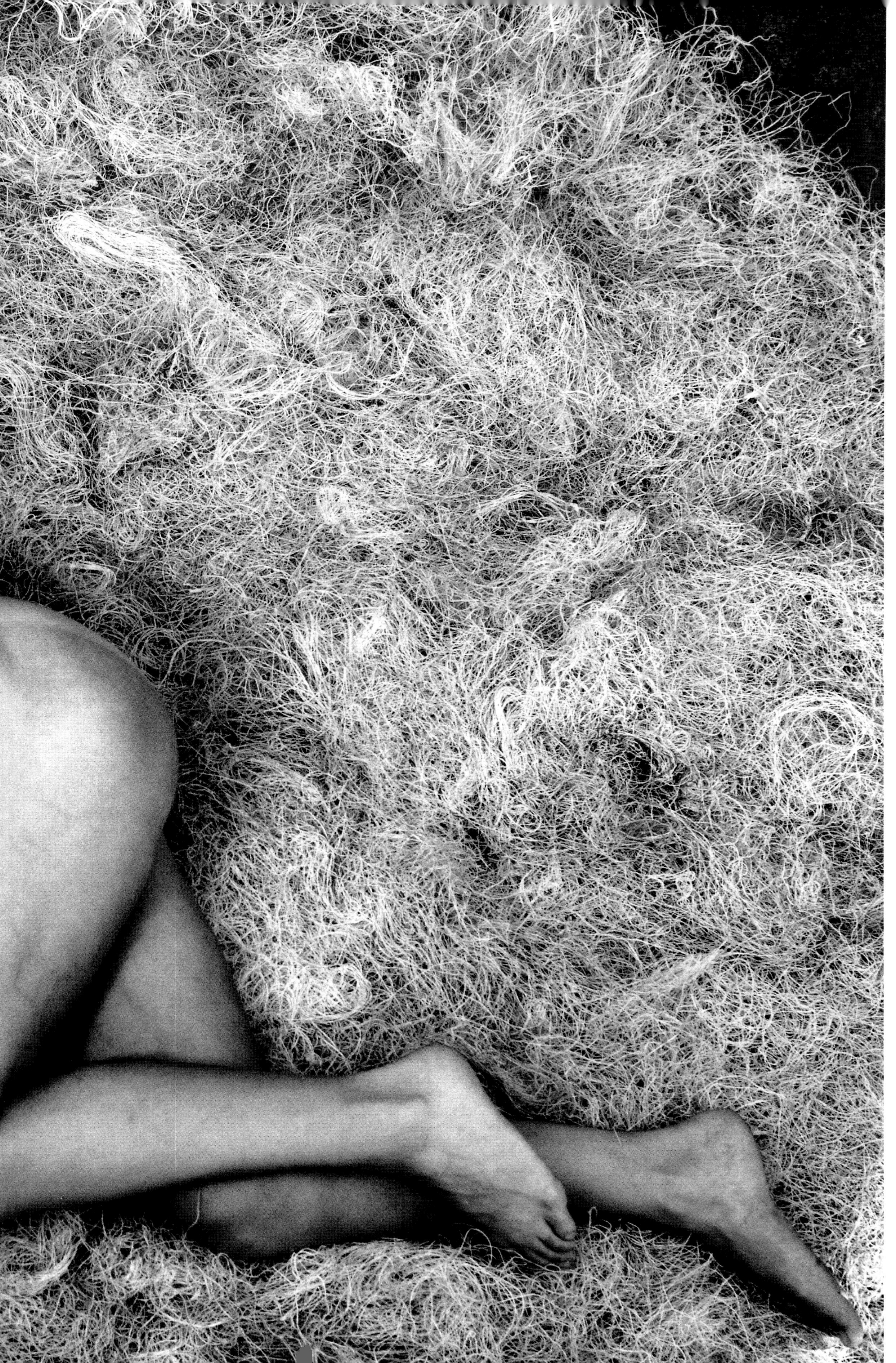

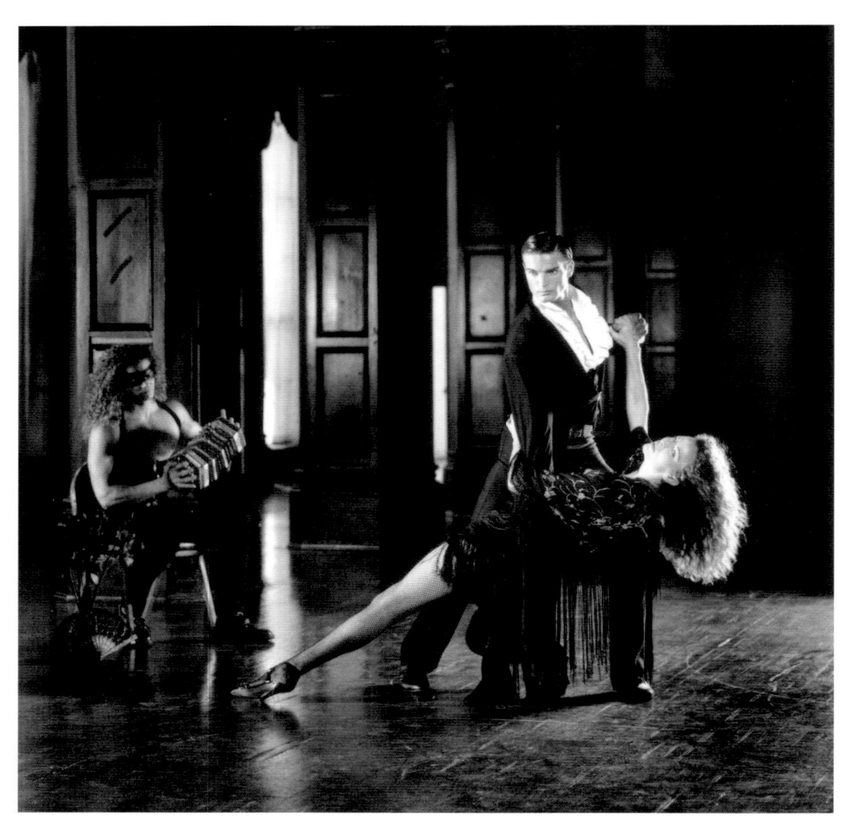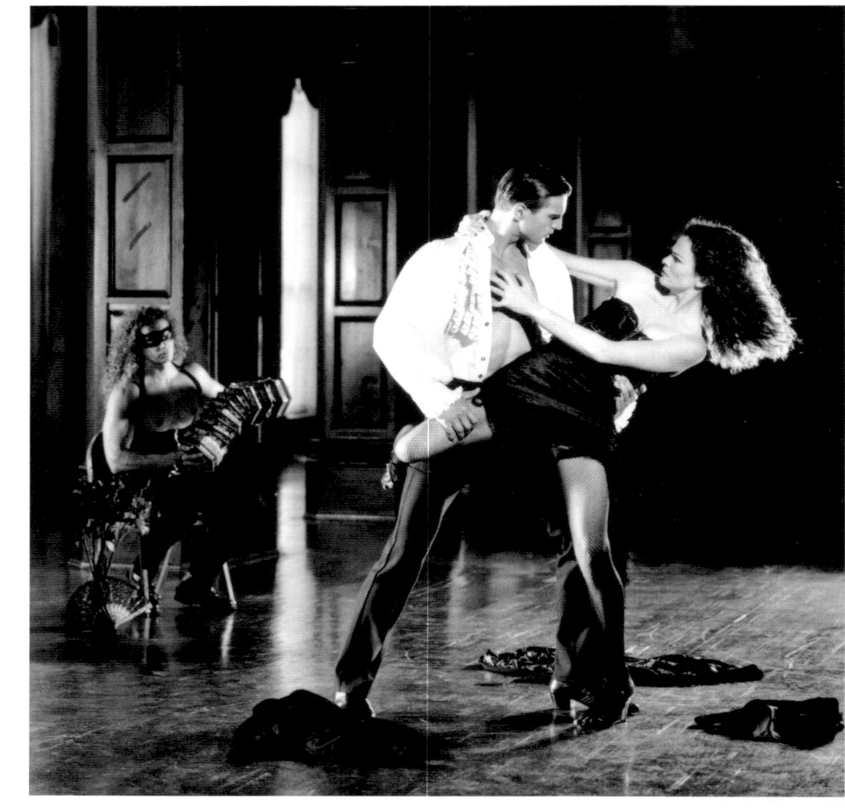

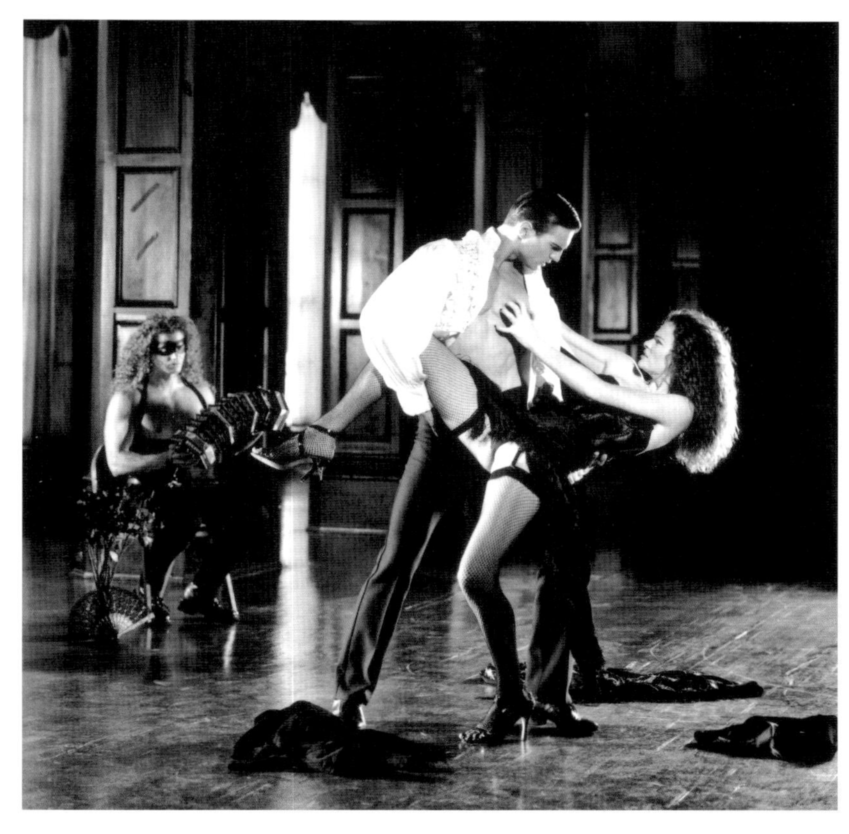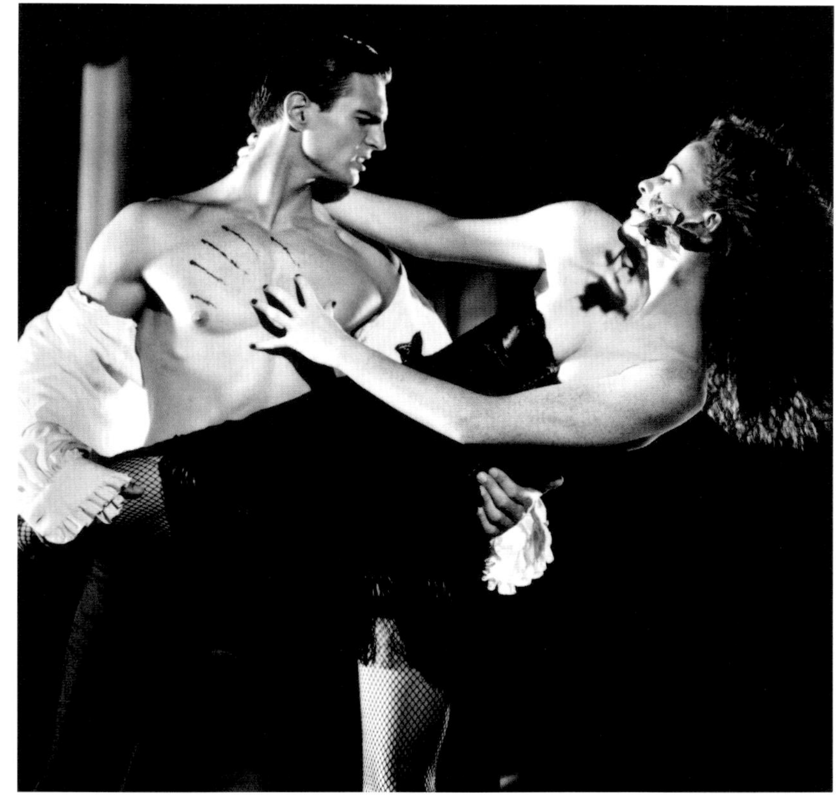

Last tango in Hollywood

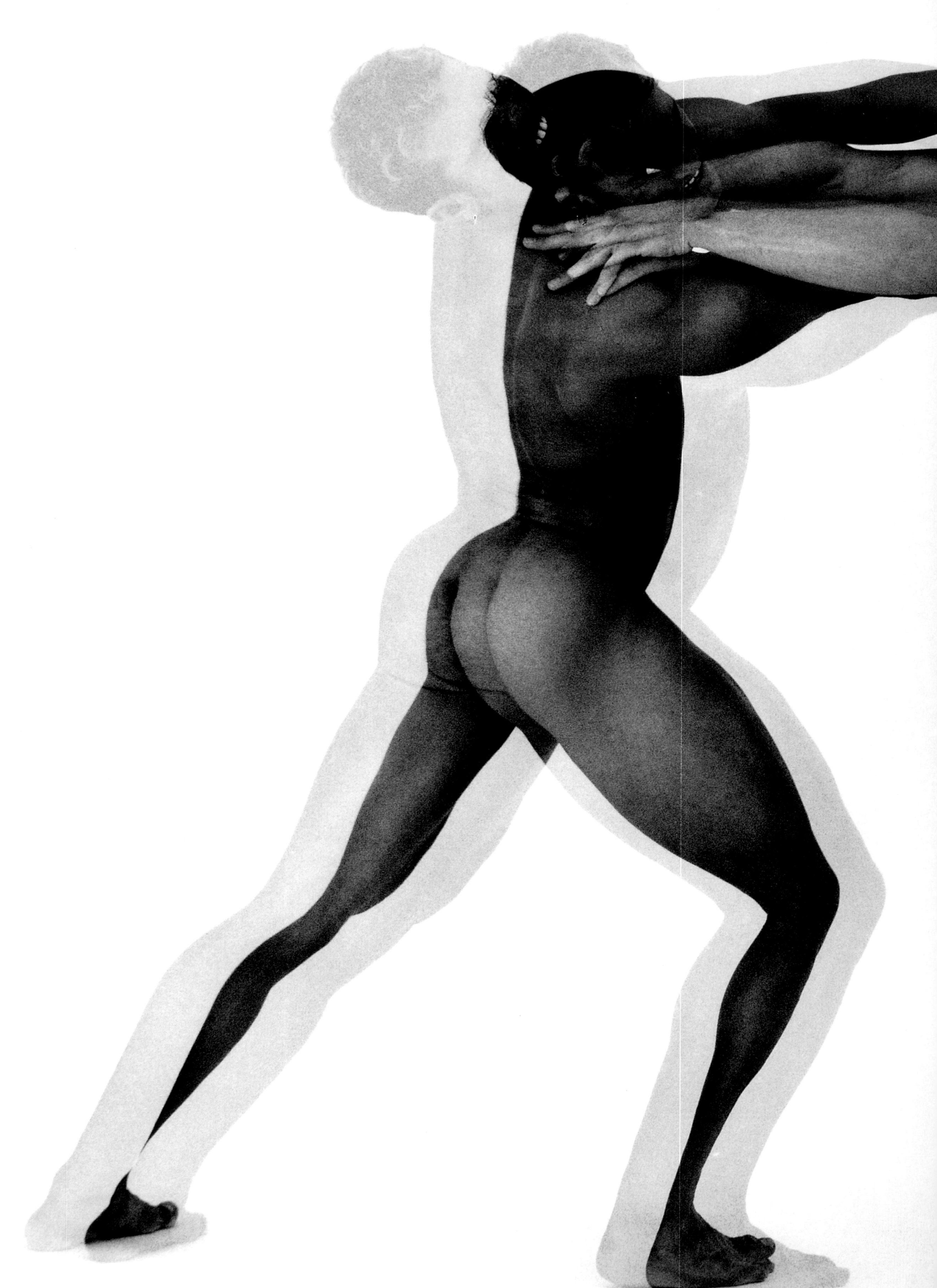

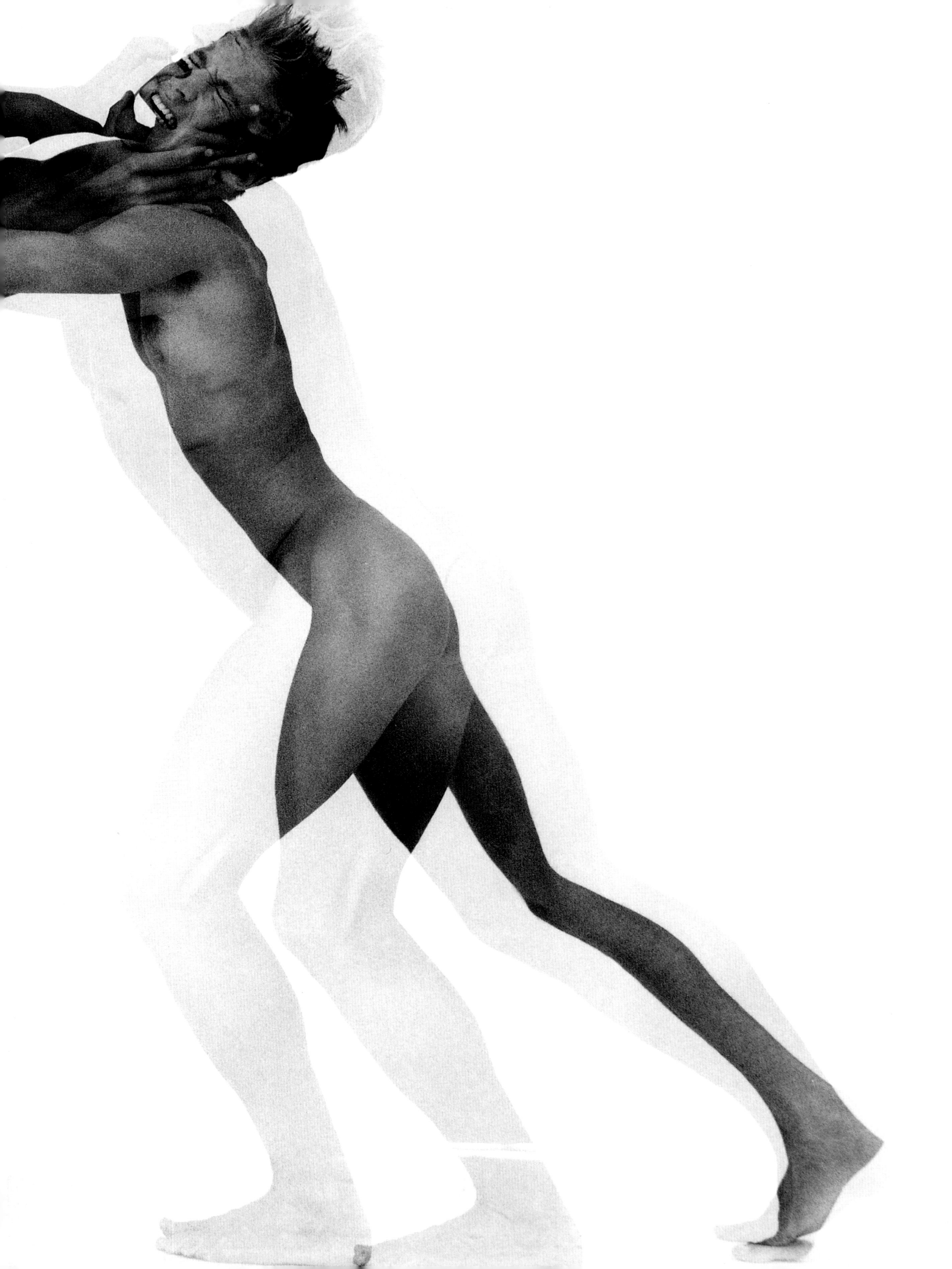

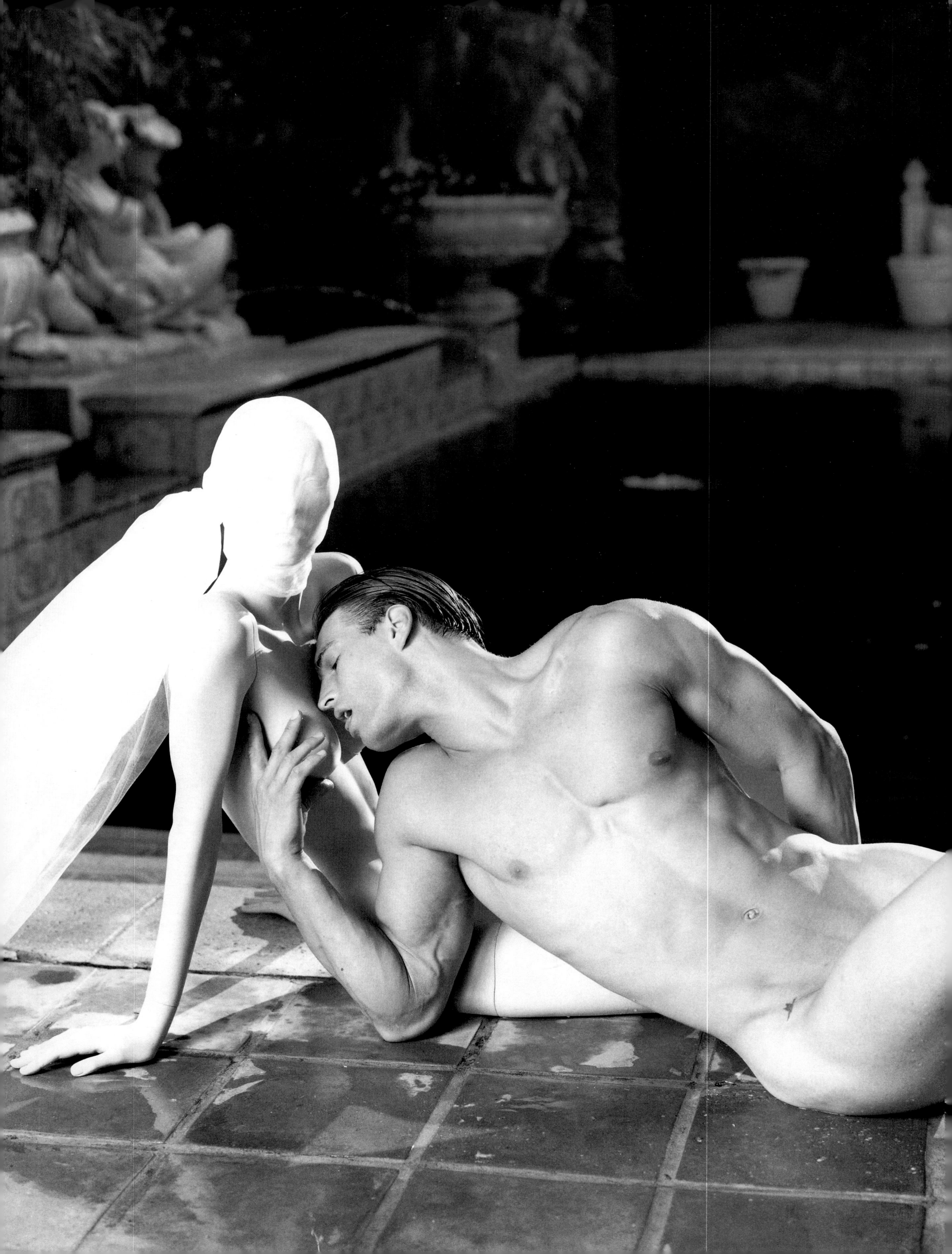

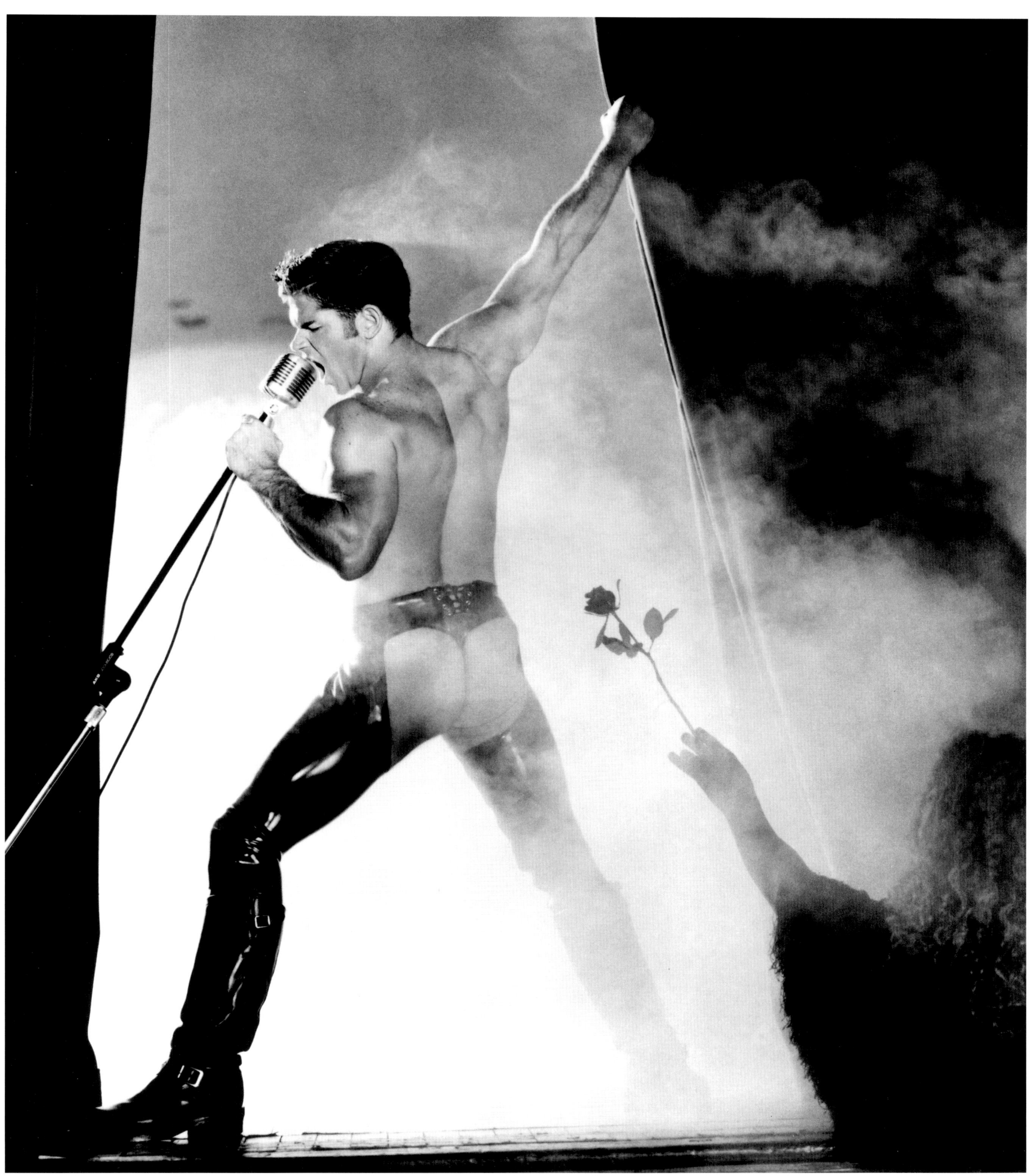

Matt Zarley Performer

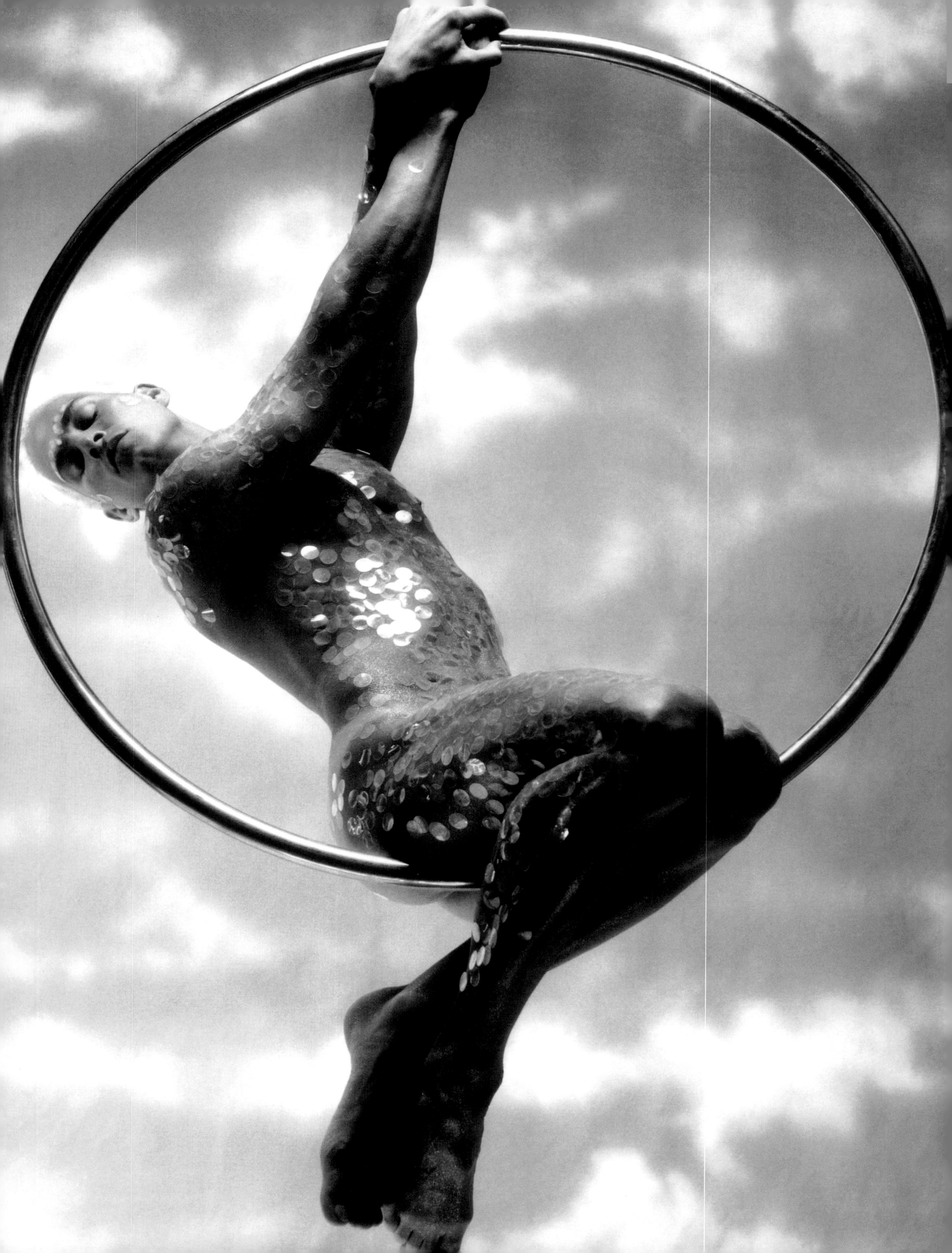

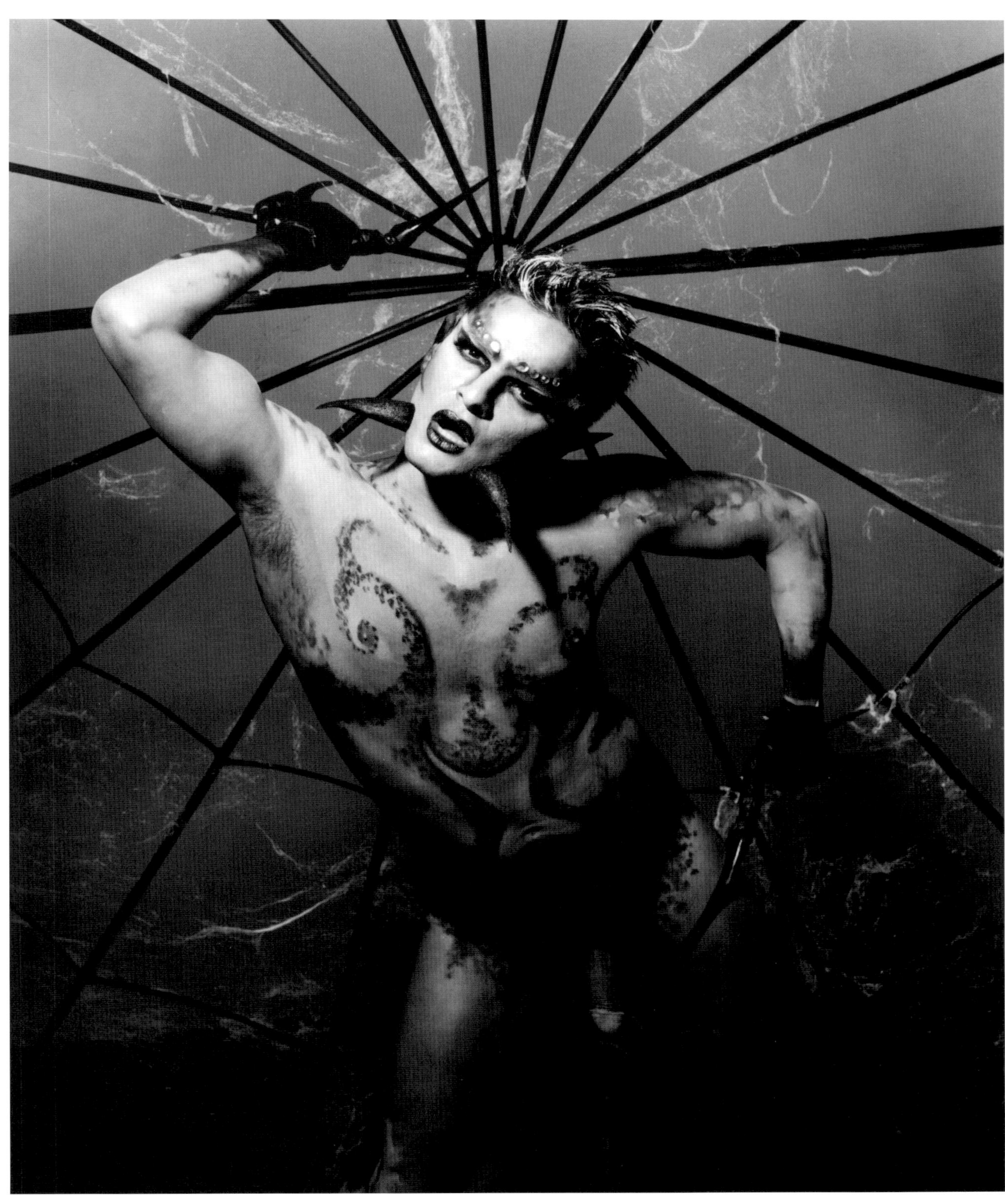

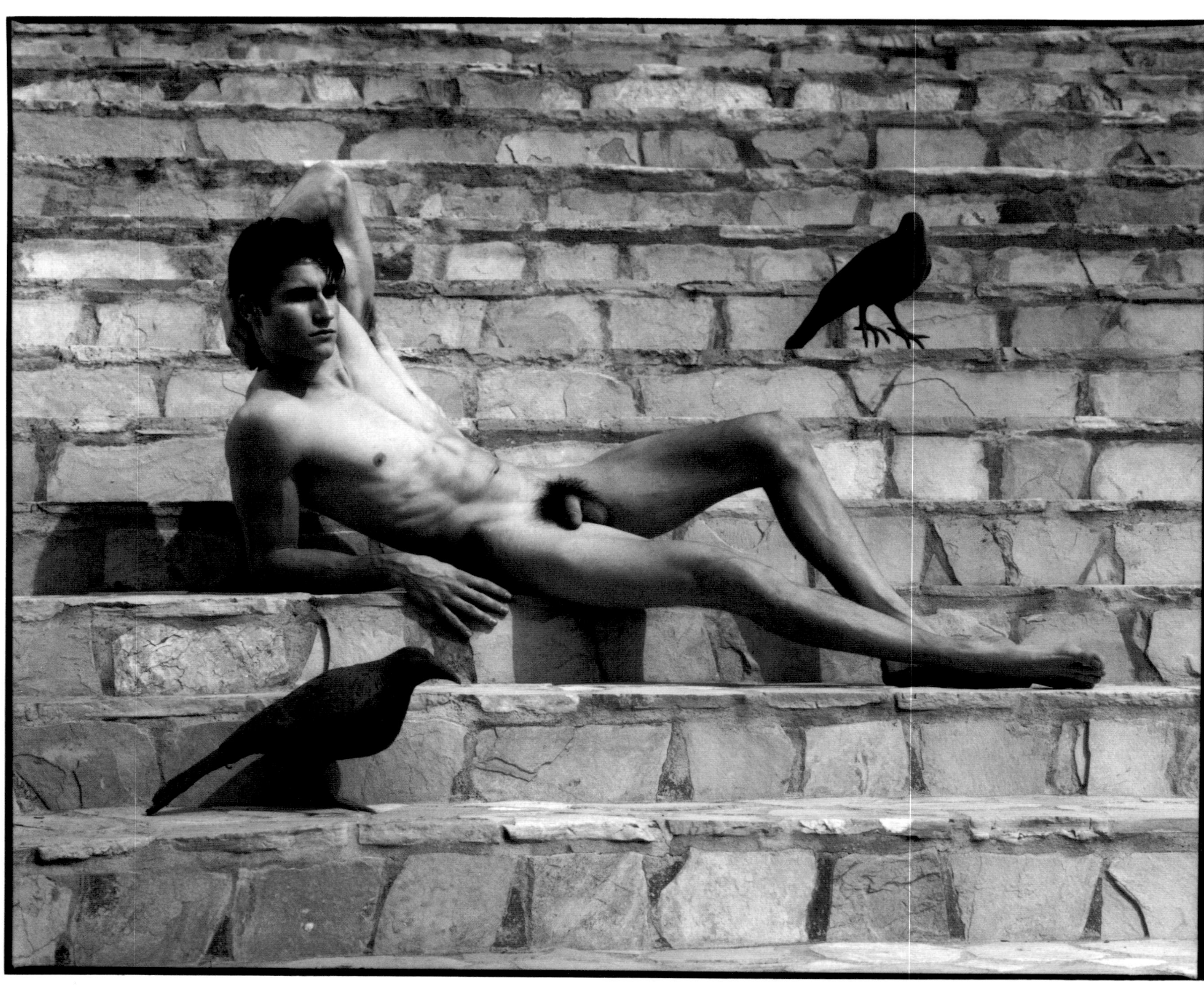

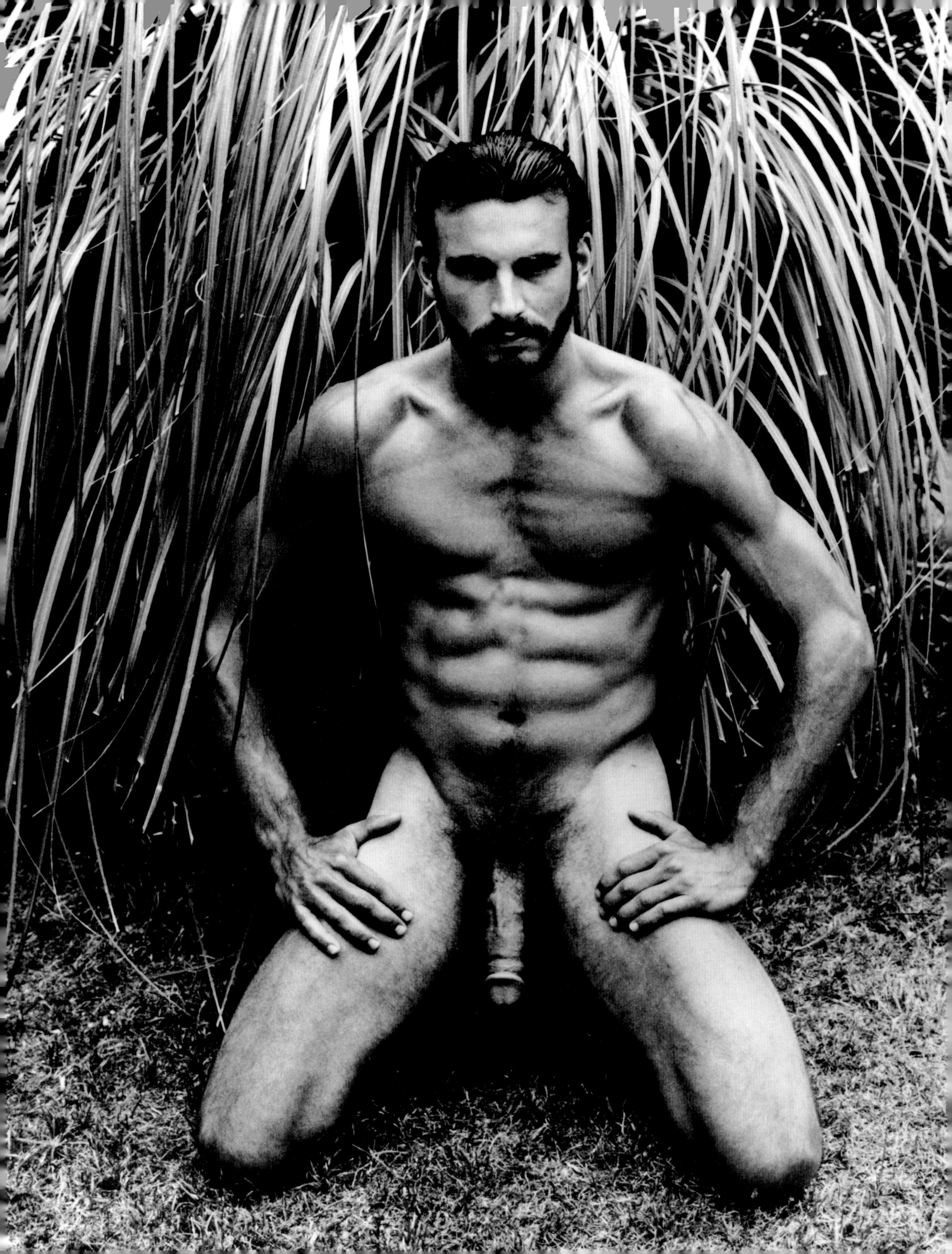

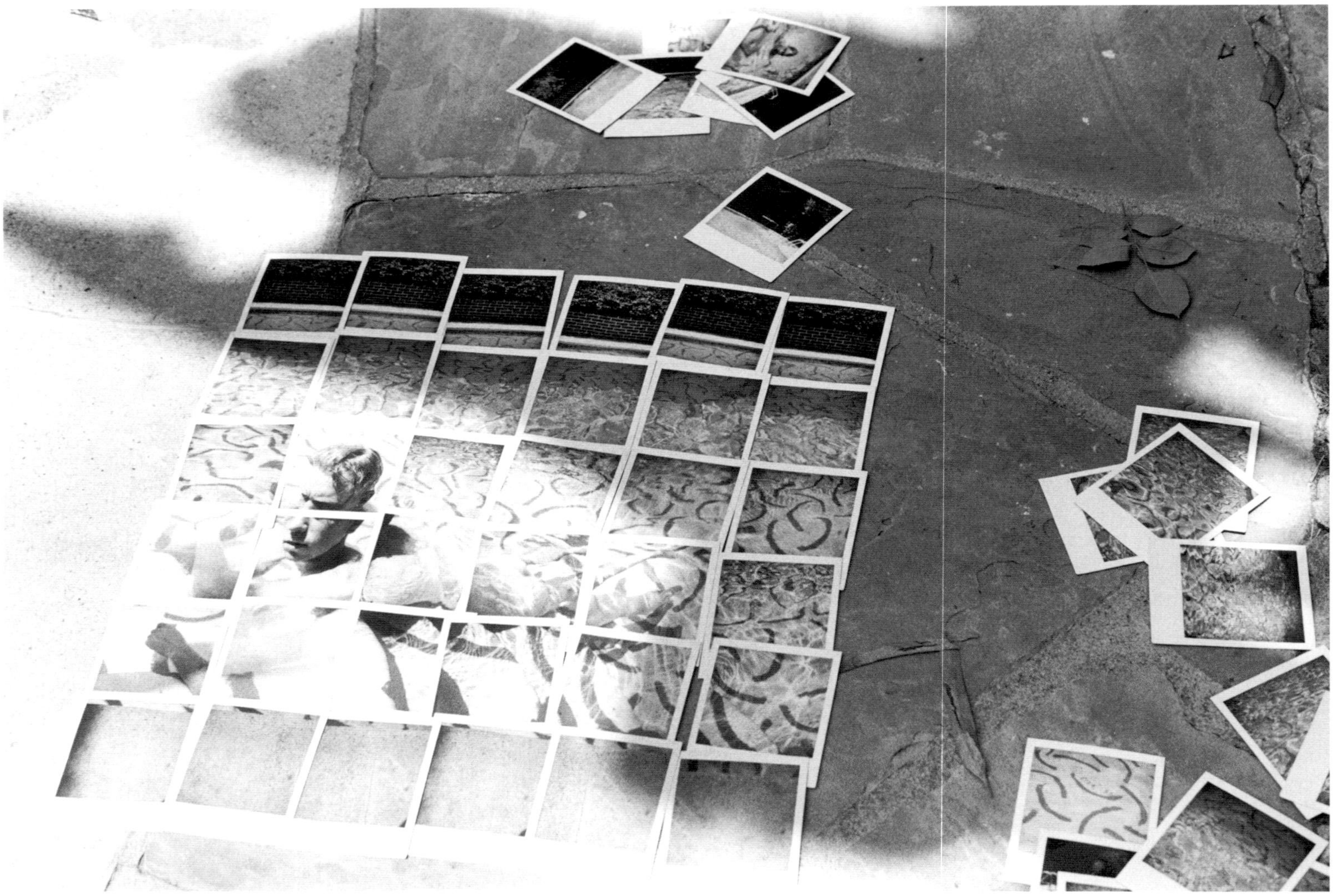

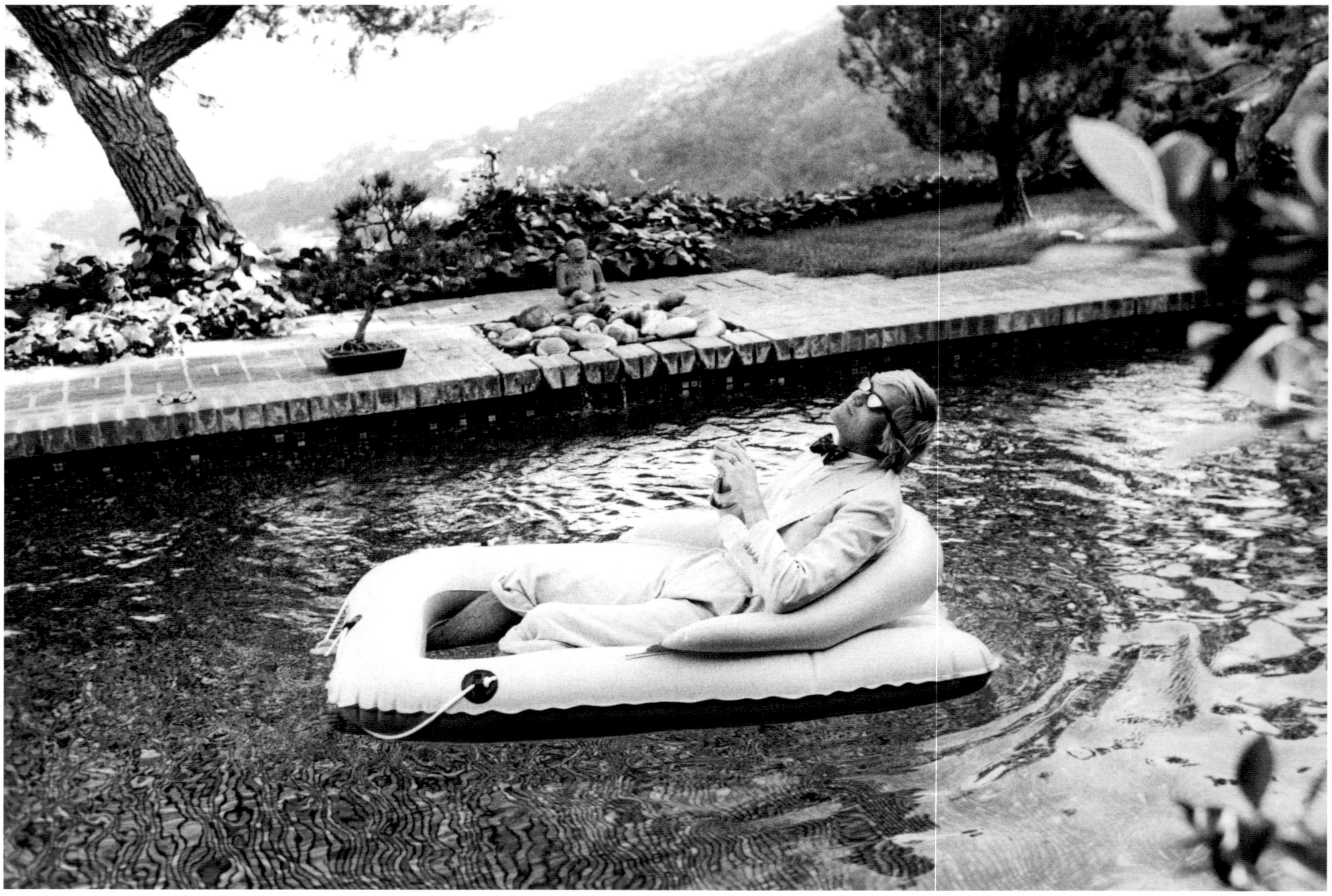

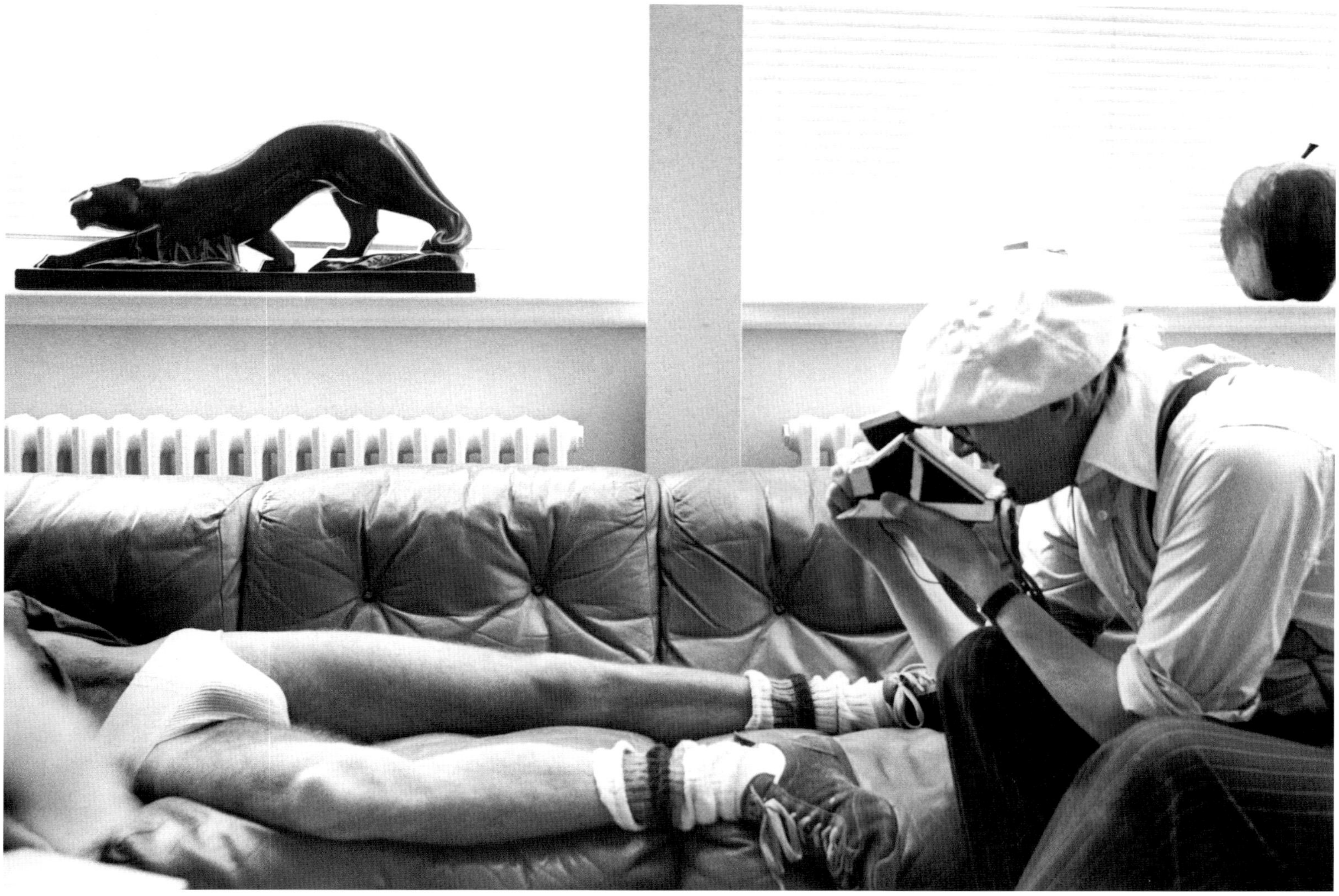

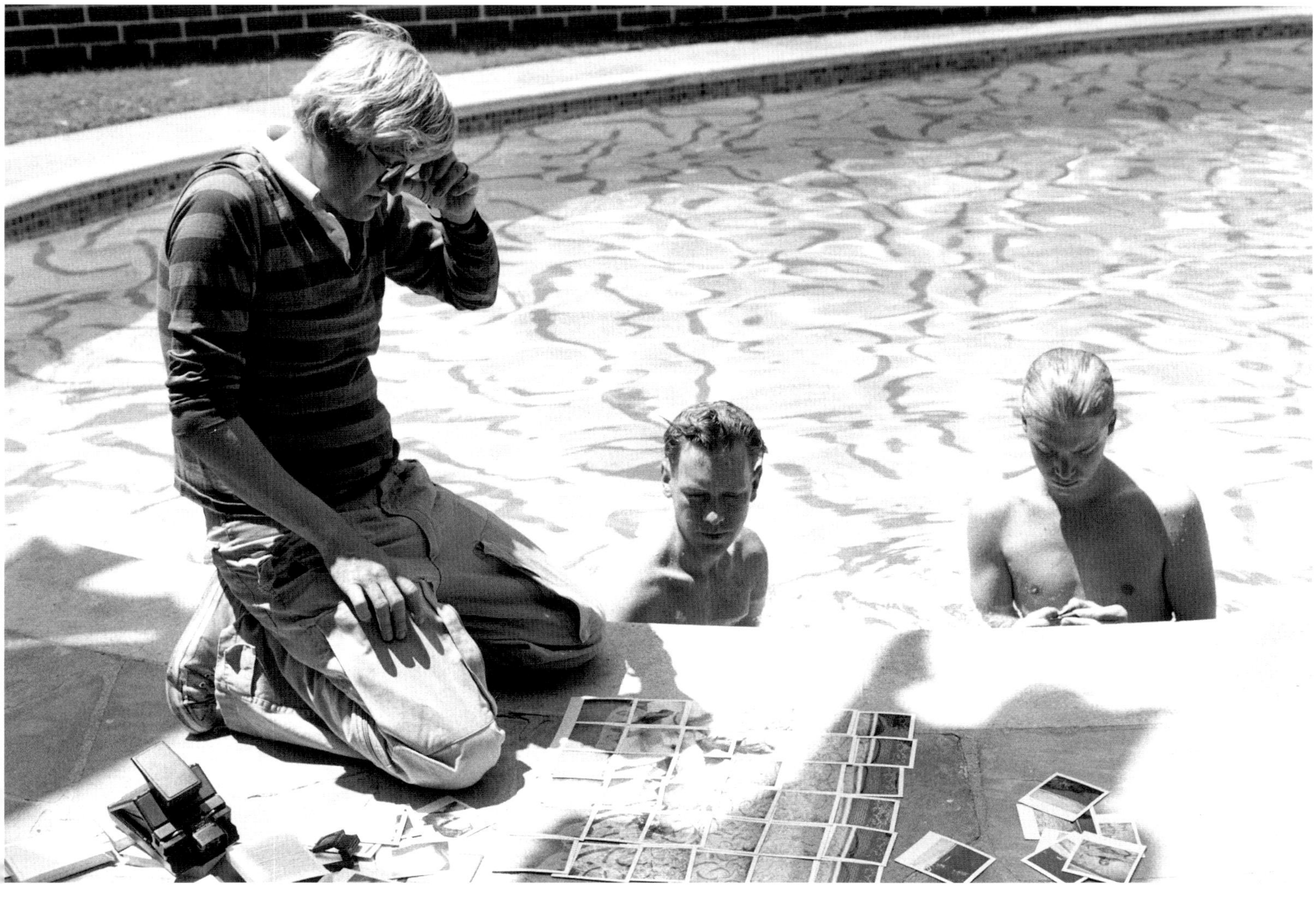

David Hockney at work

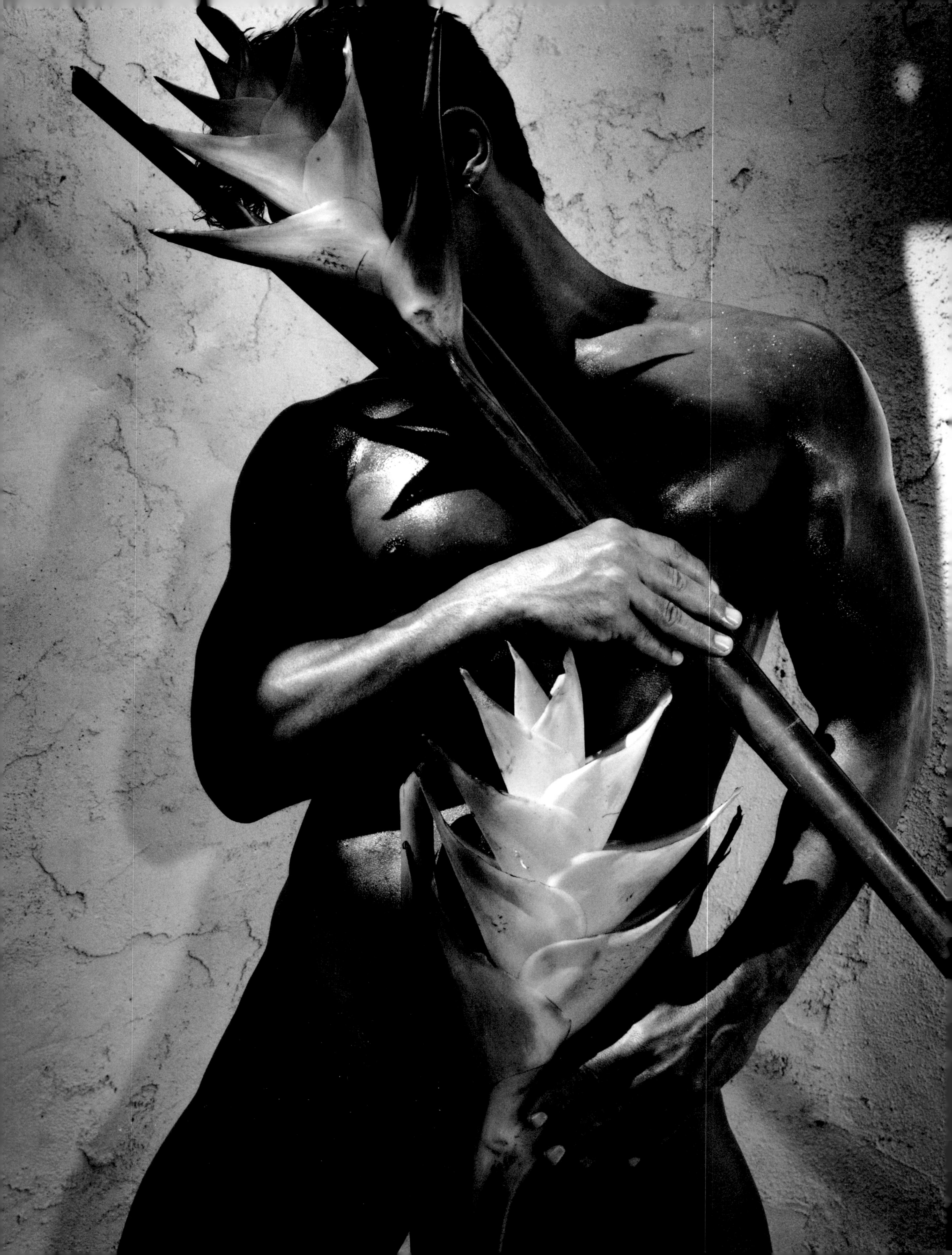

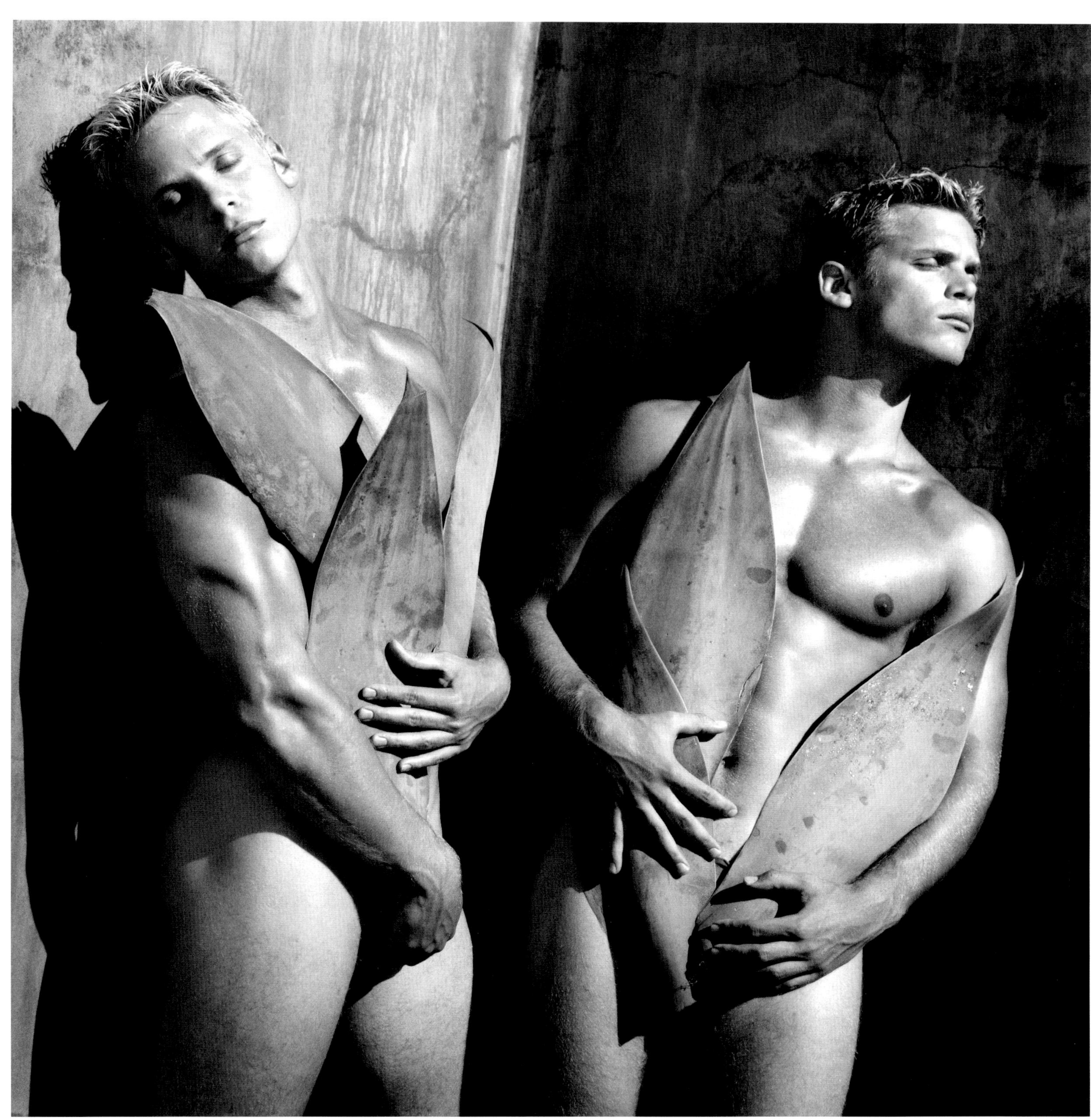

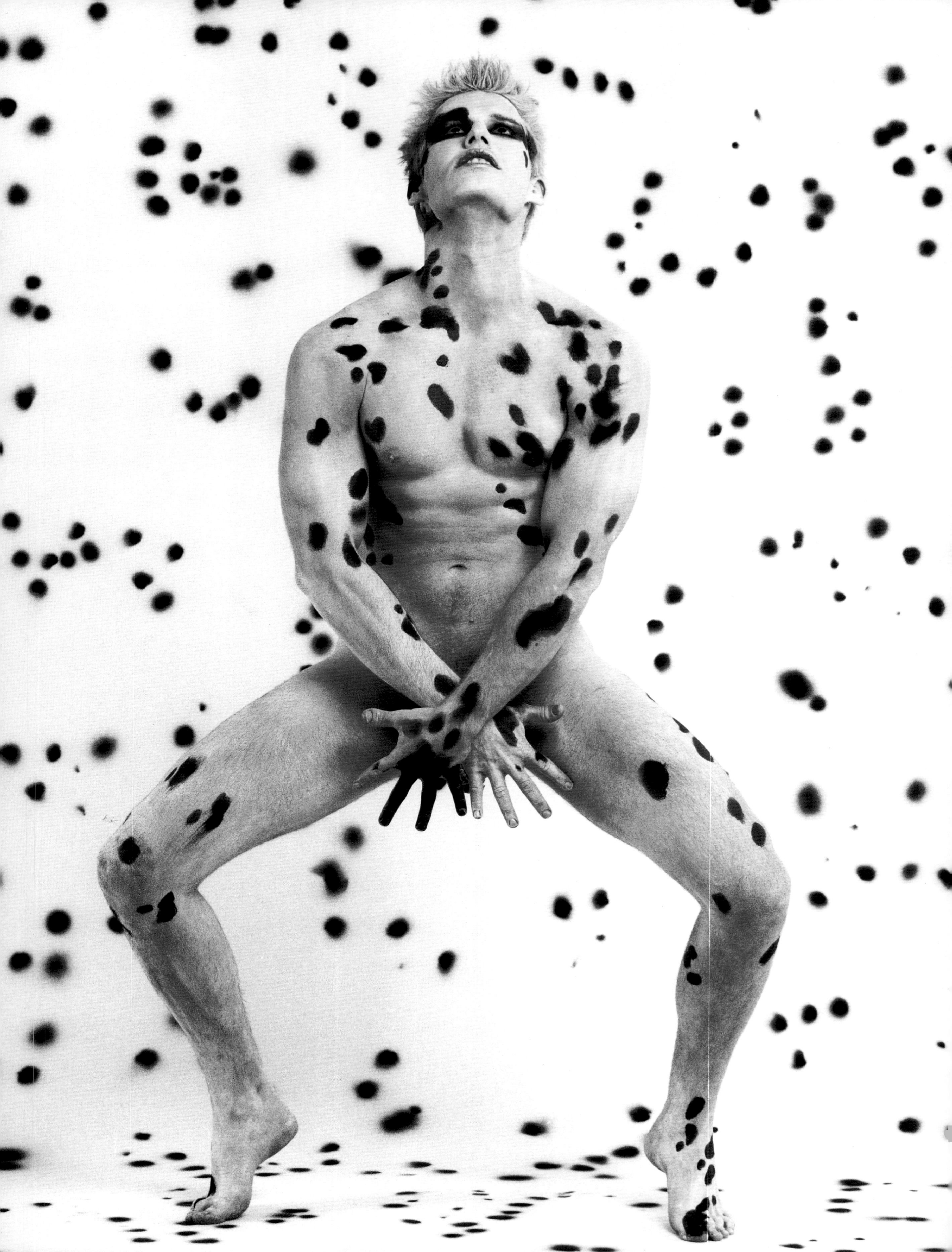

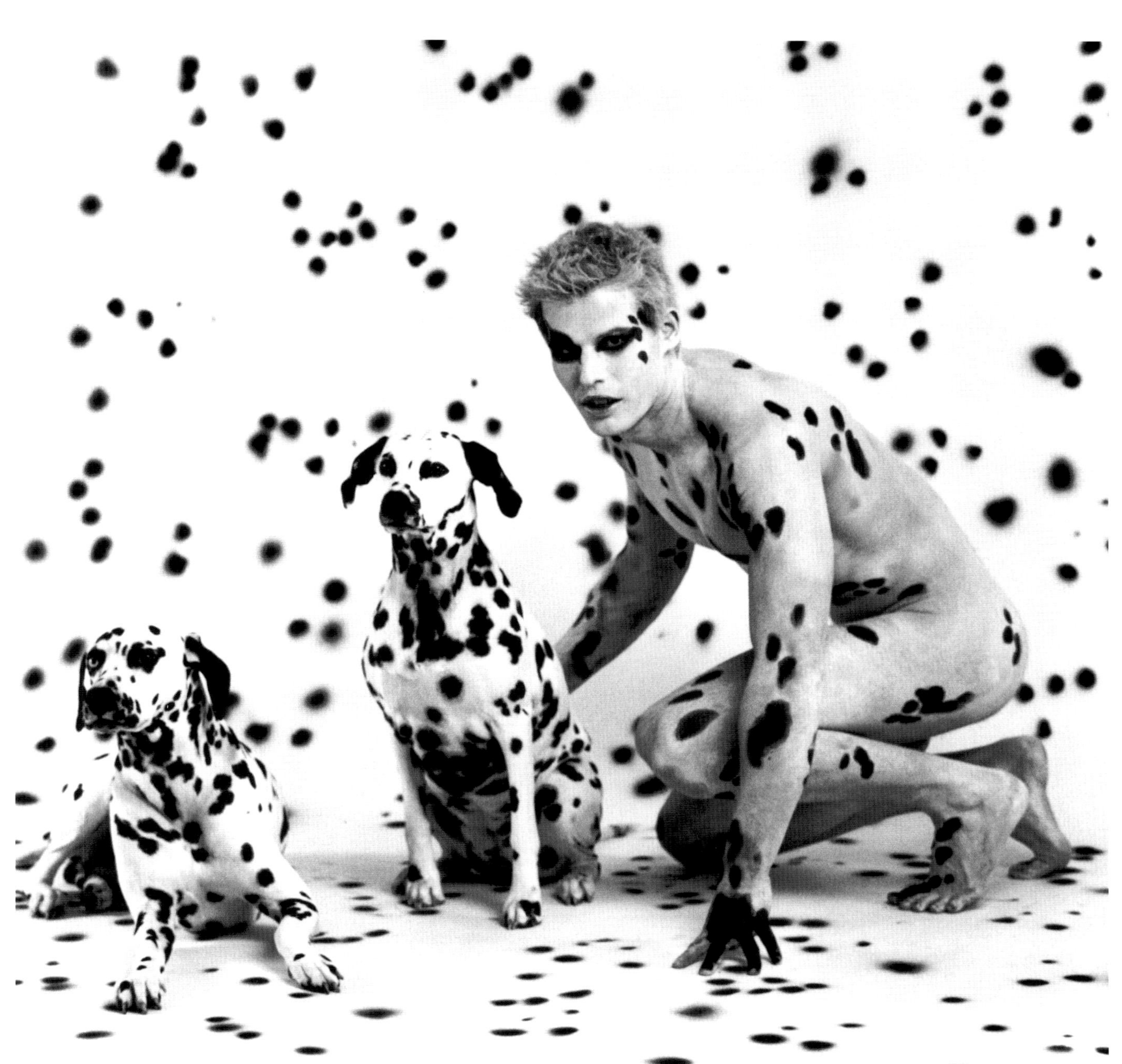

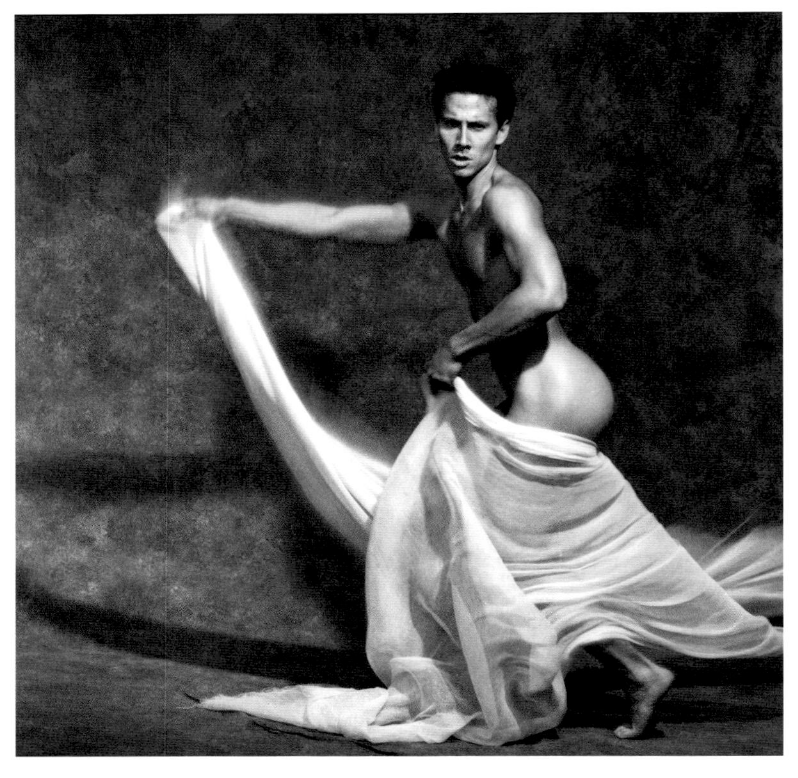
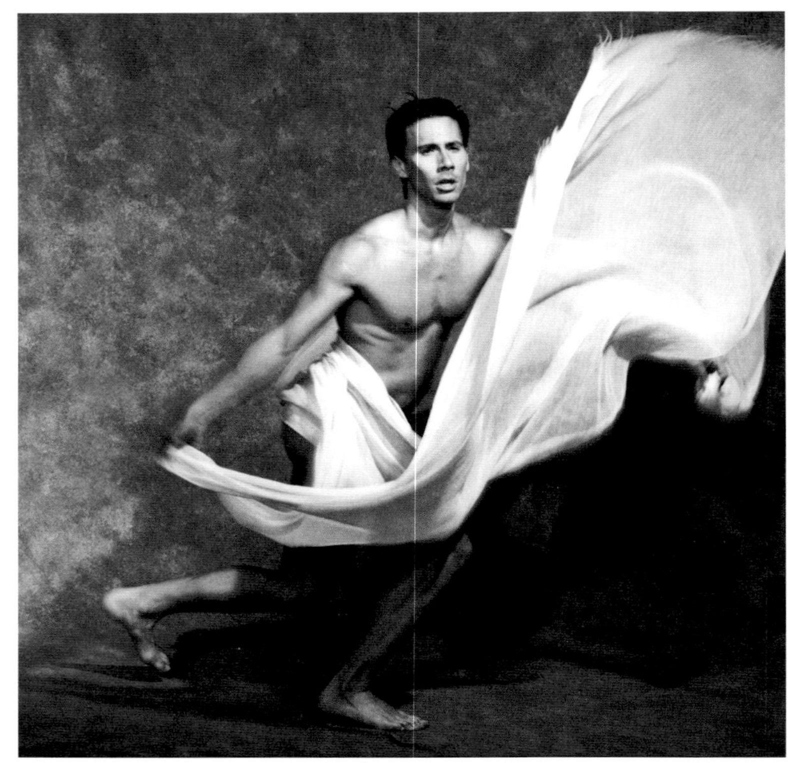
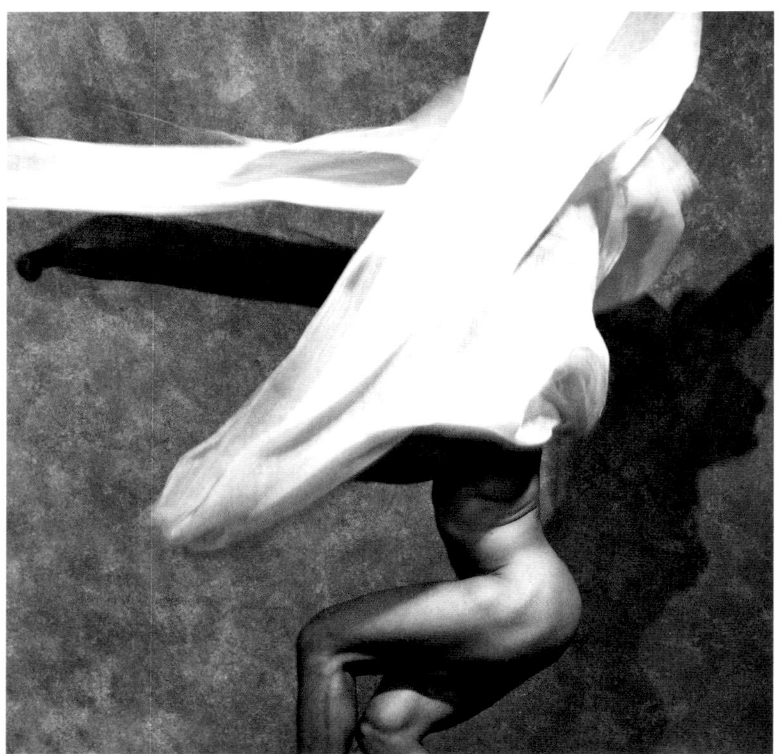
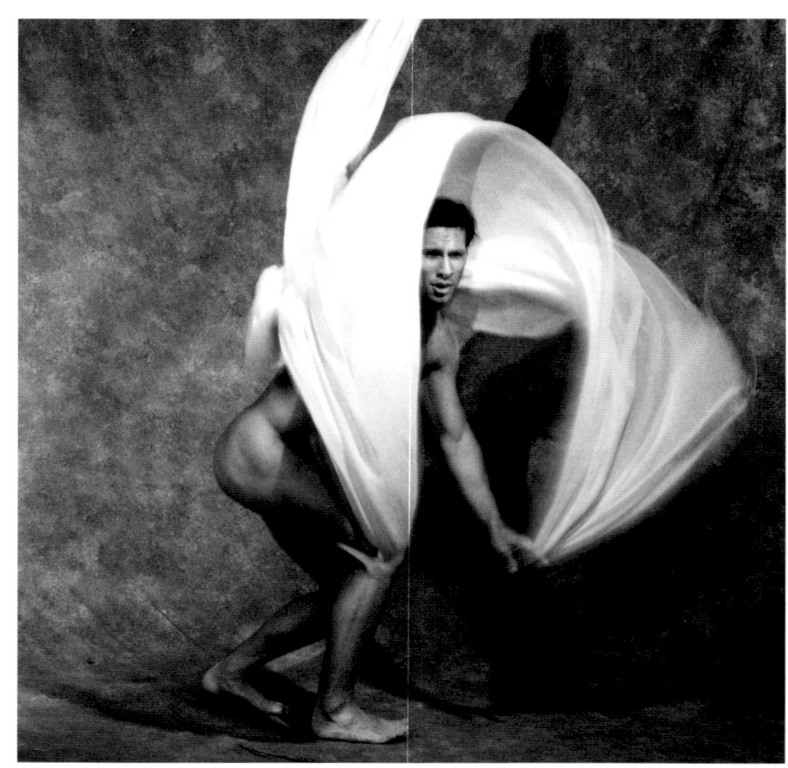

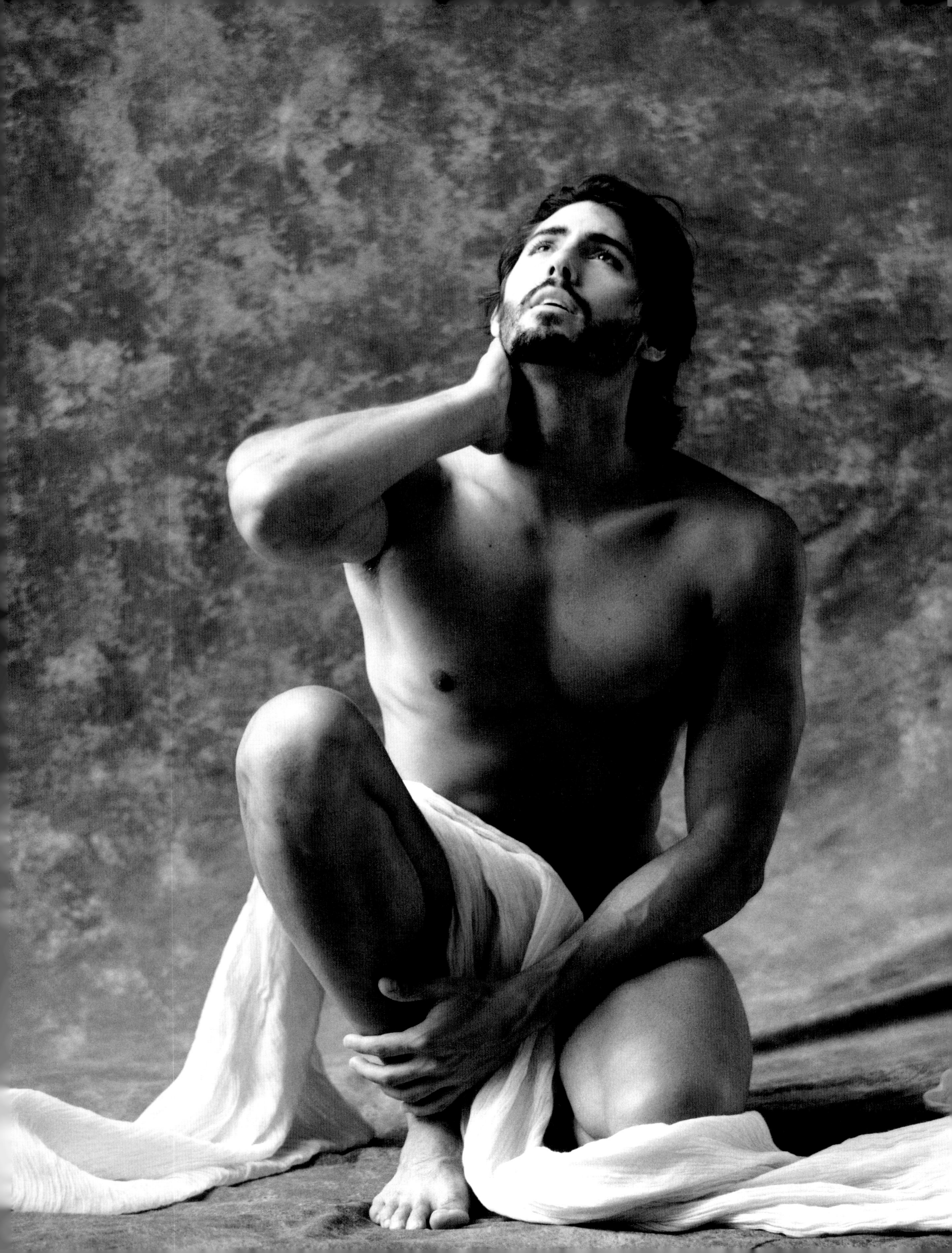

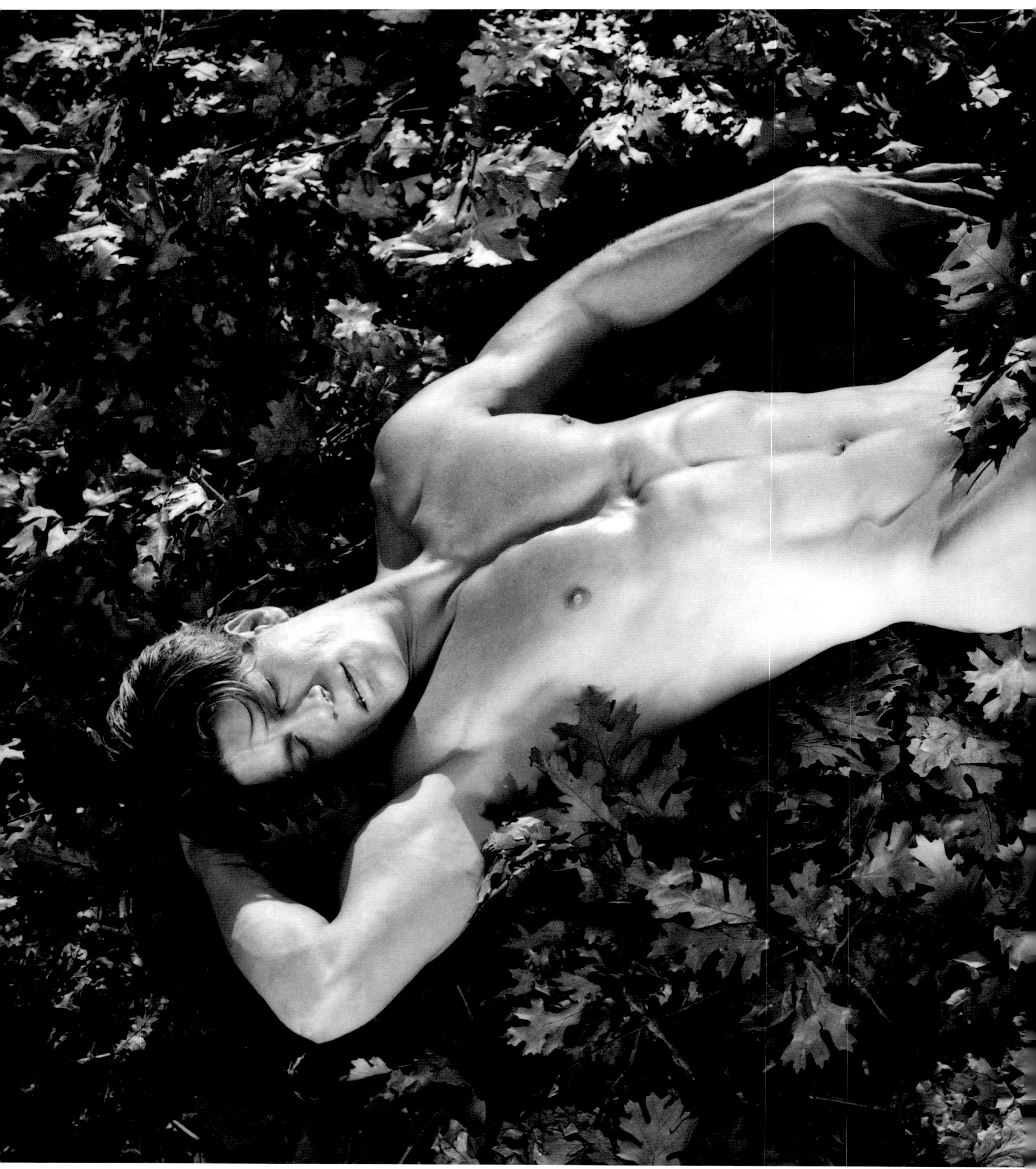

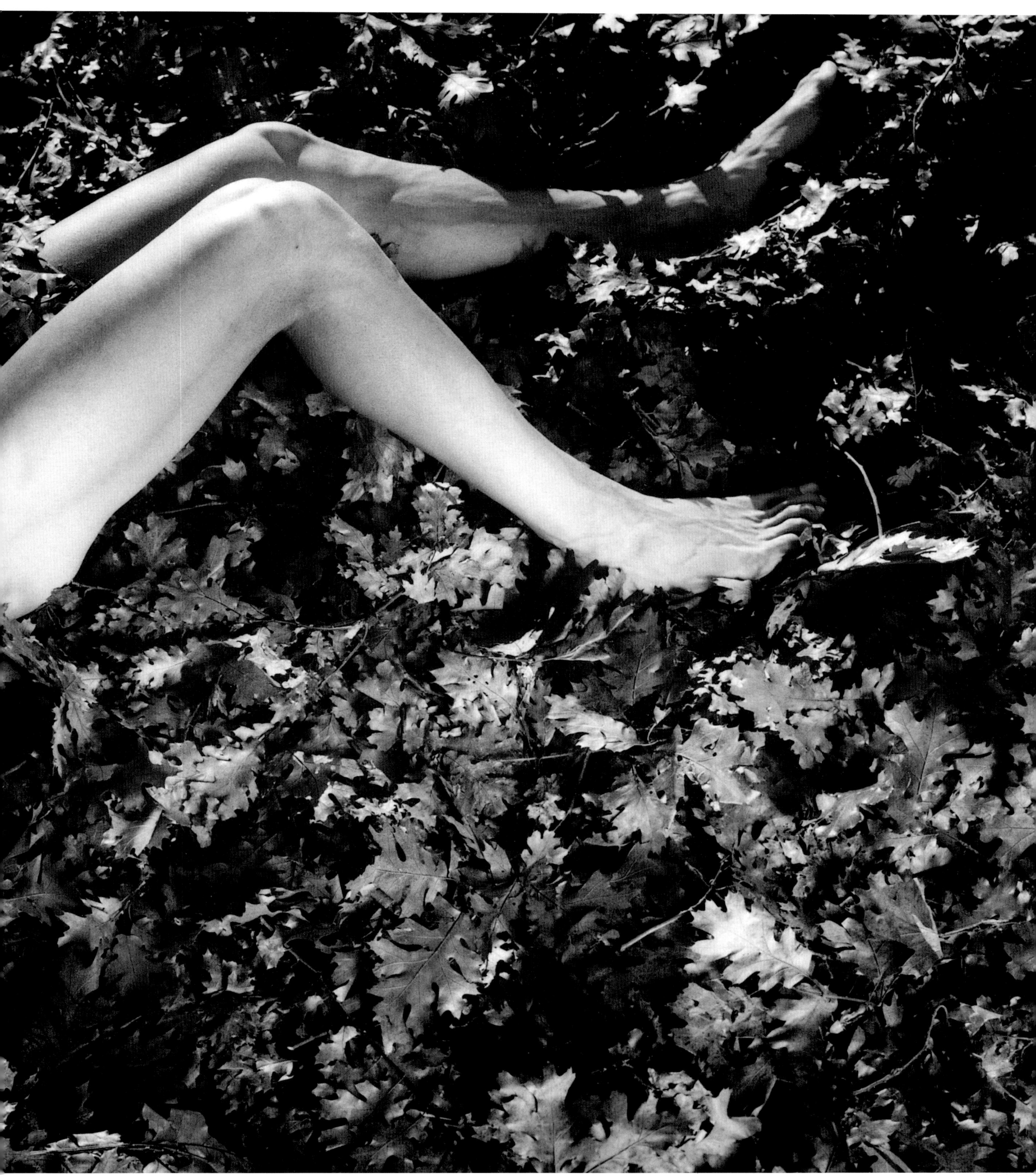

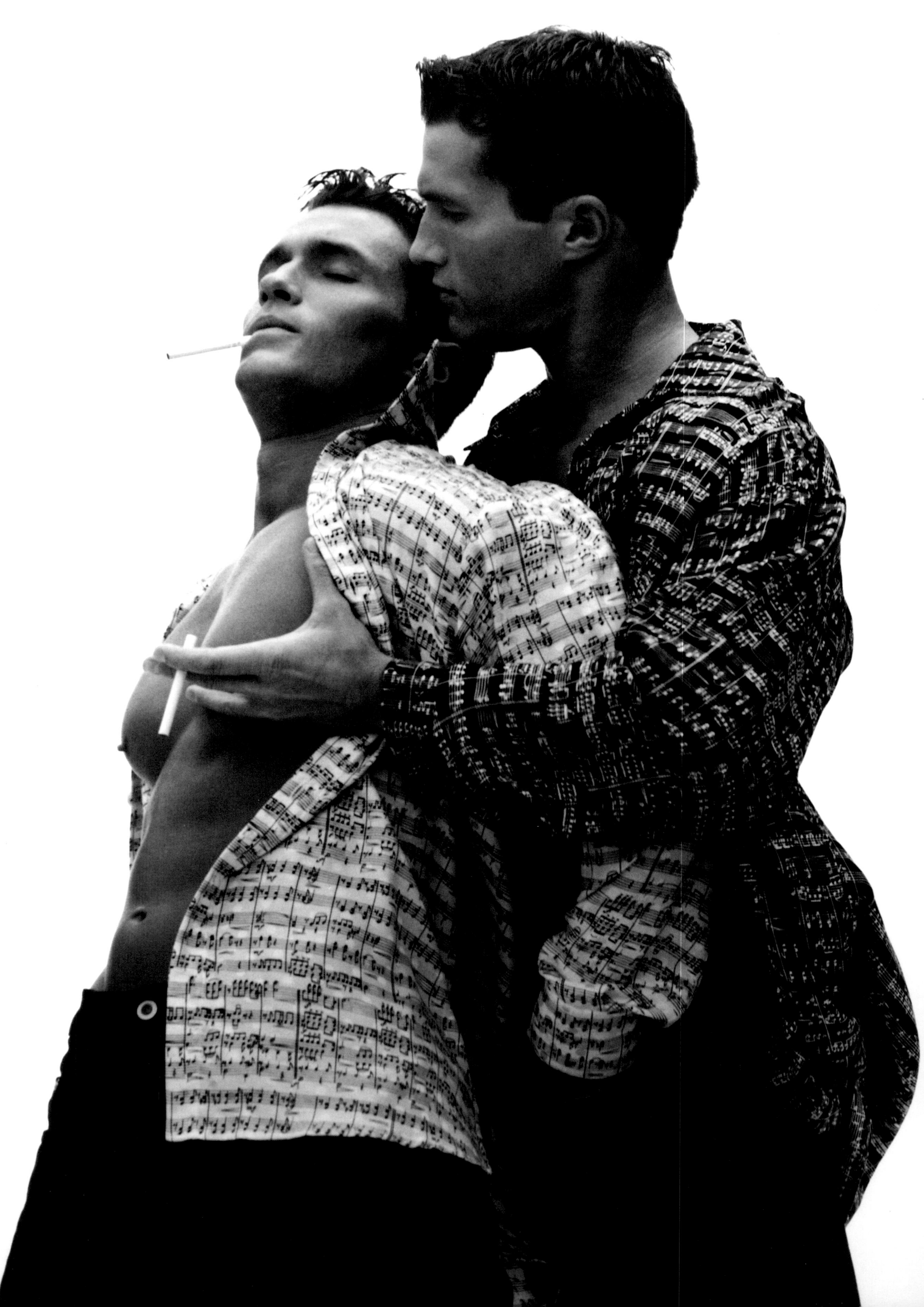

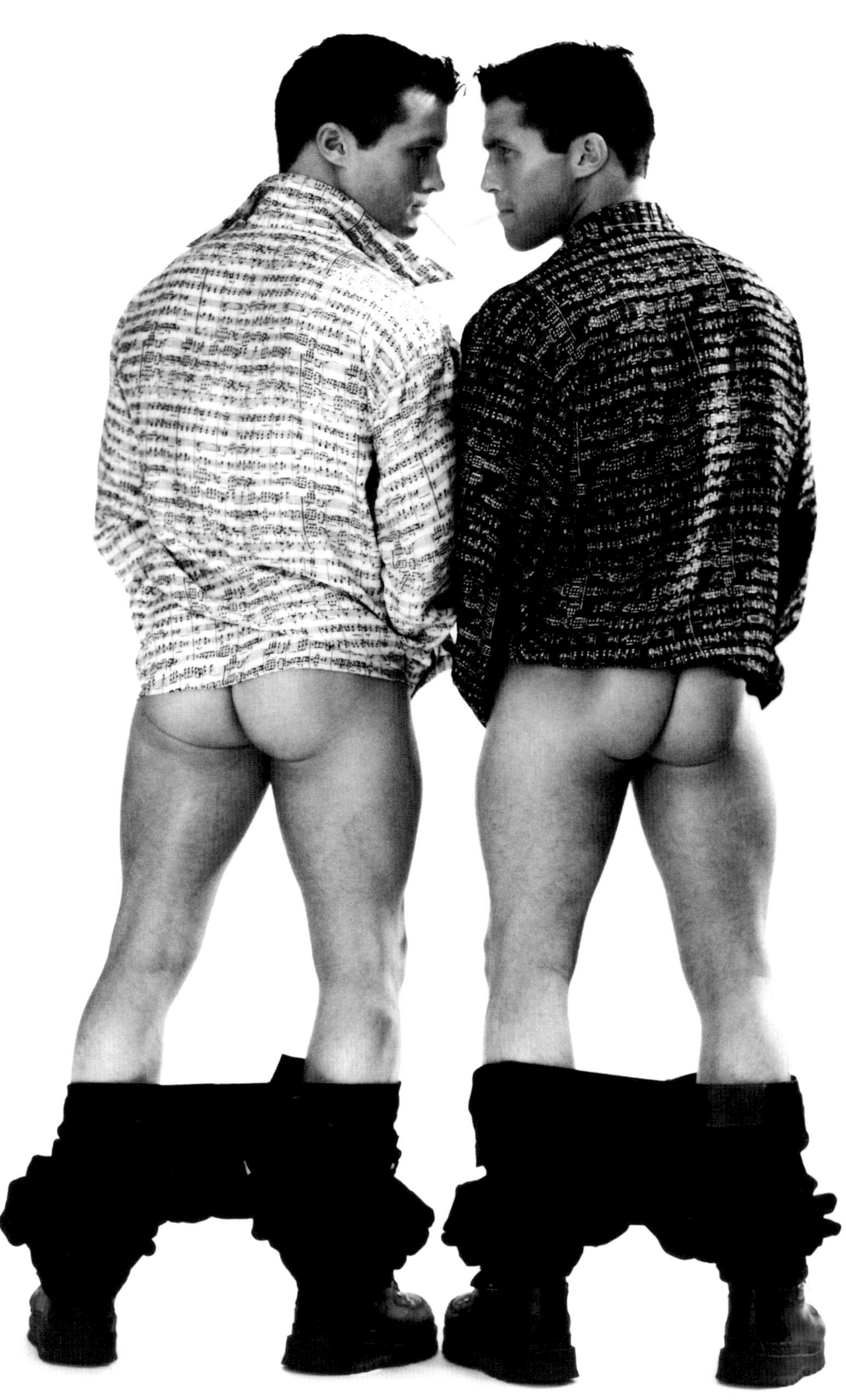

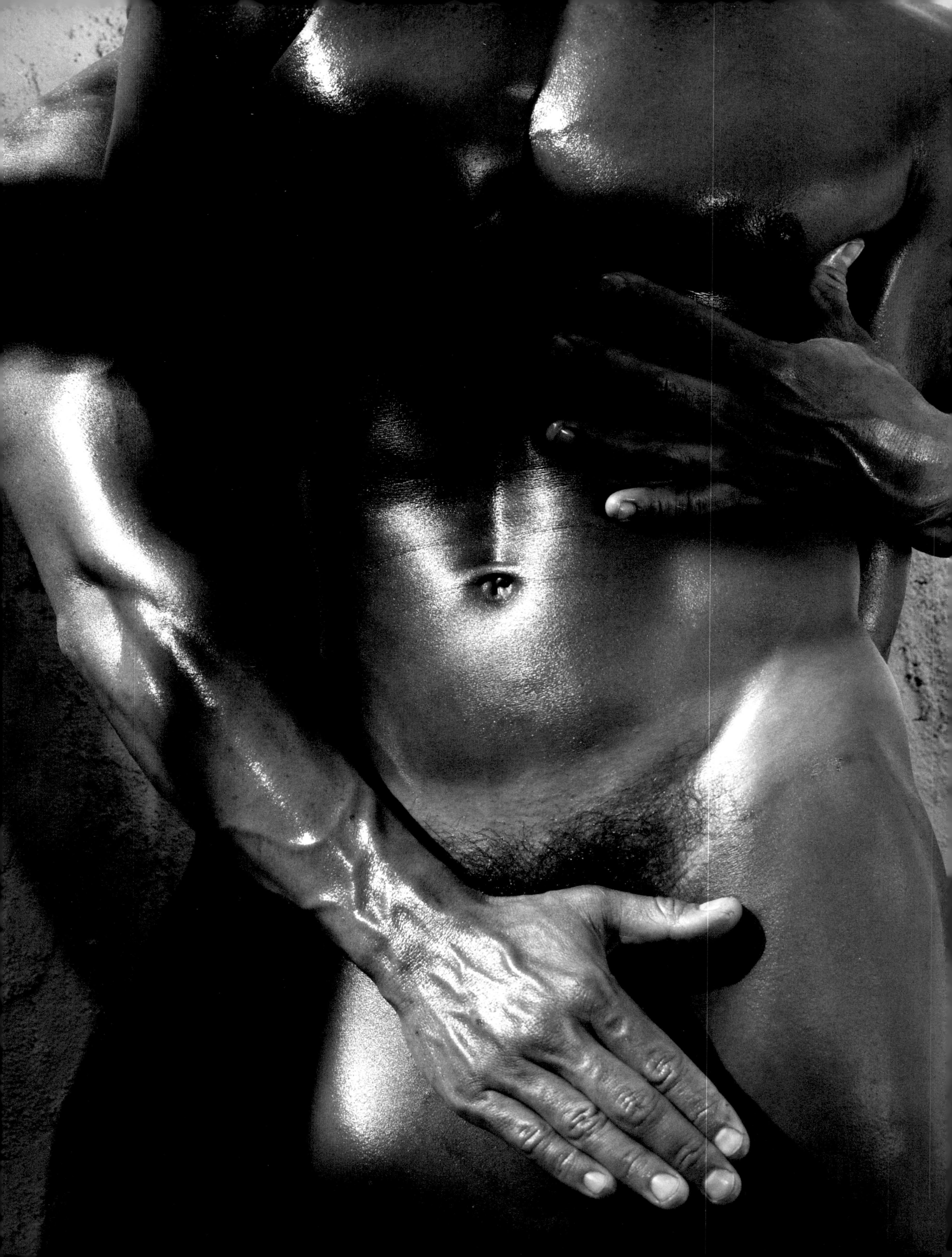

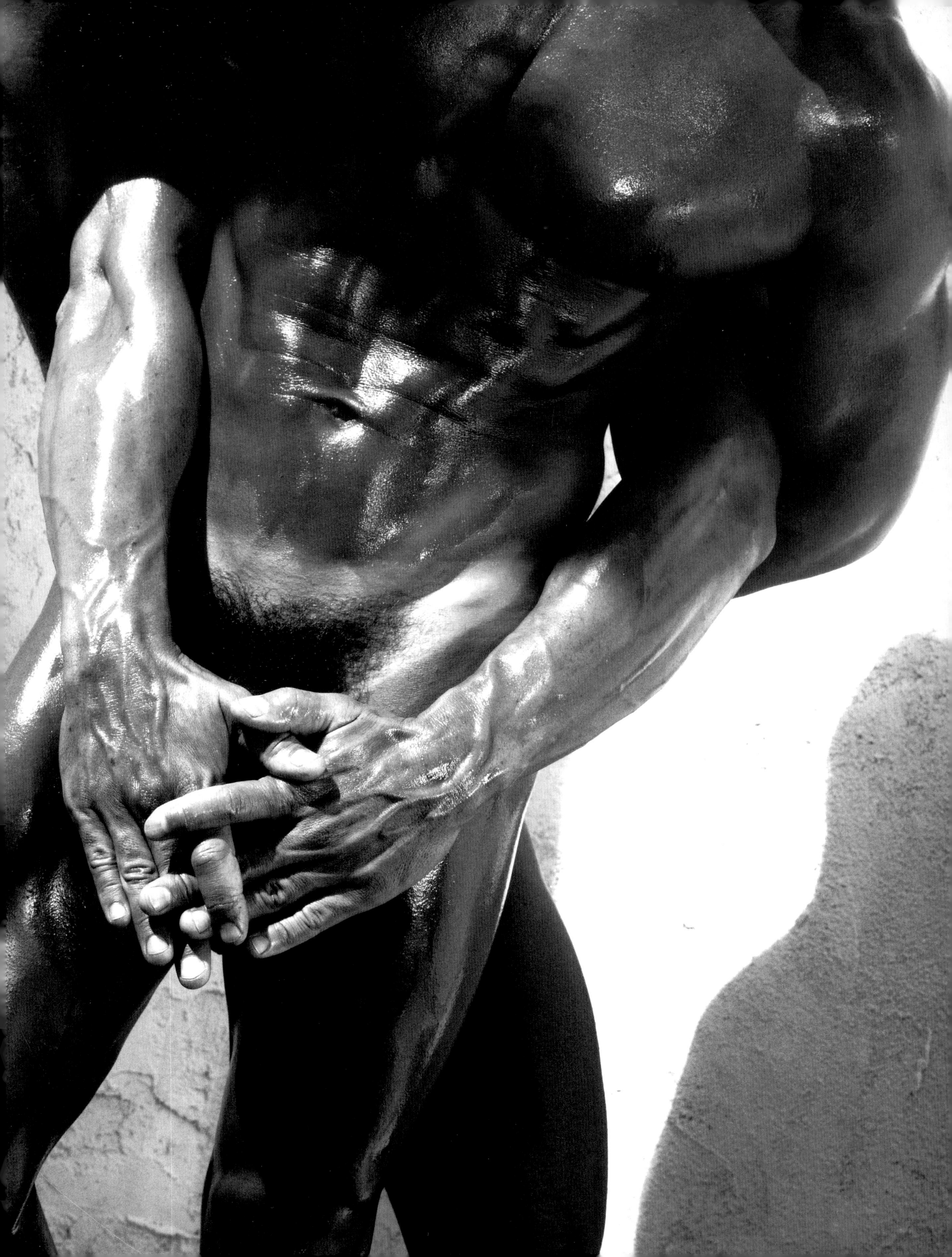

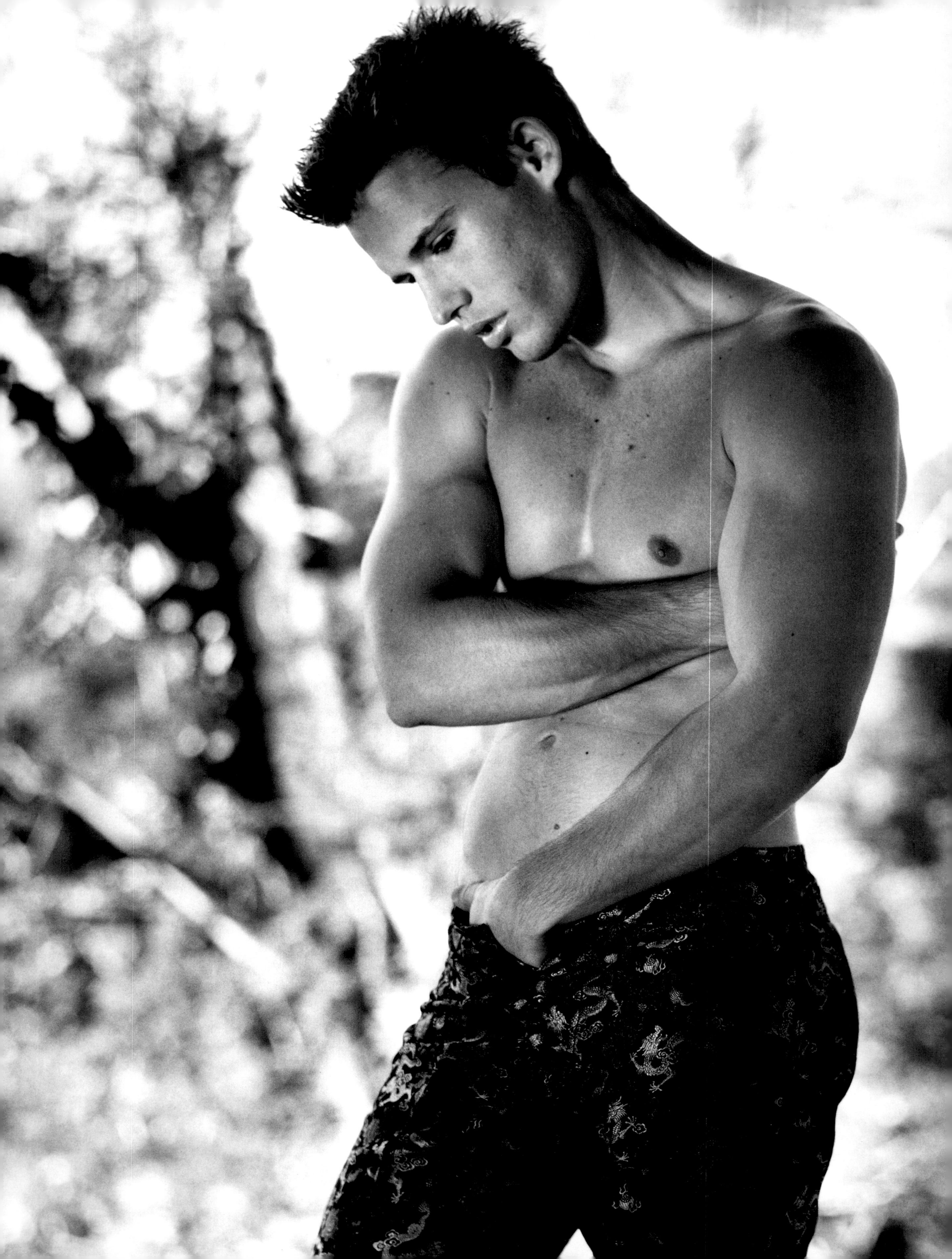

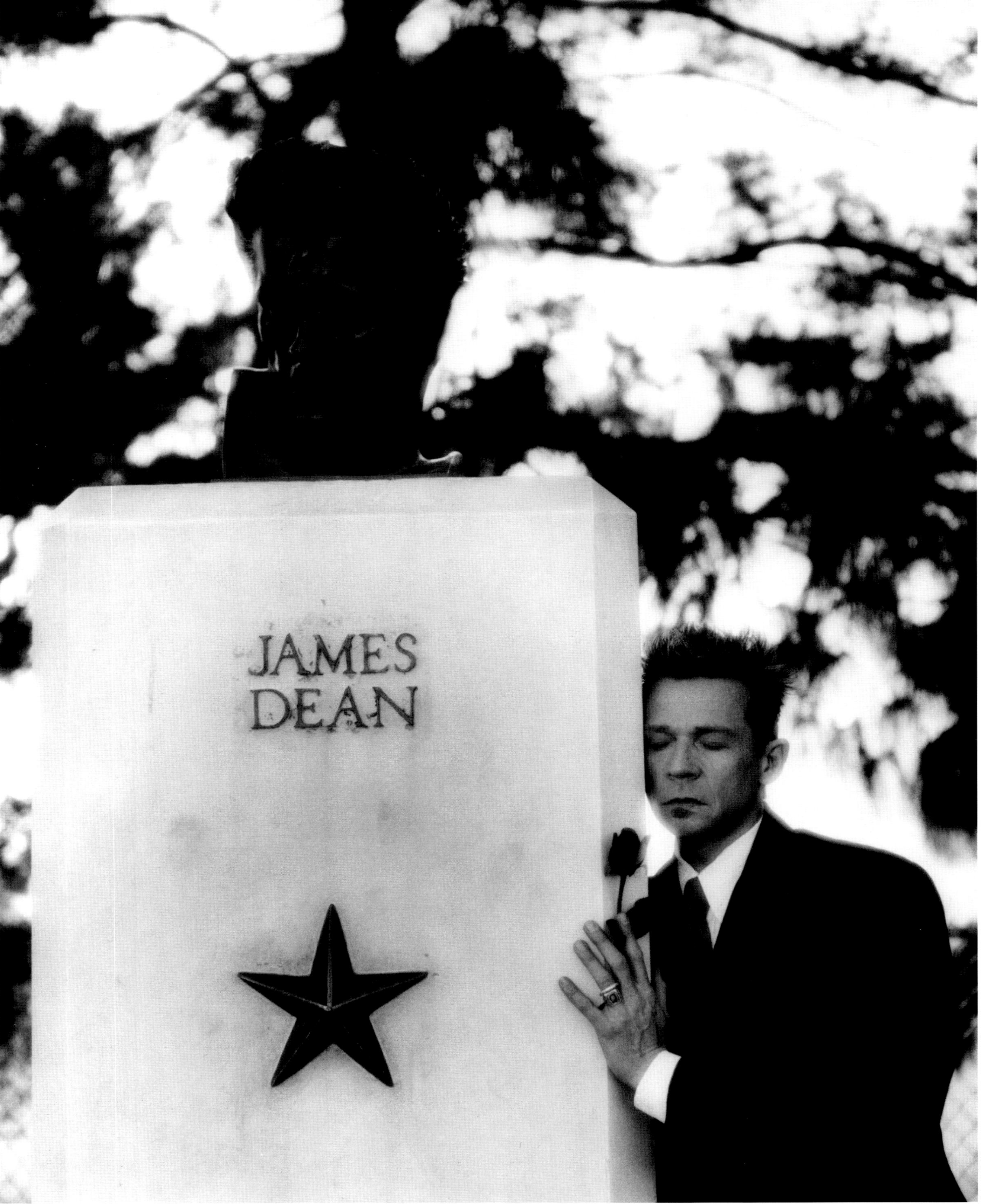
JAMES
DEAN

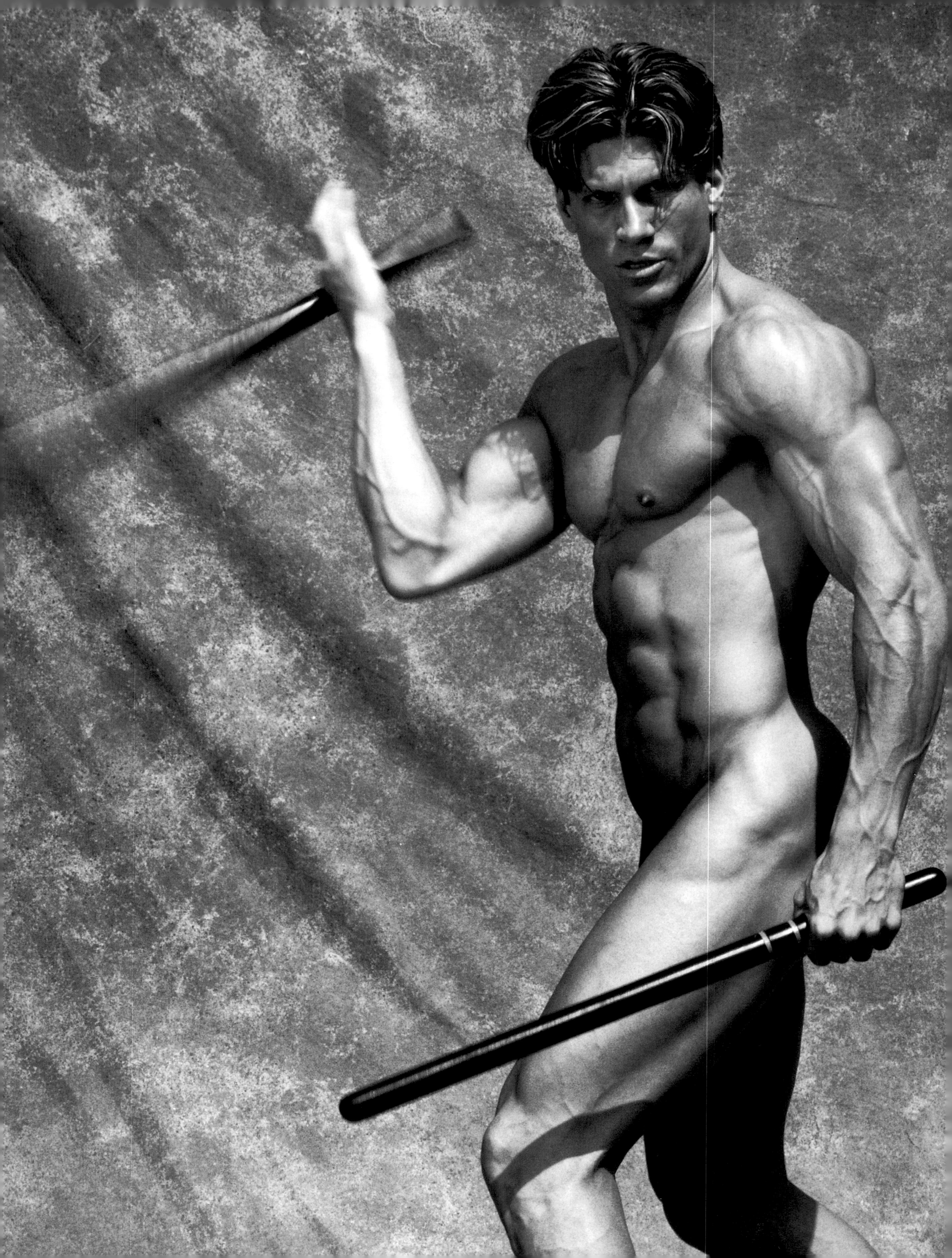

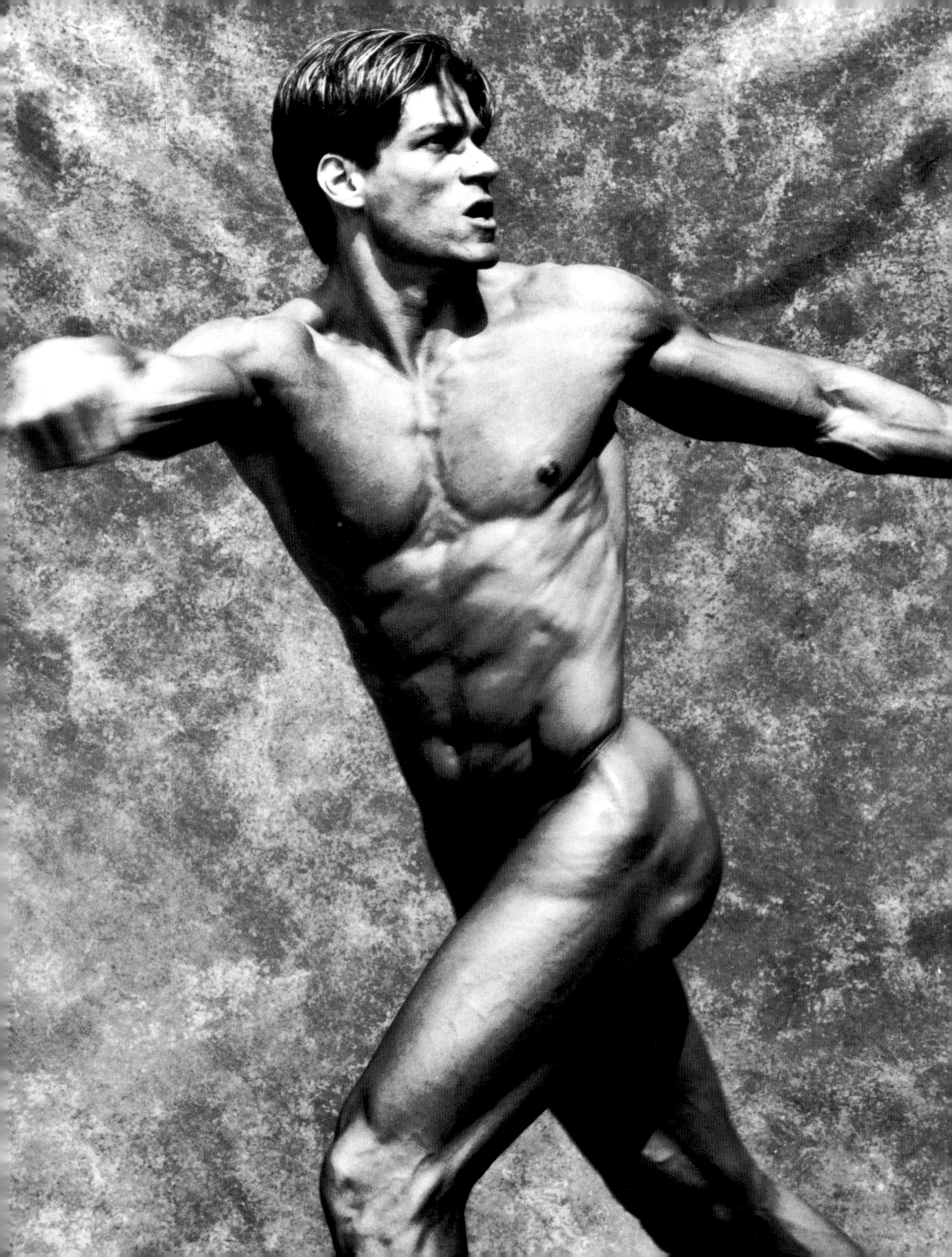

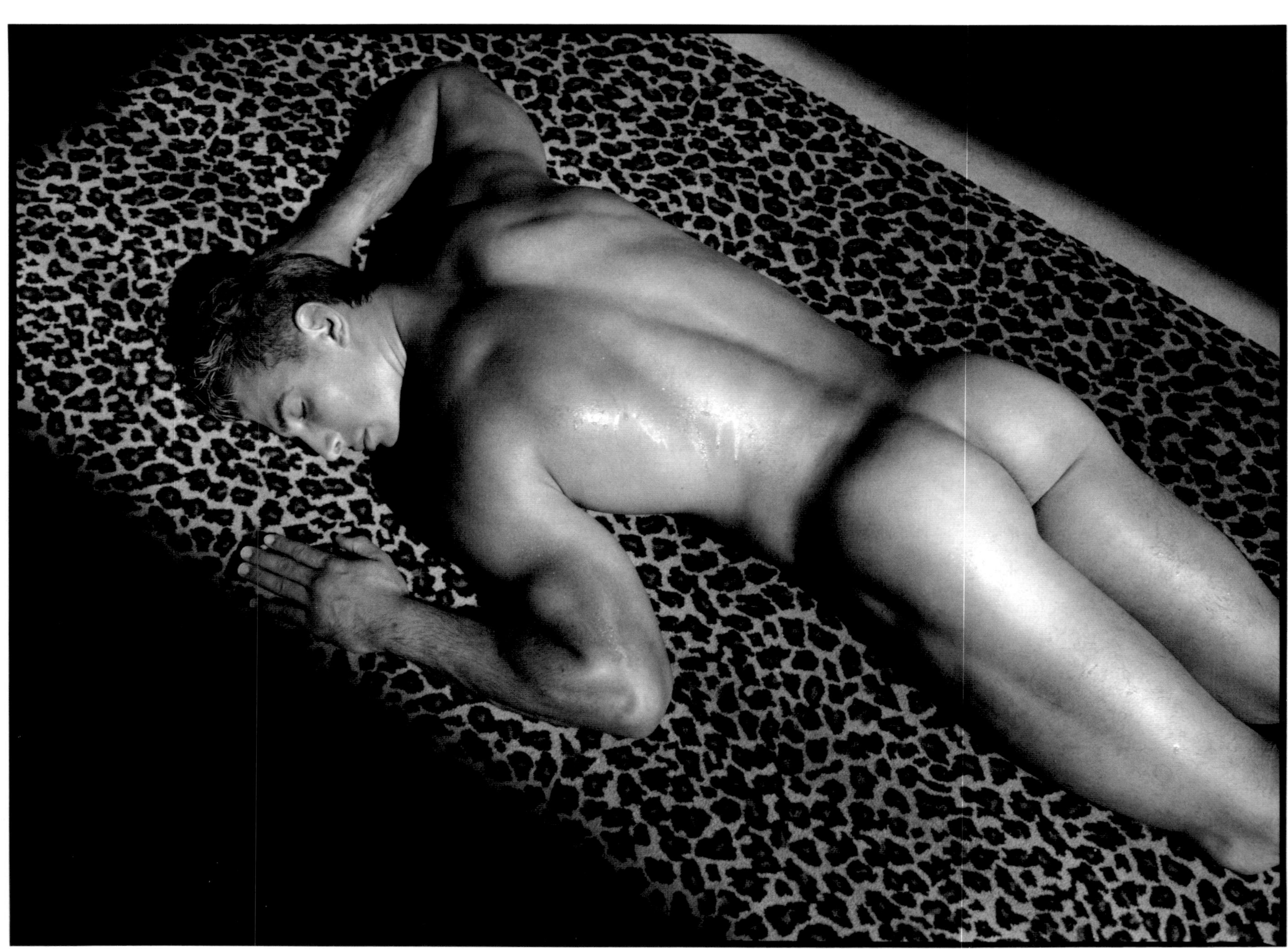

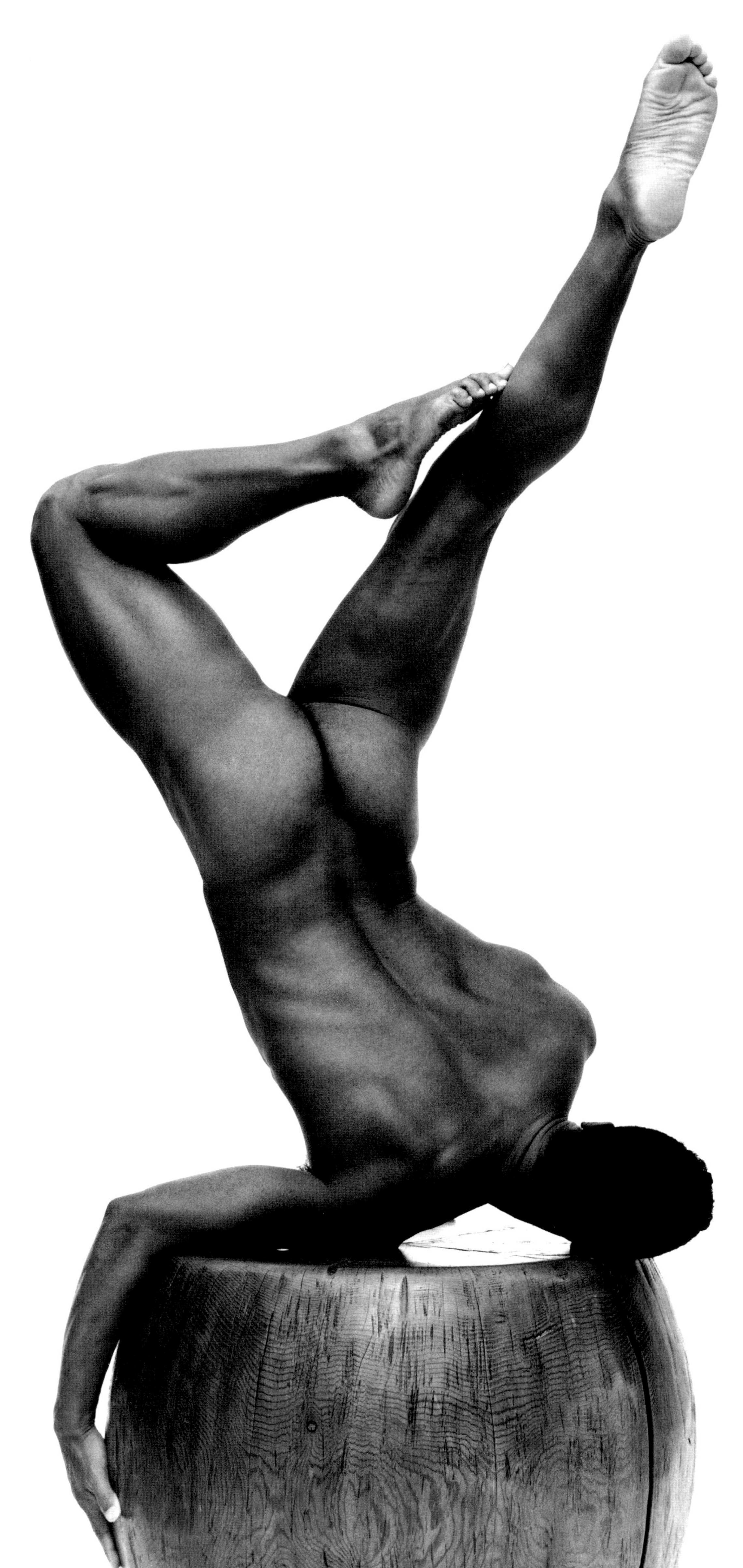

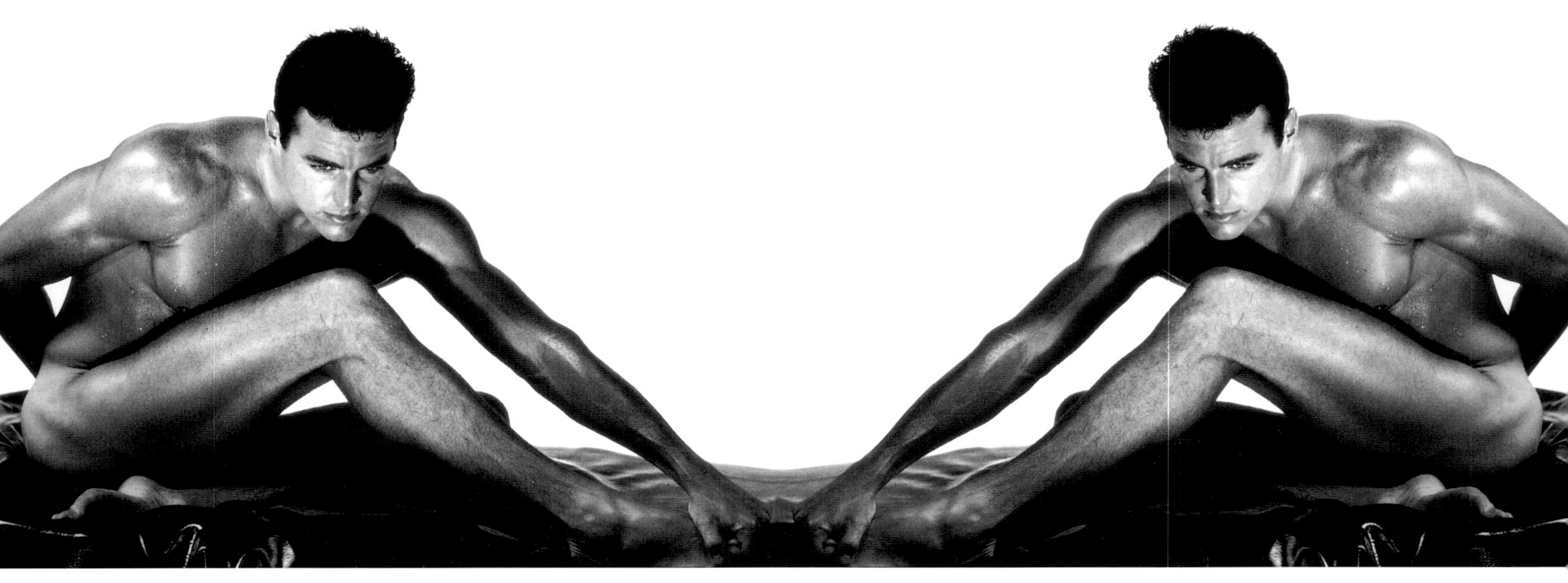

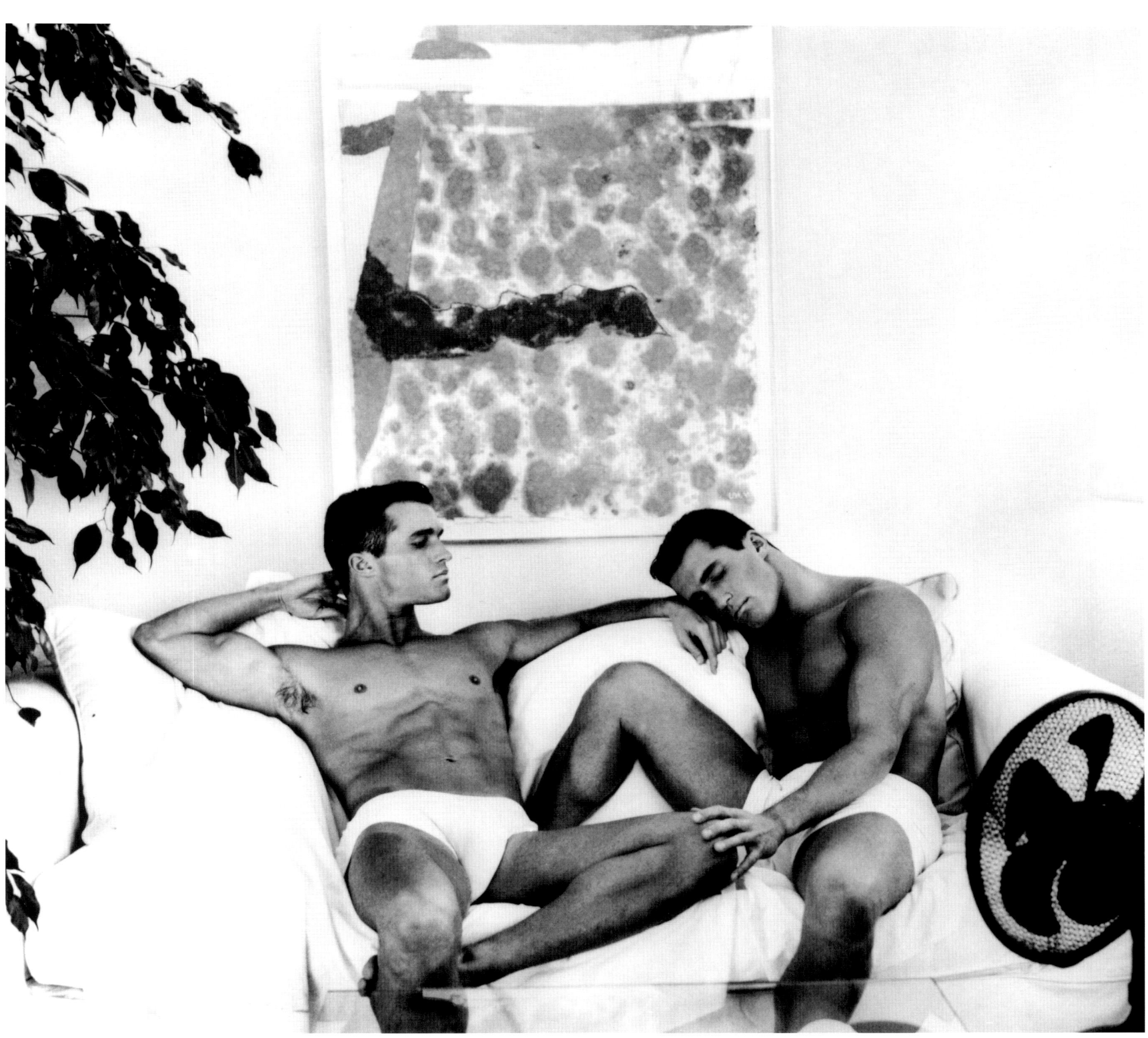

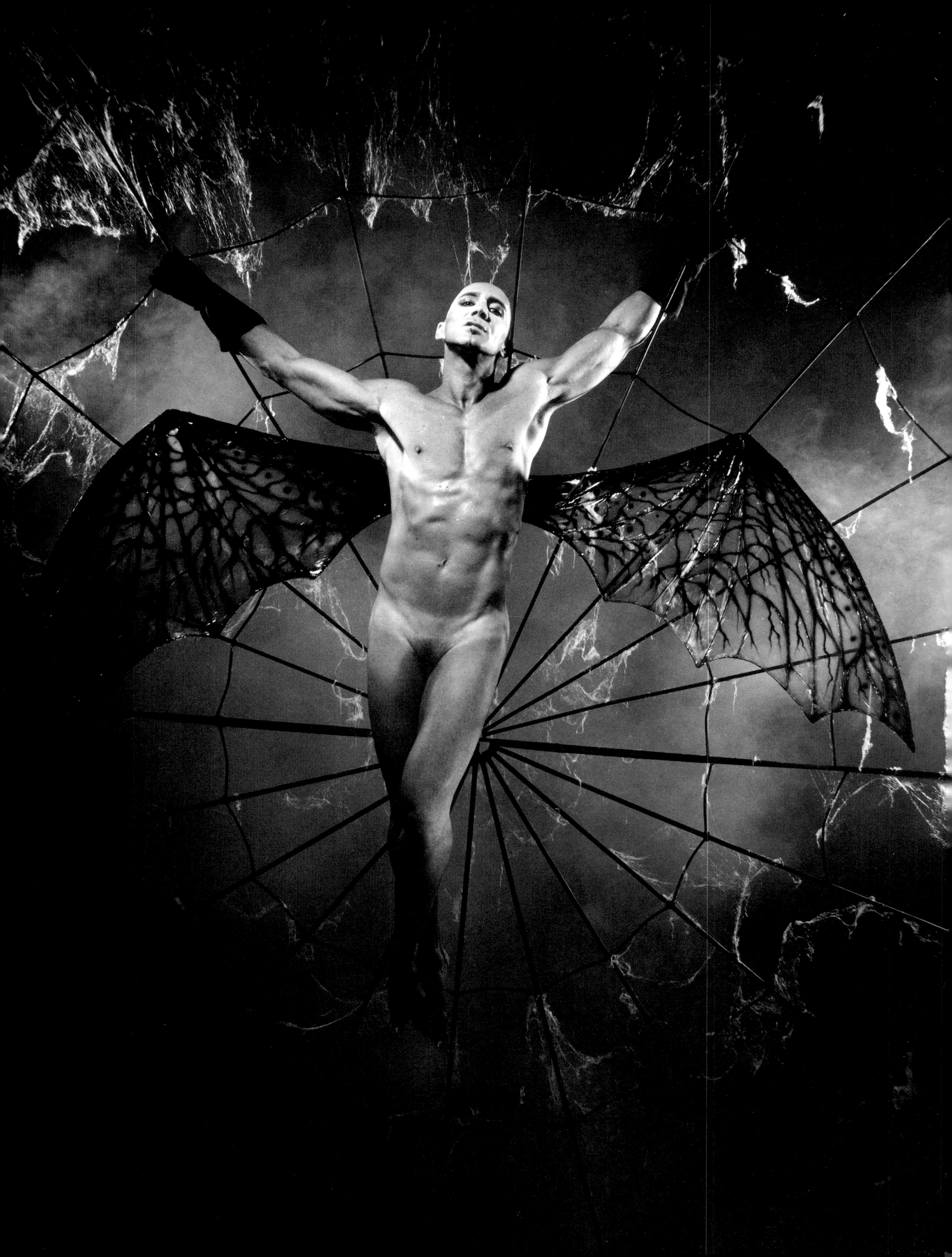

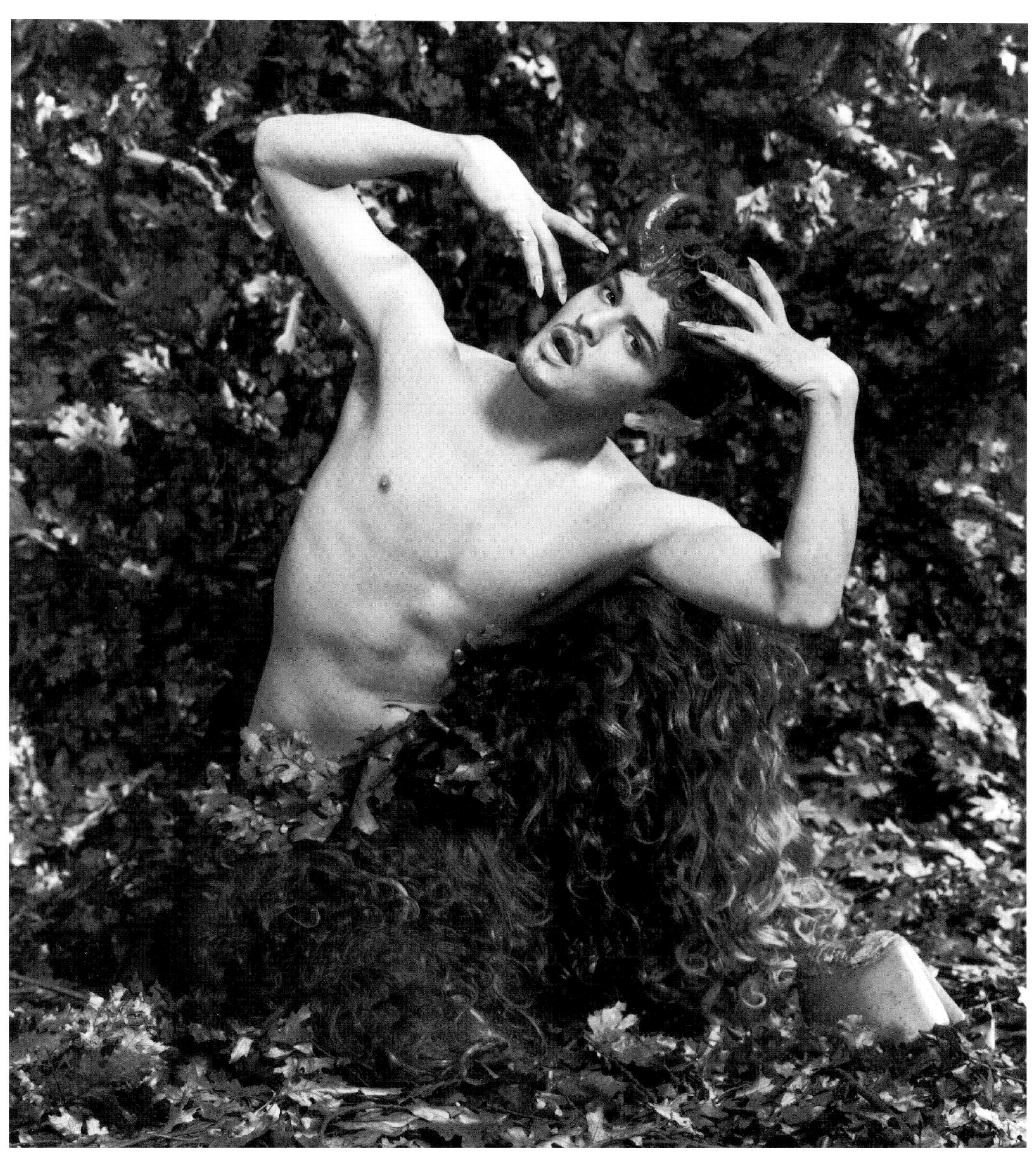

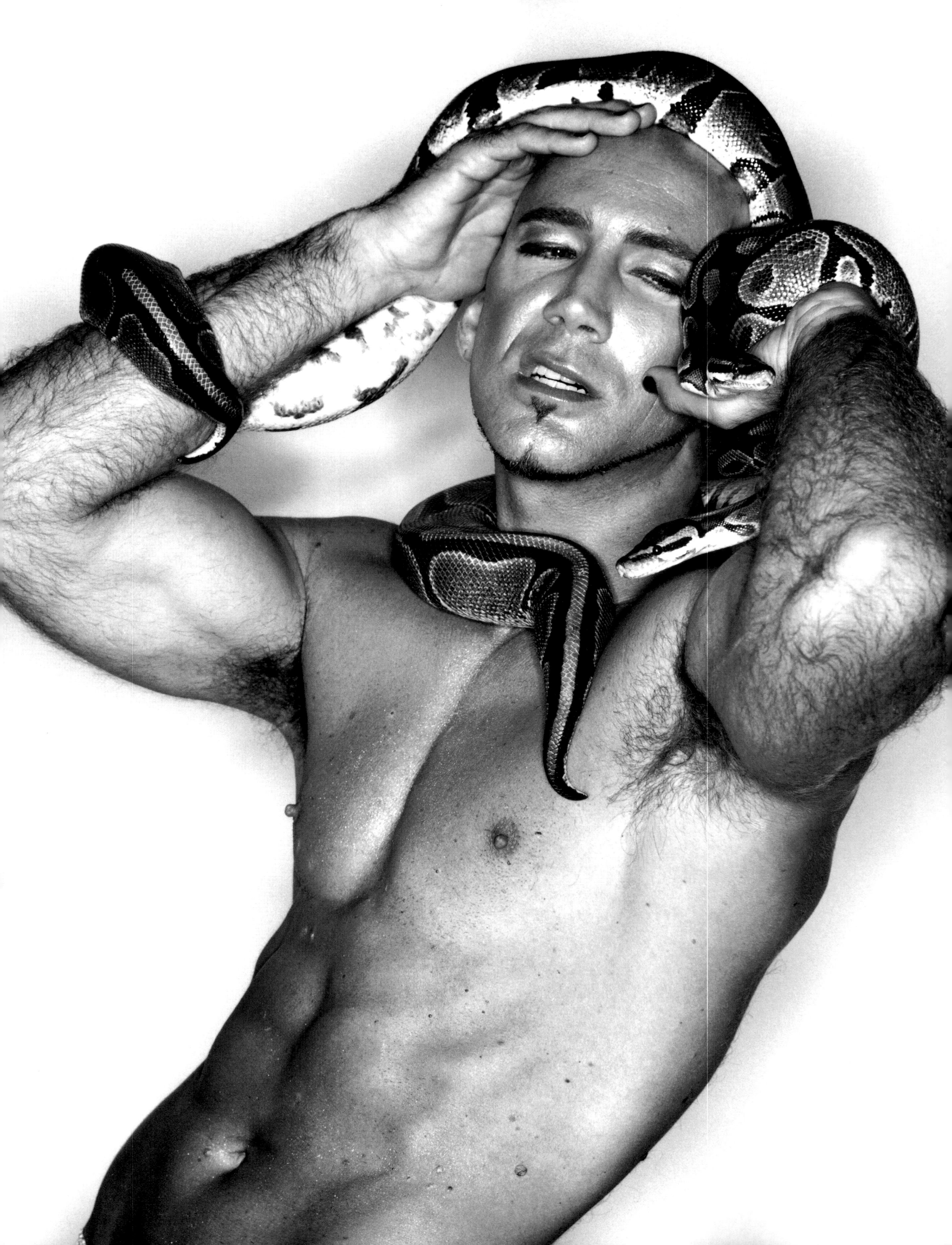

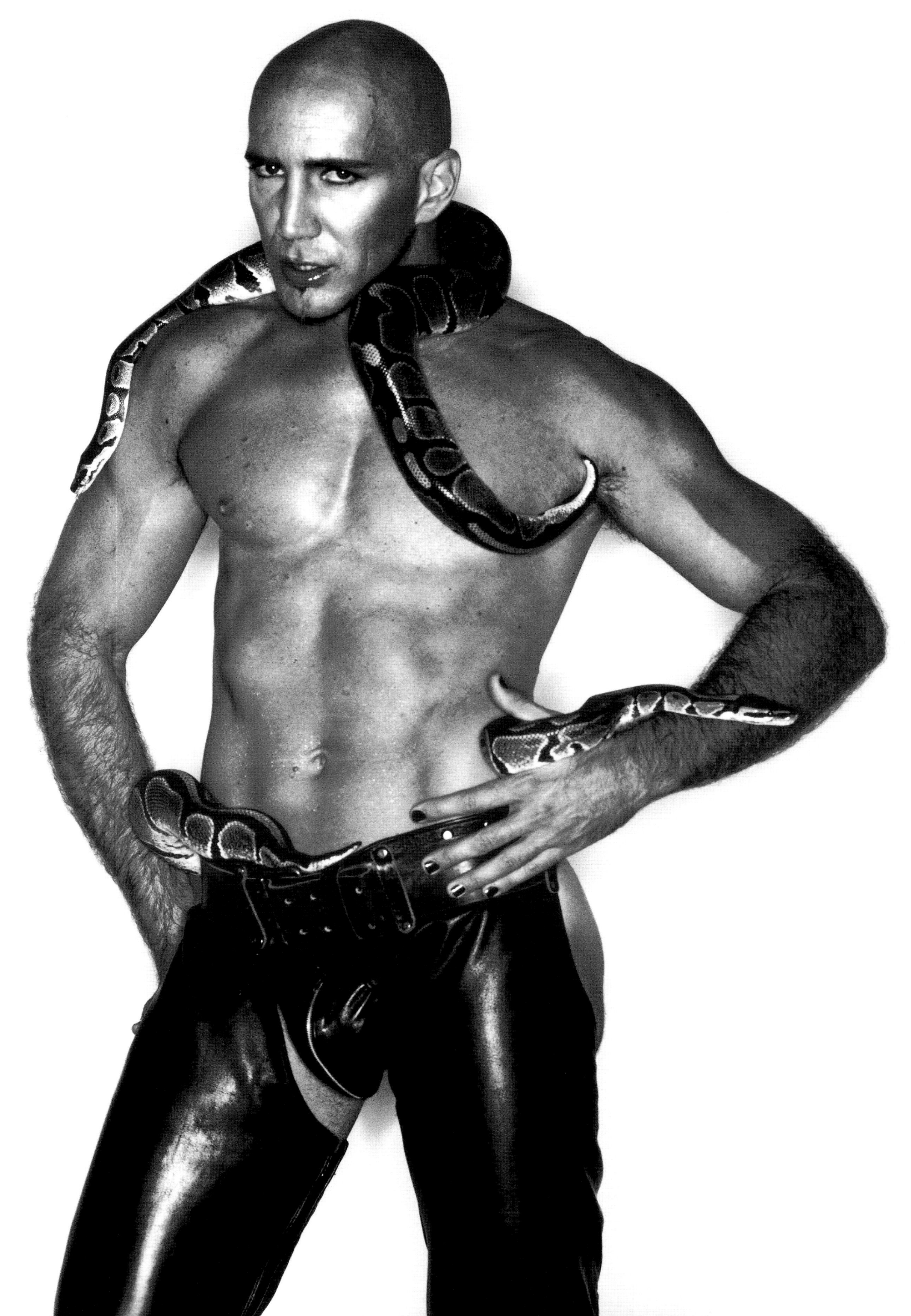

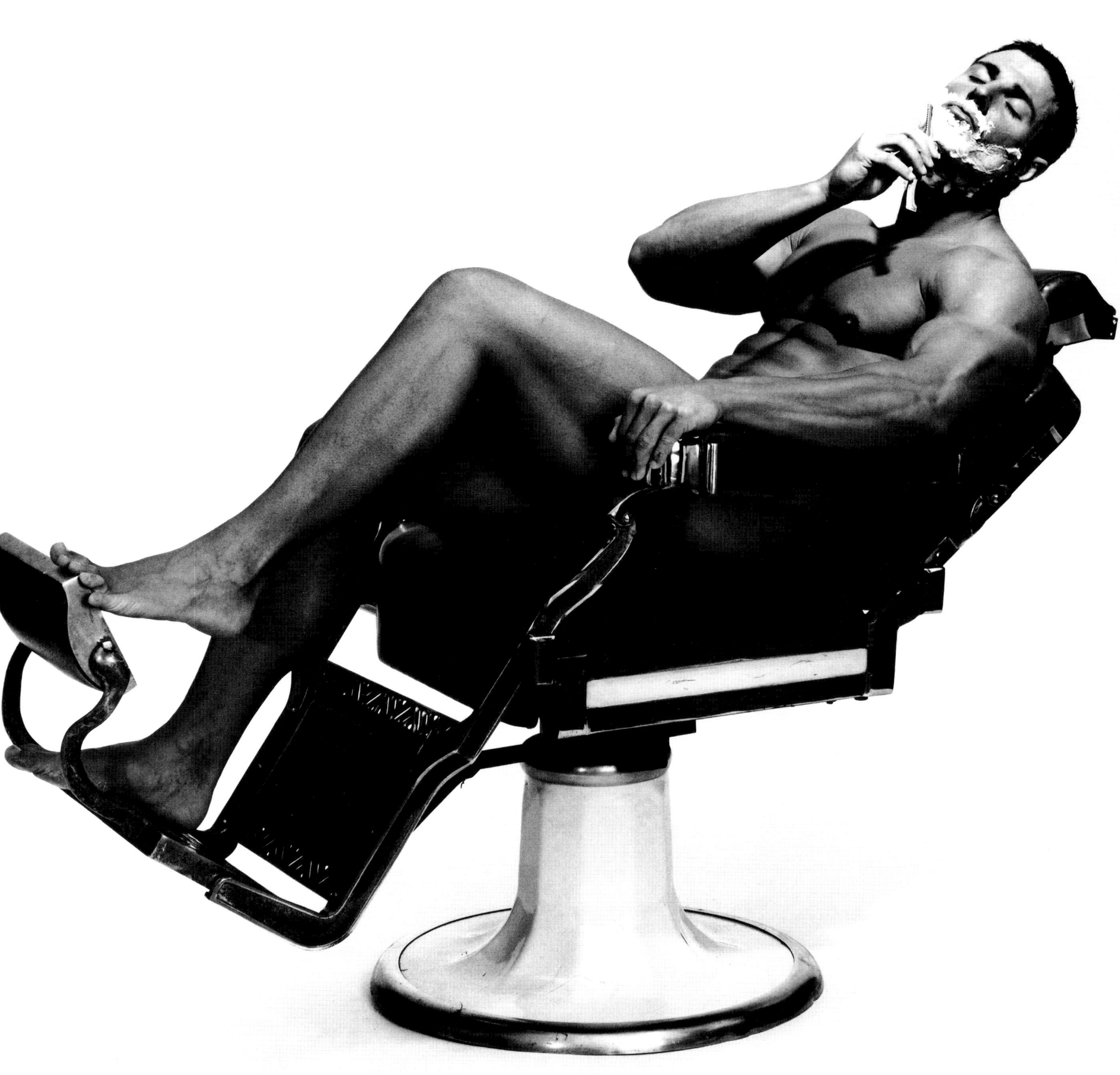

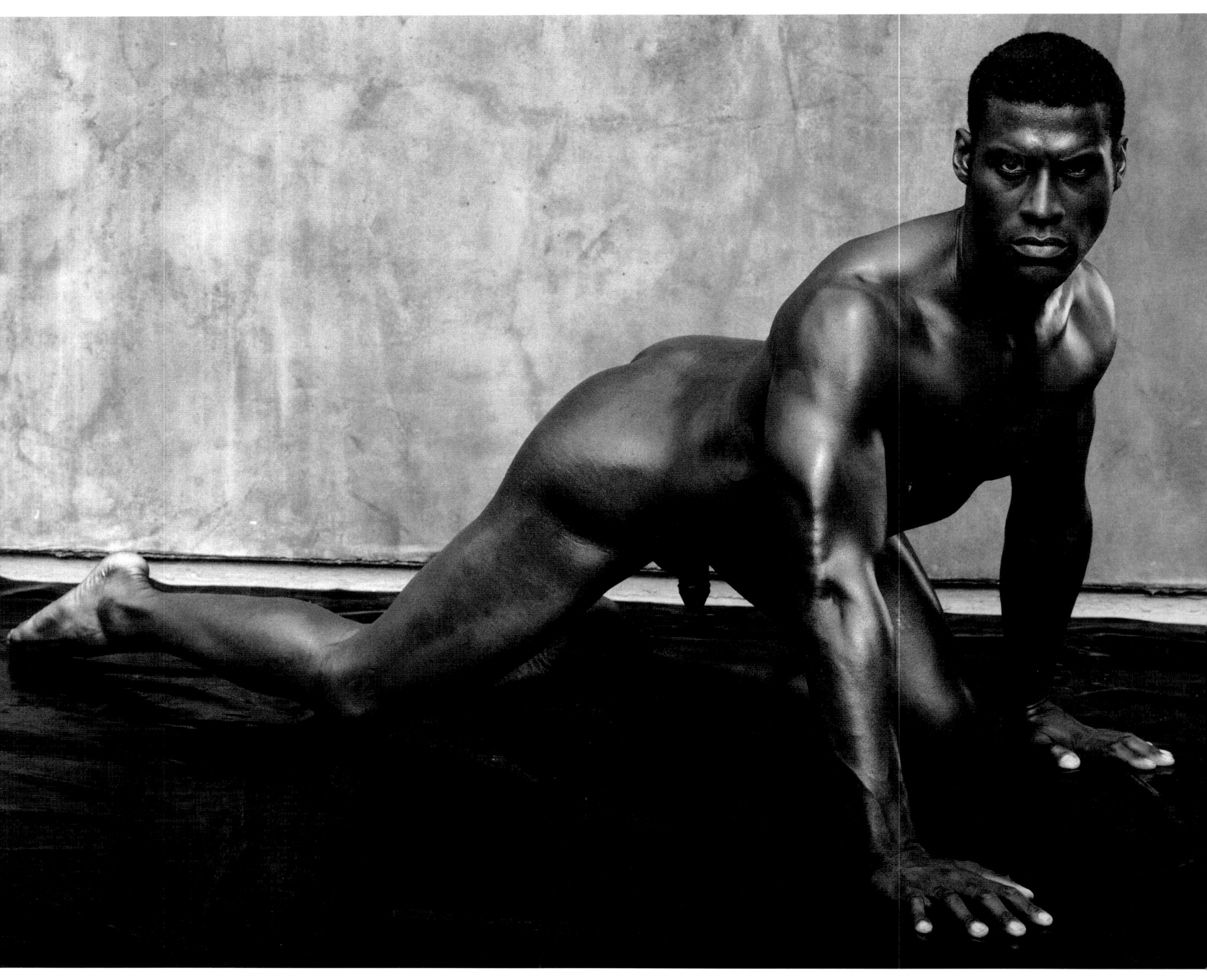

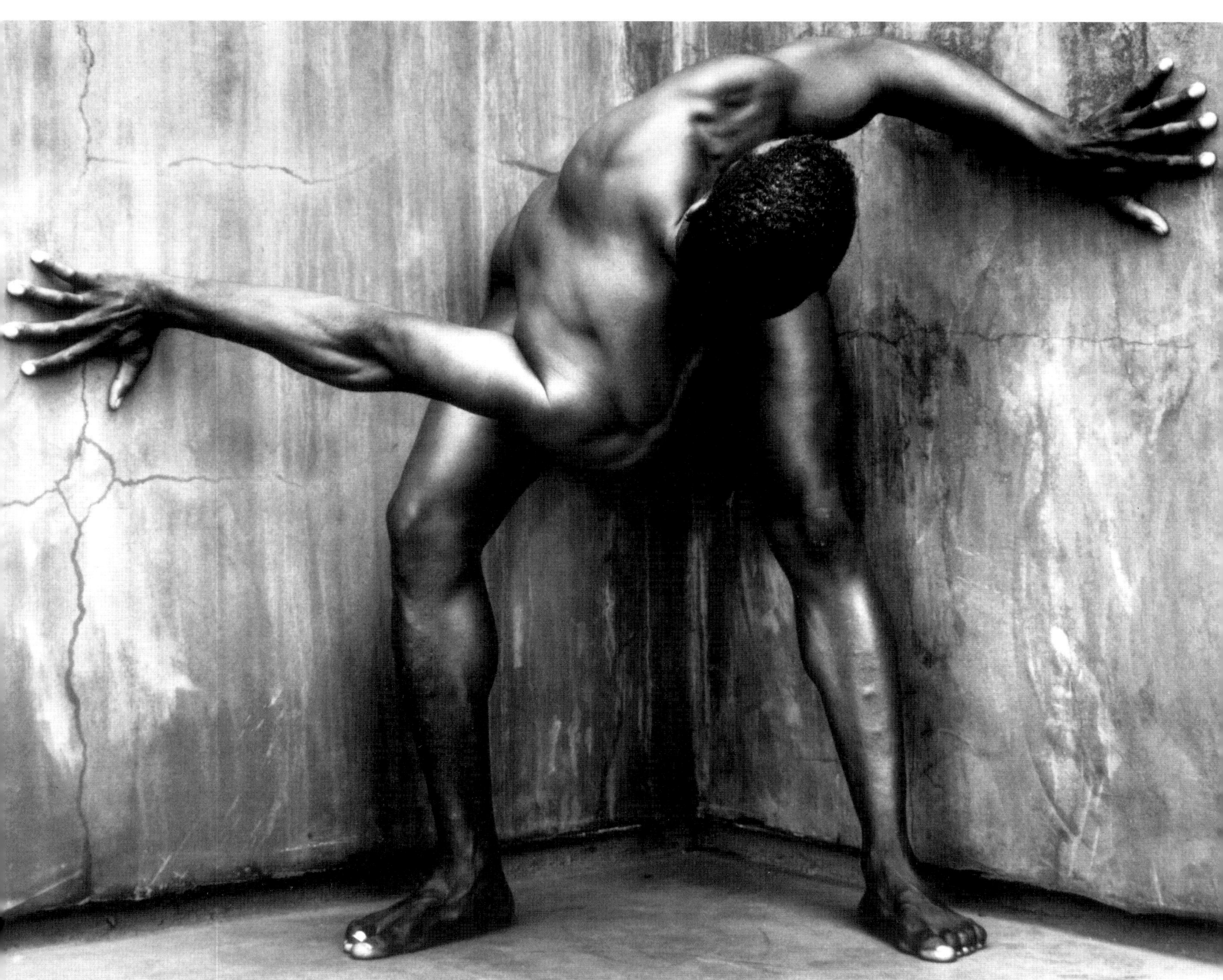

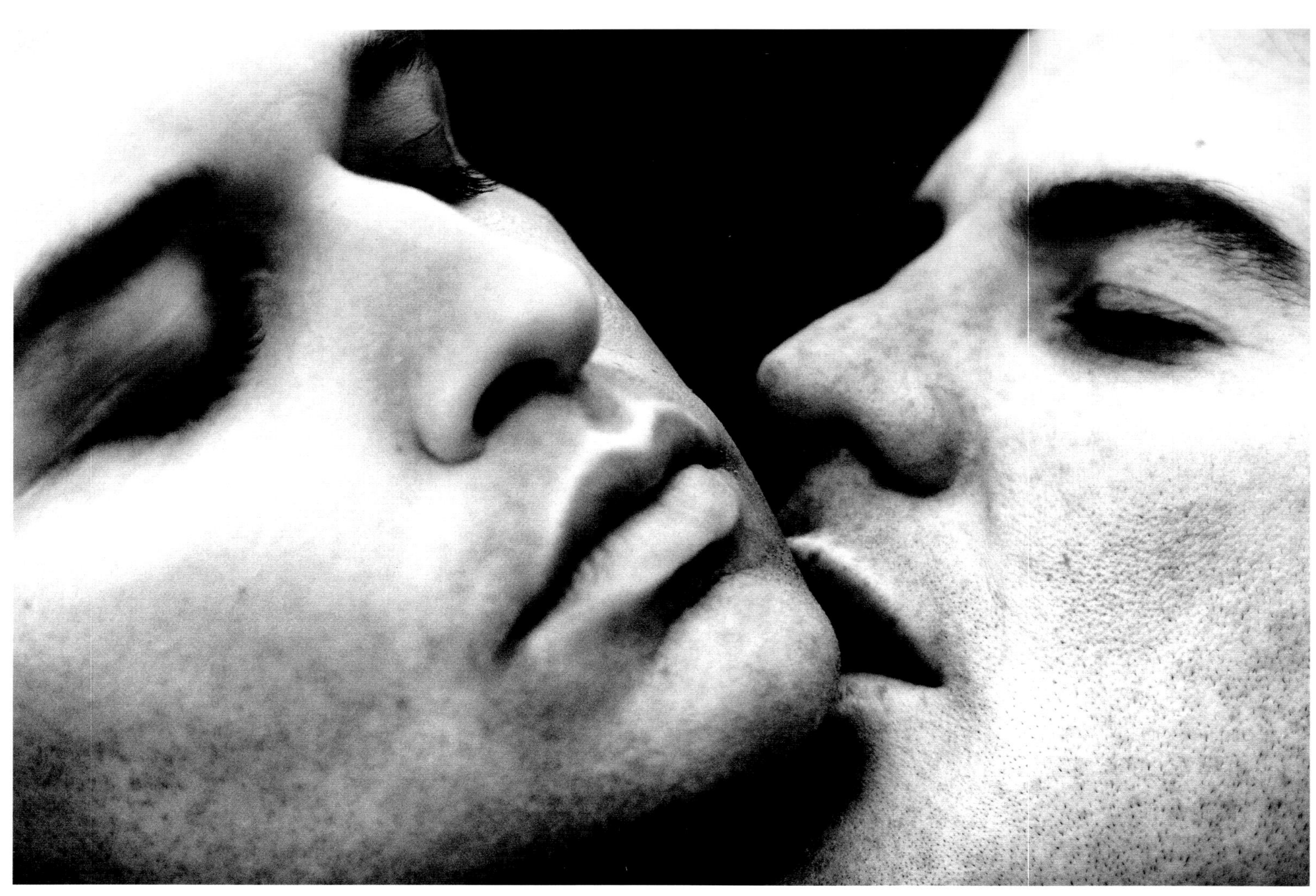

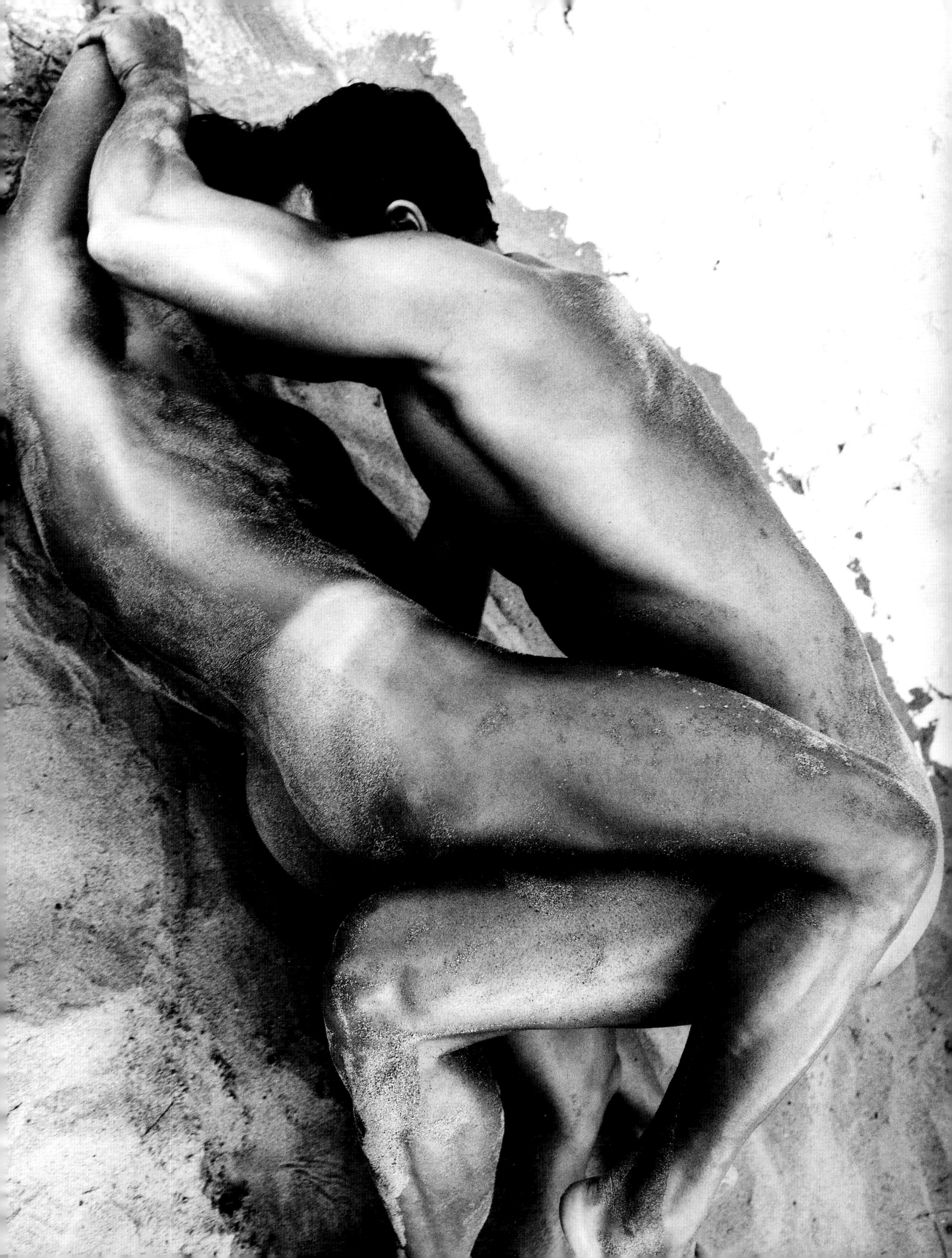

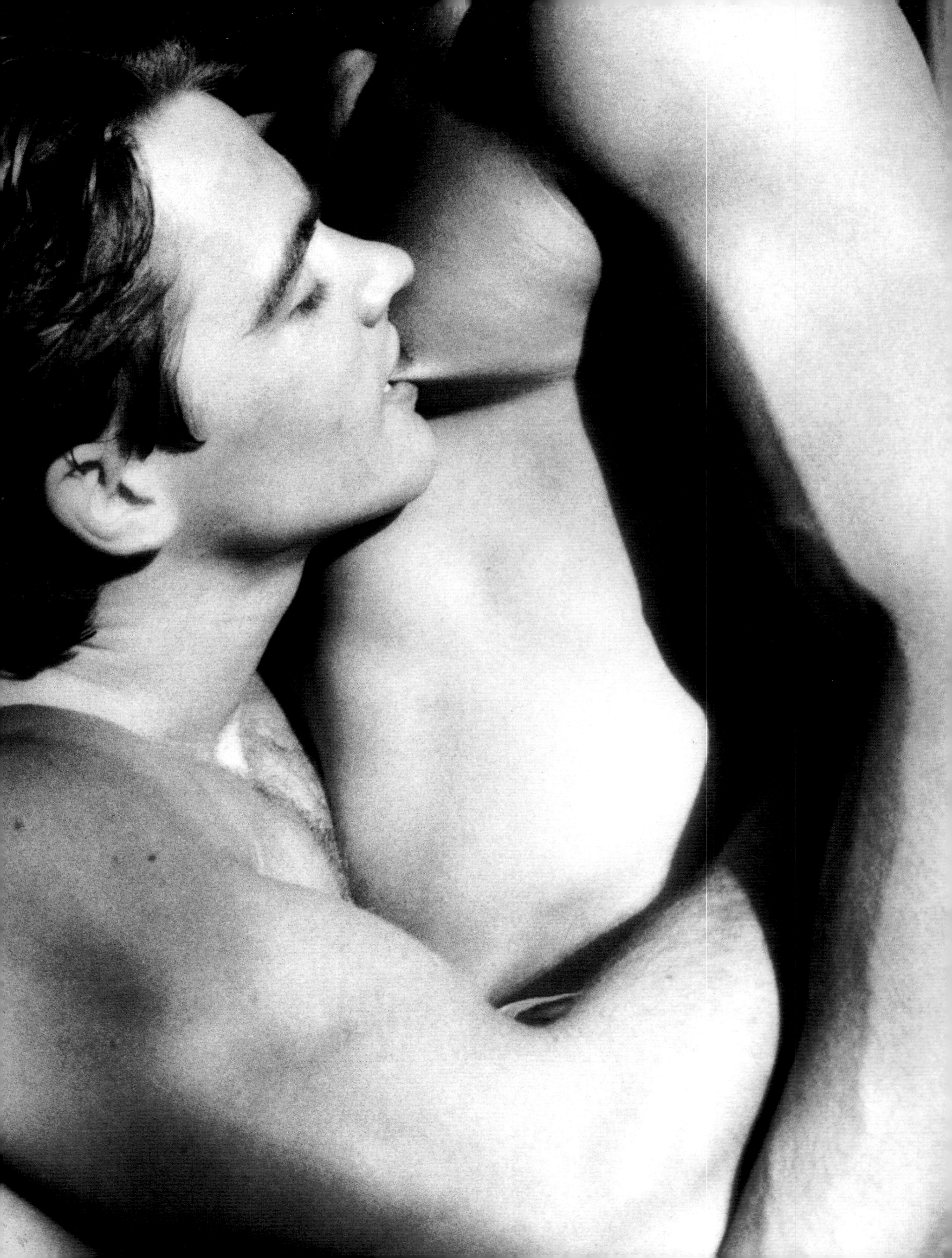

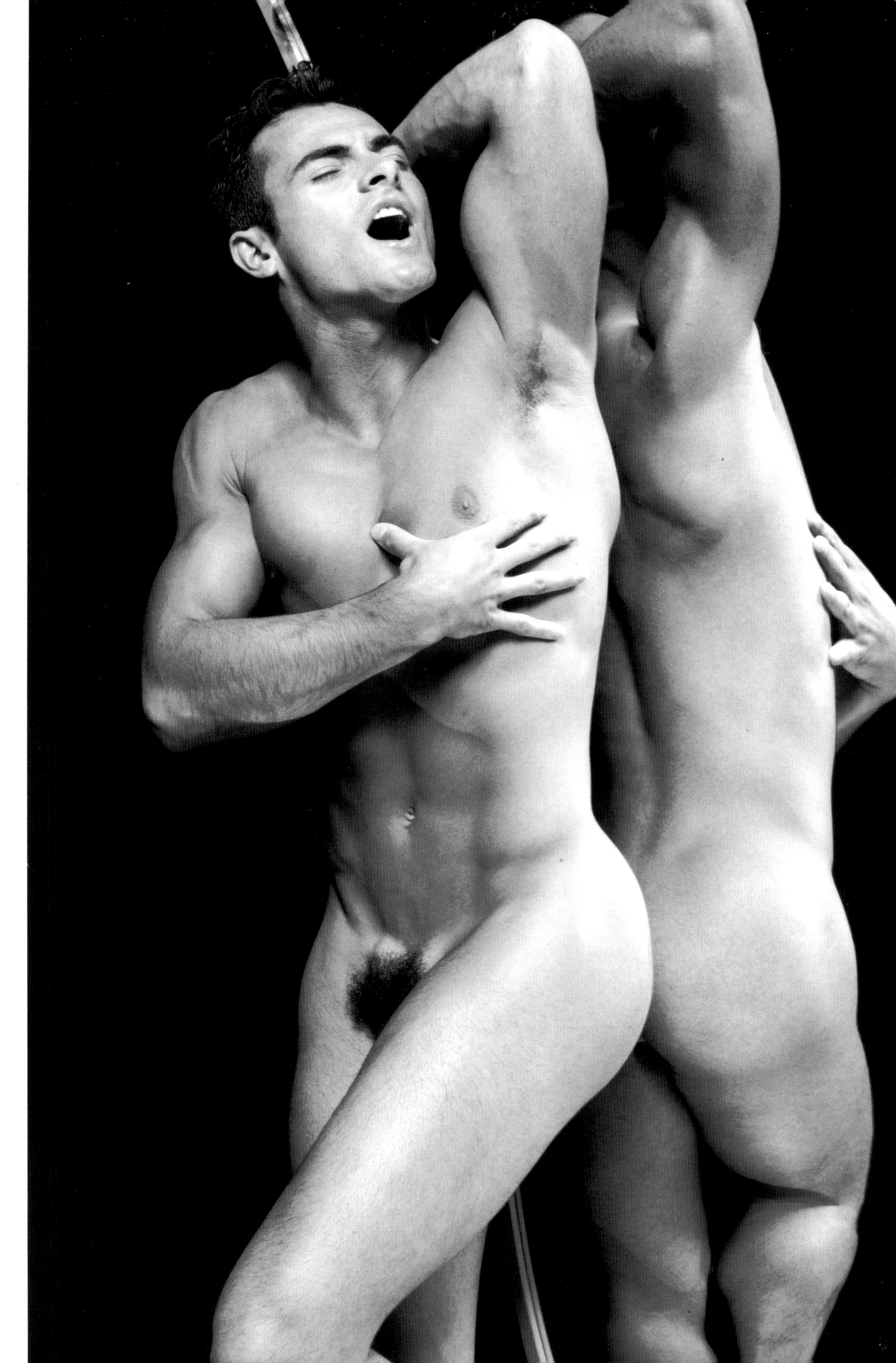

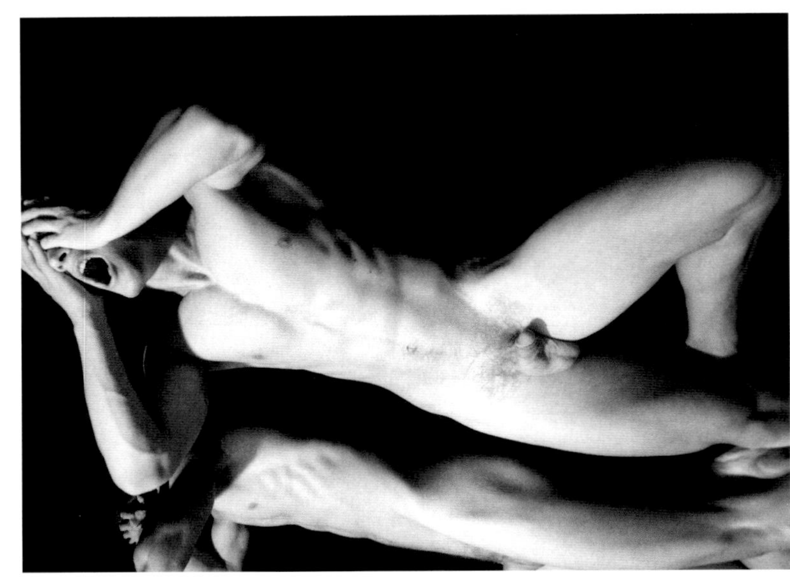

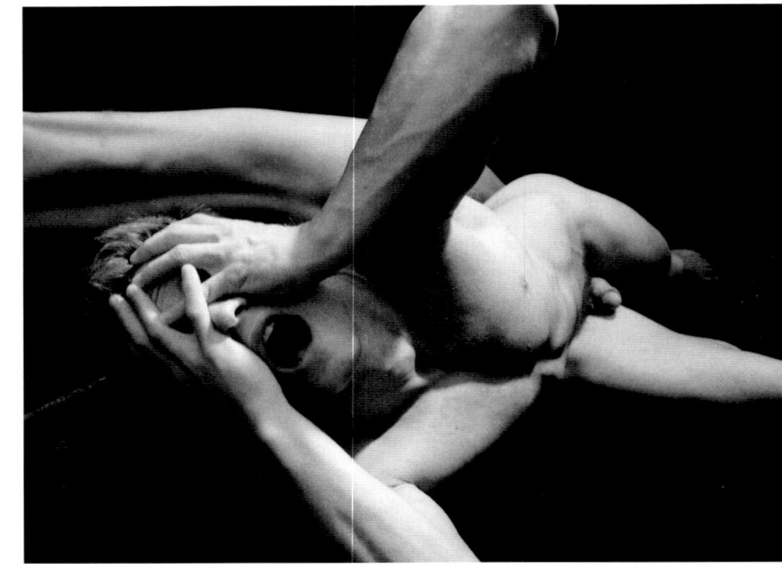

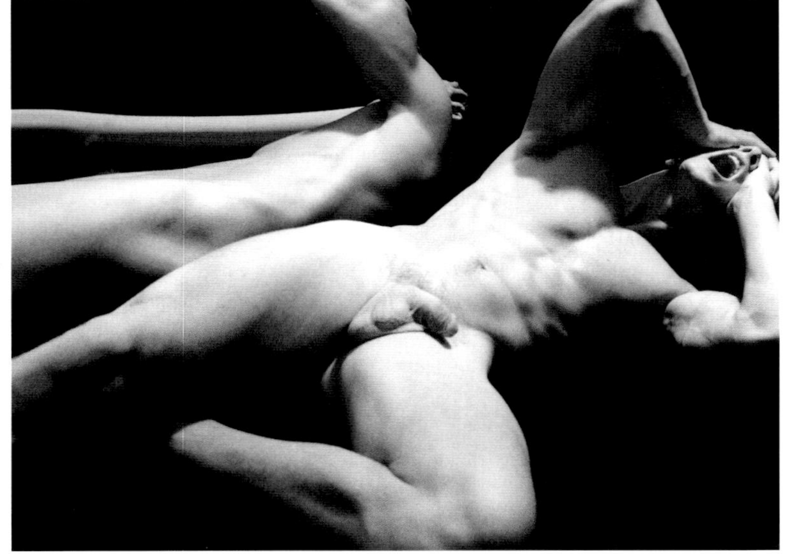

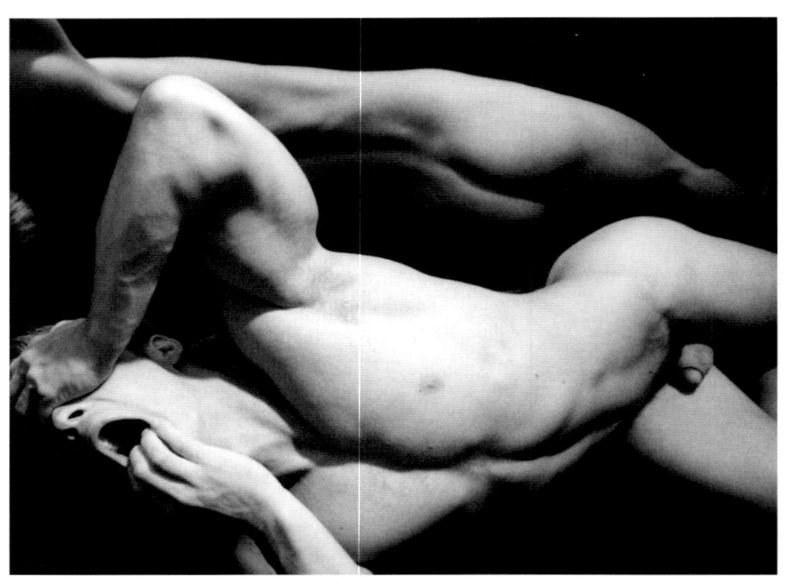

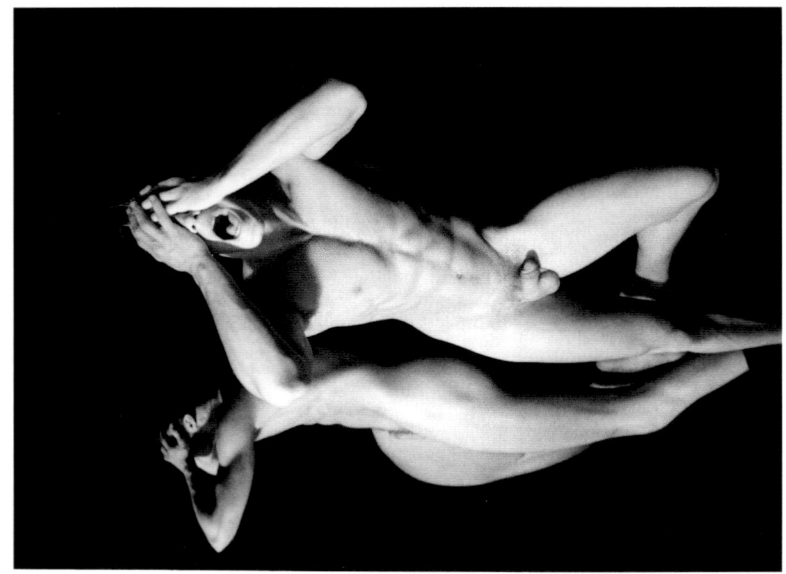

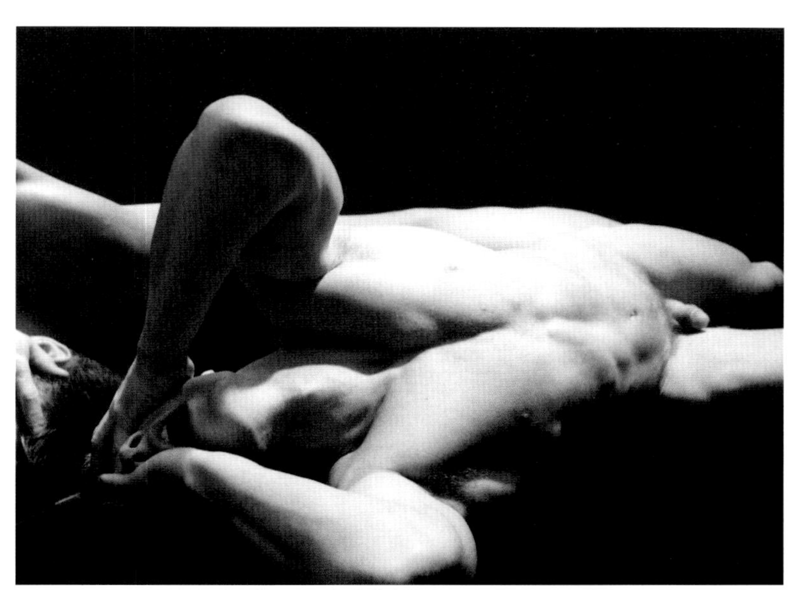
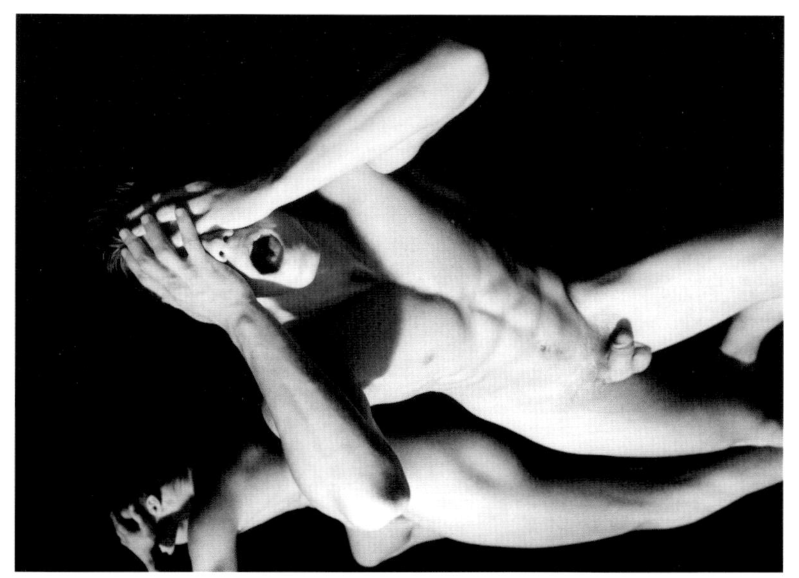
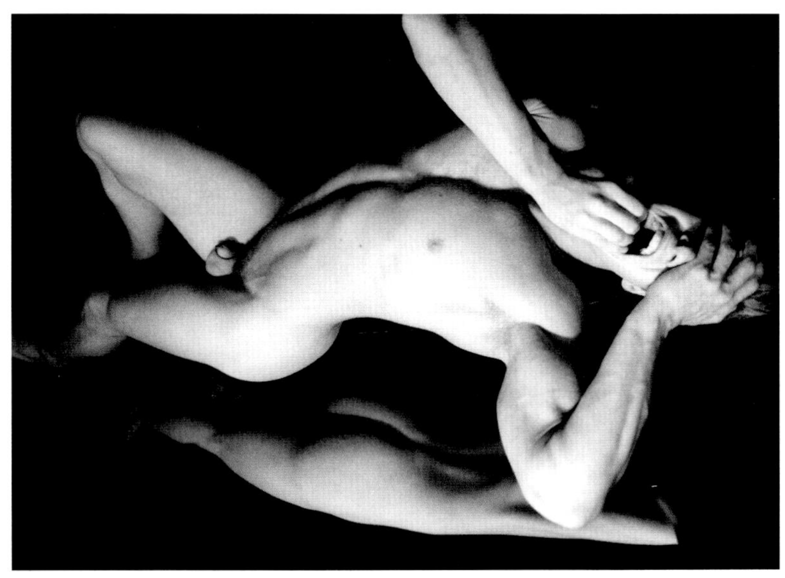
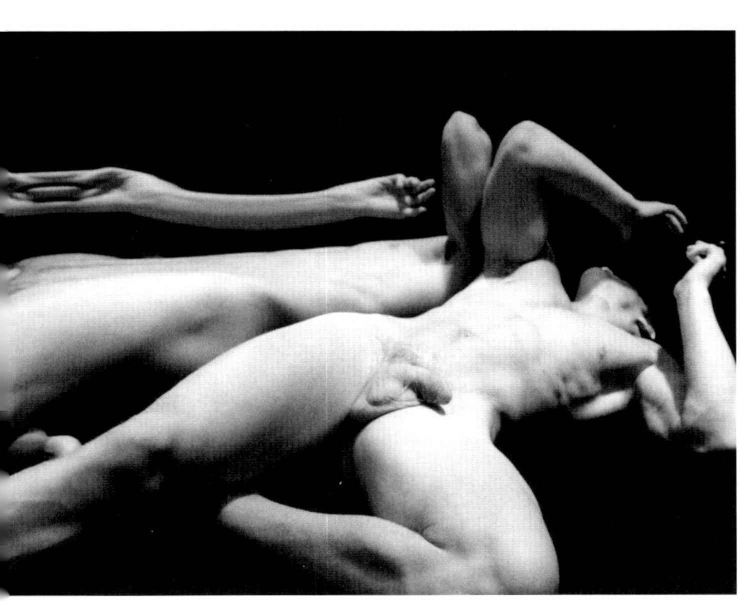
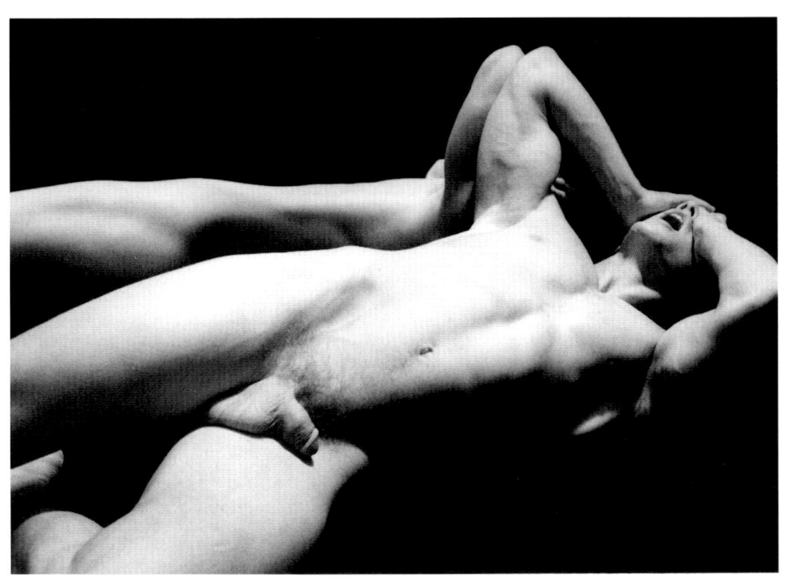

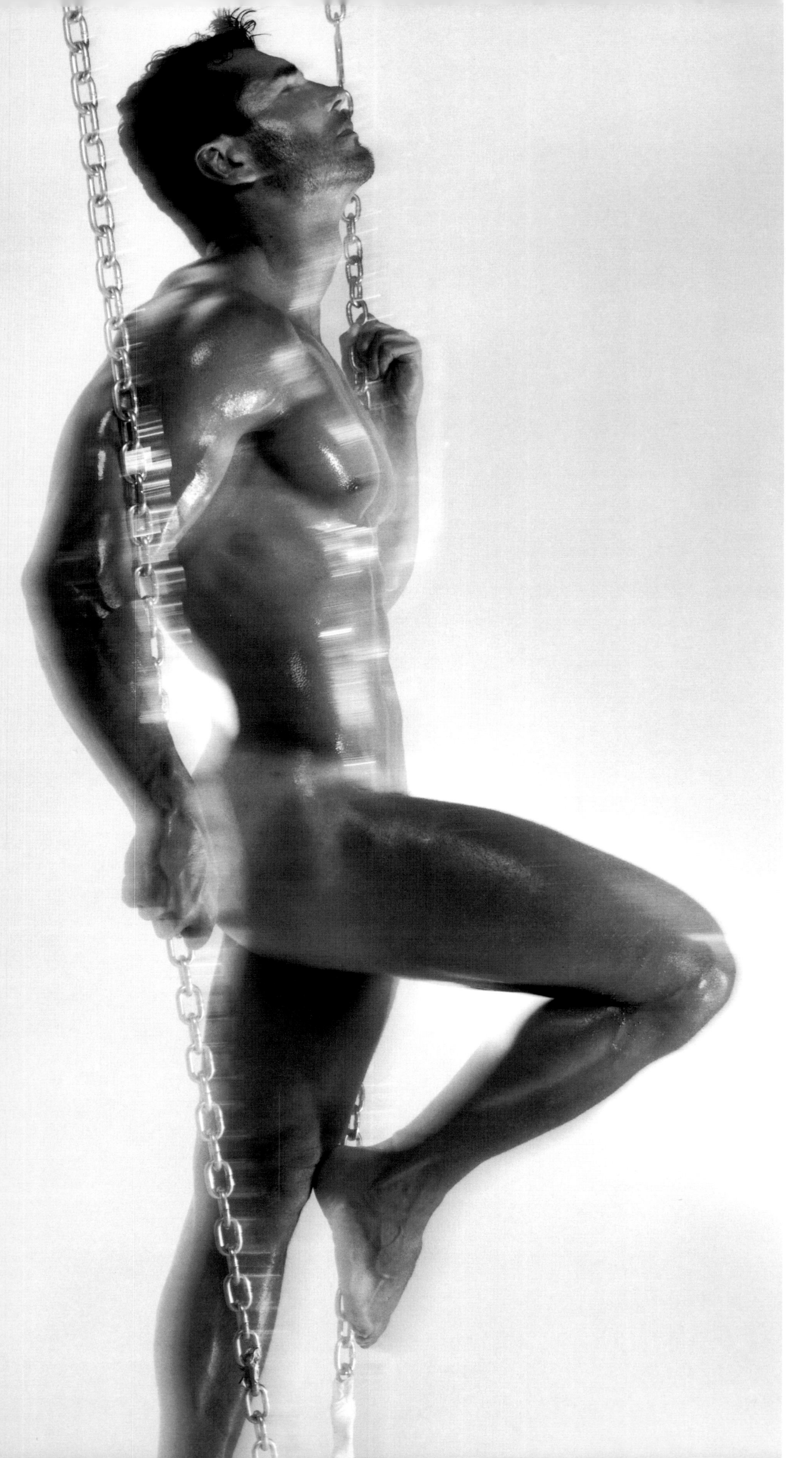

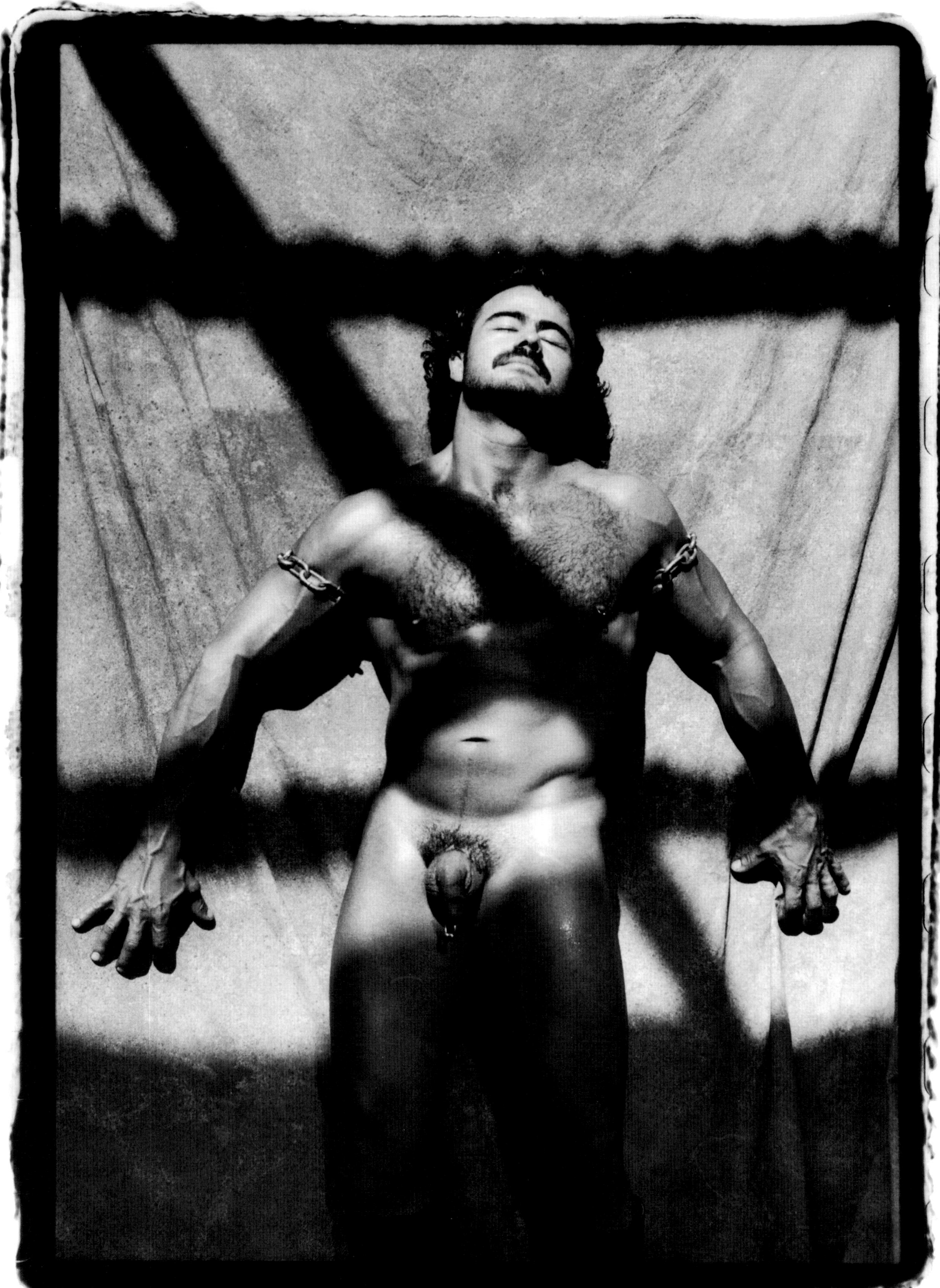

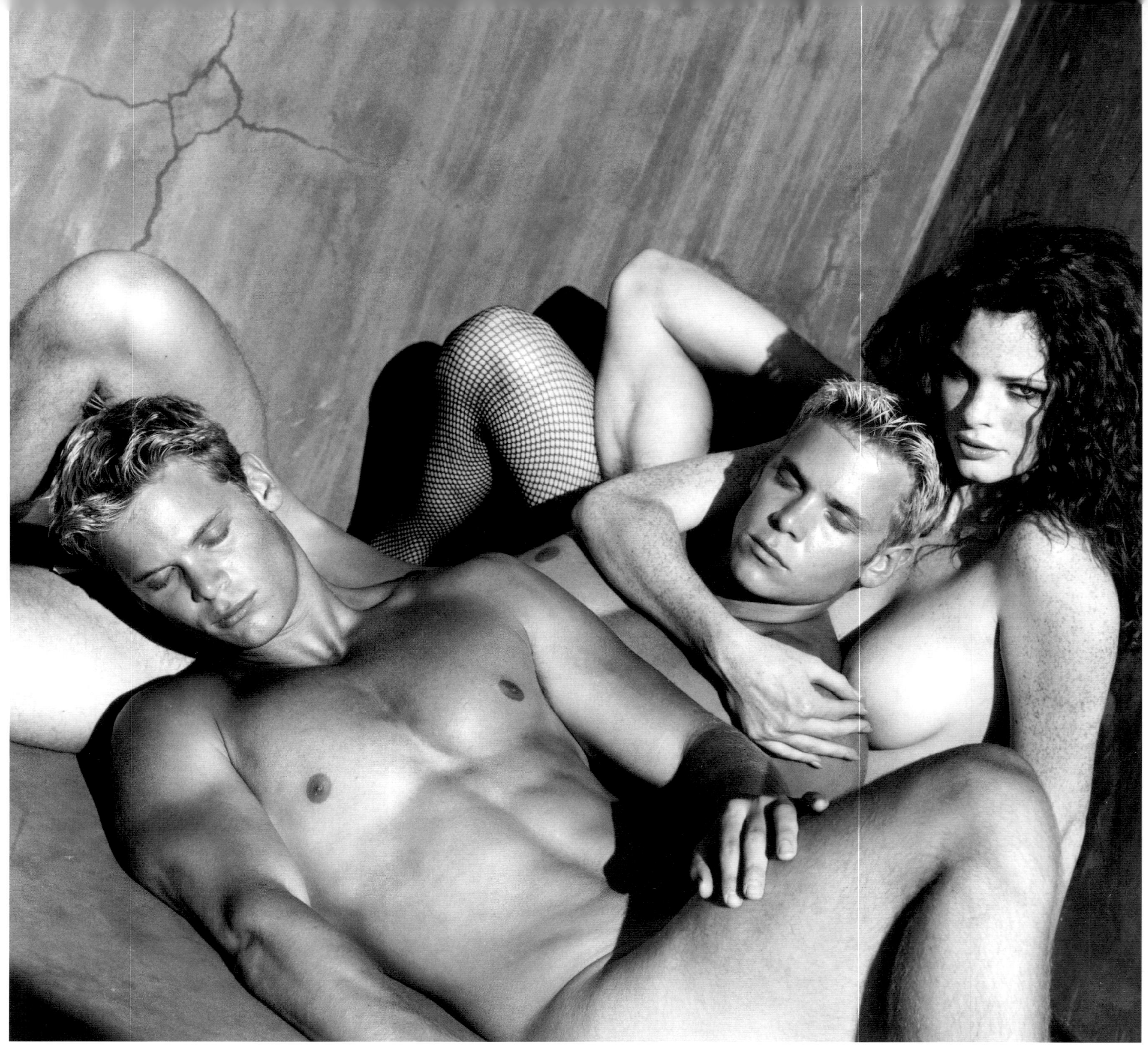

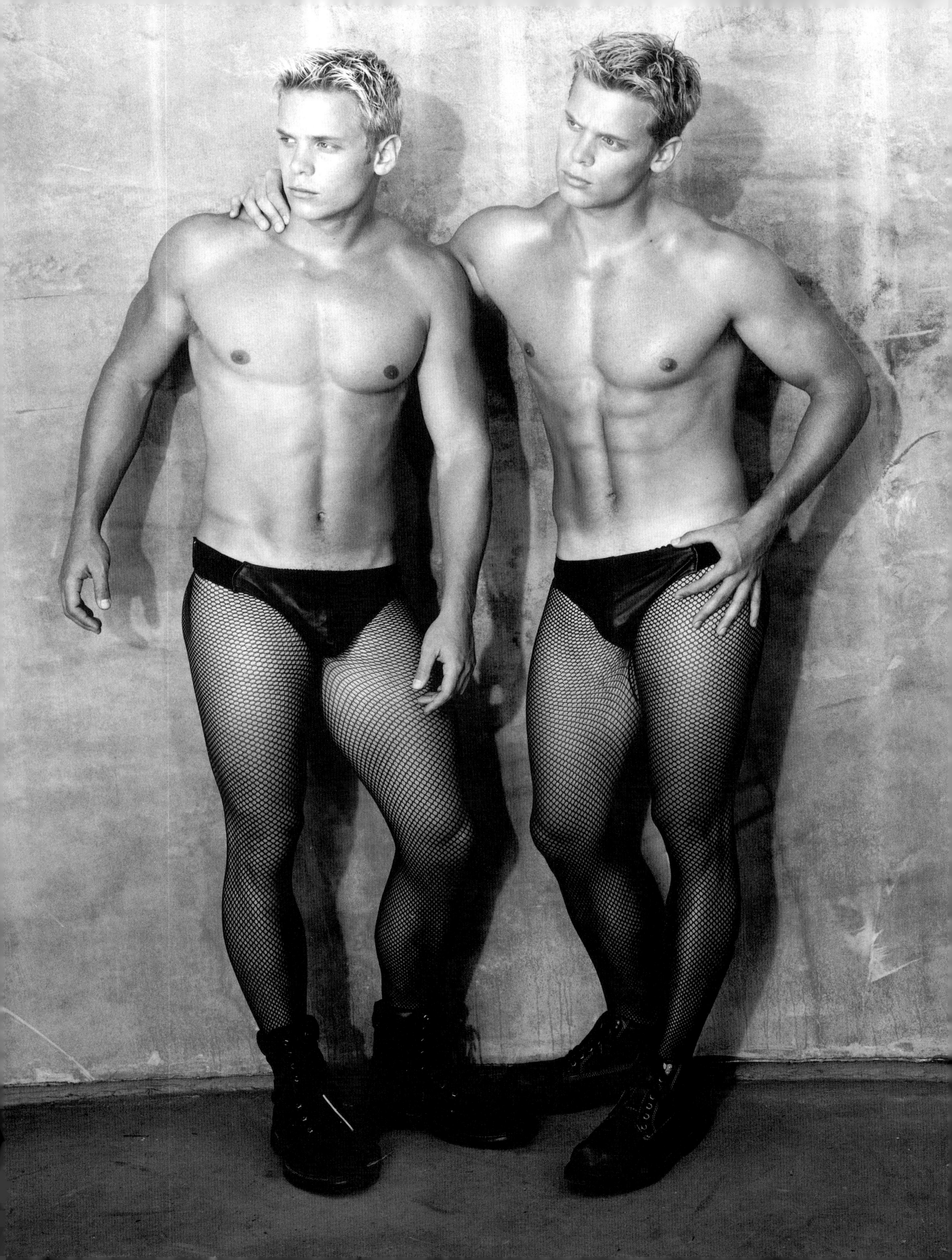

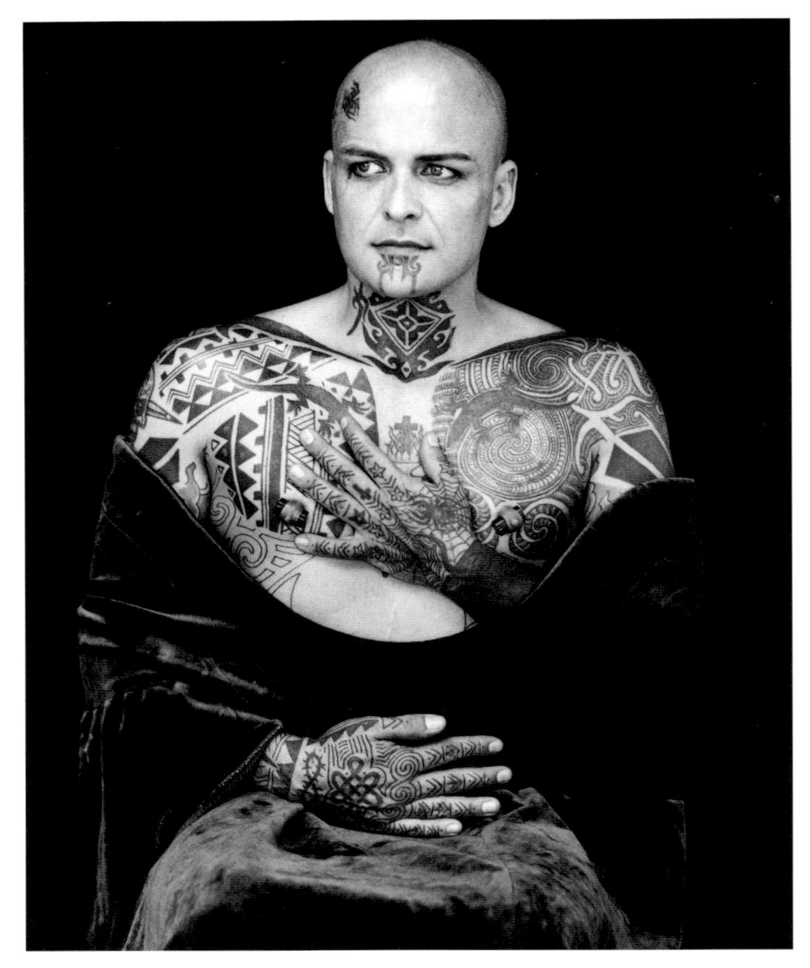

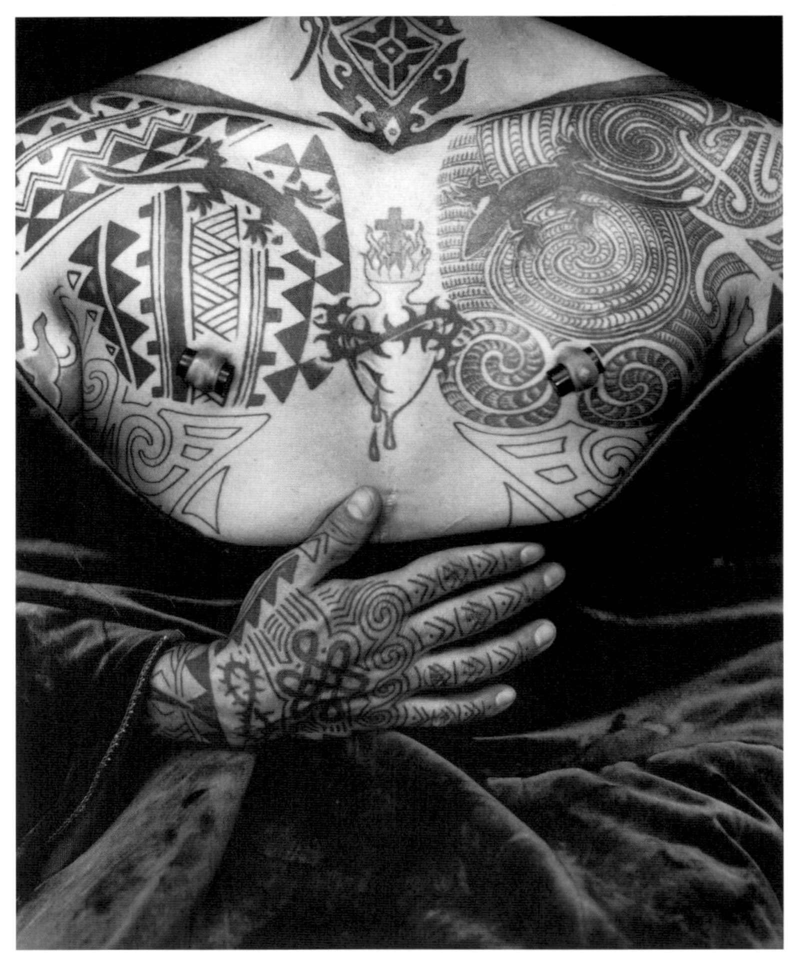

Ron Athey Performance Artist

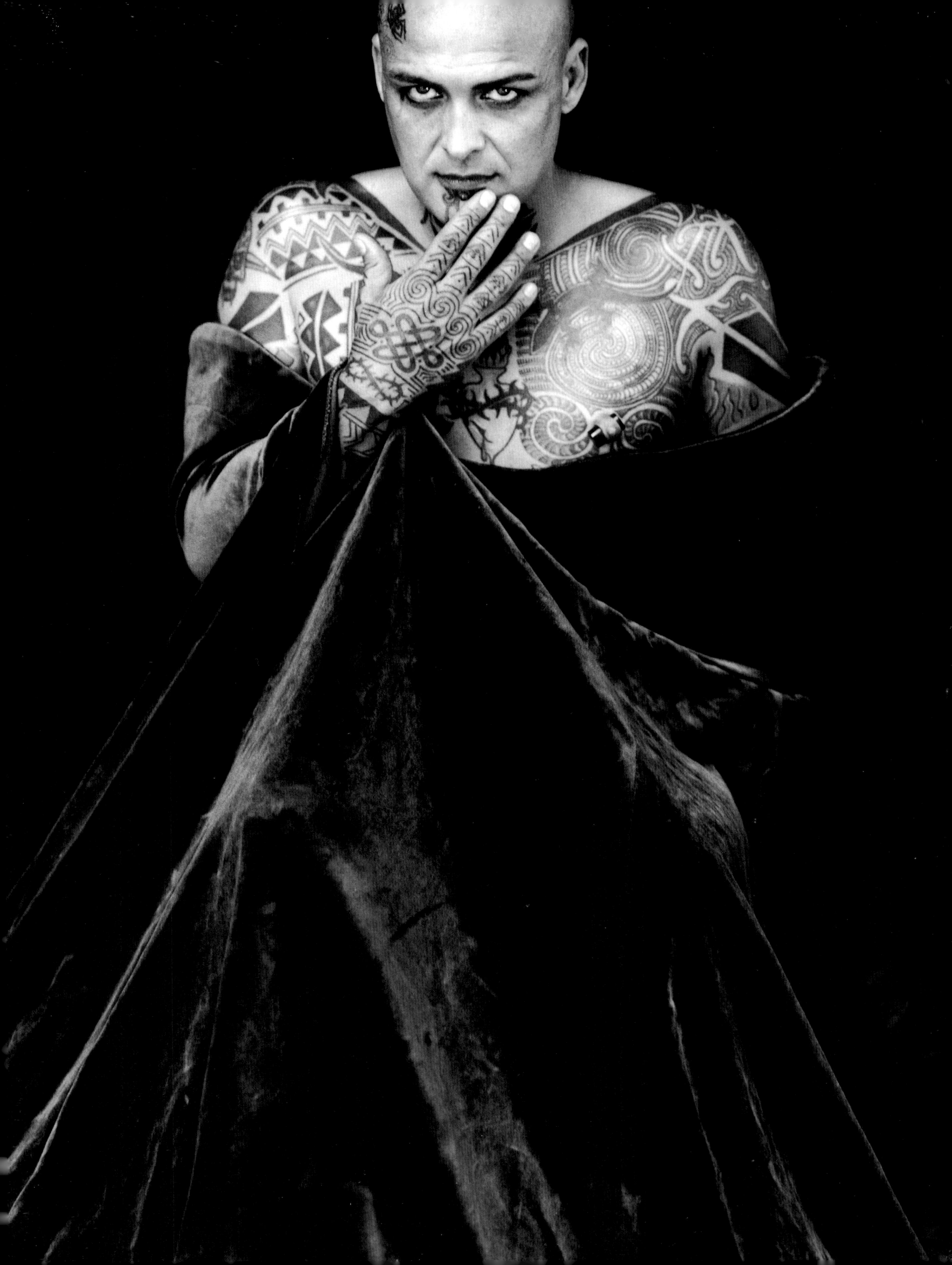

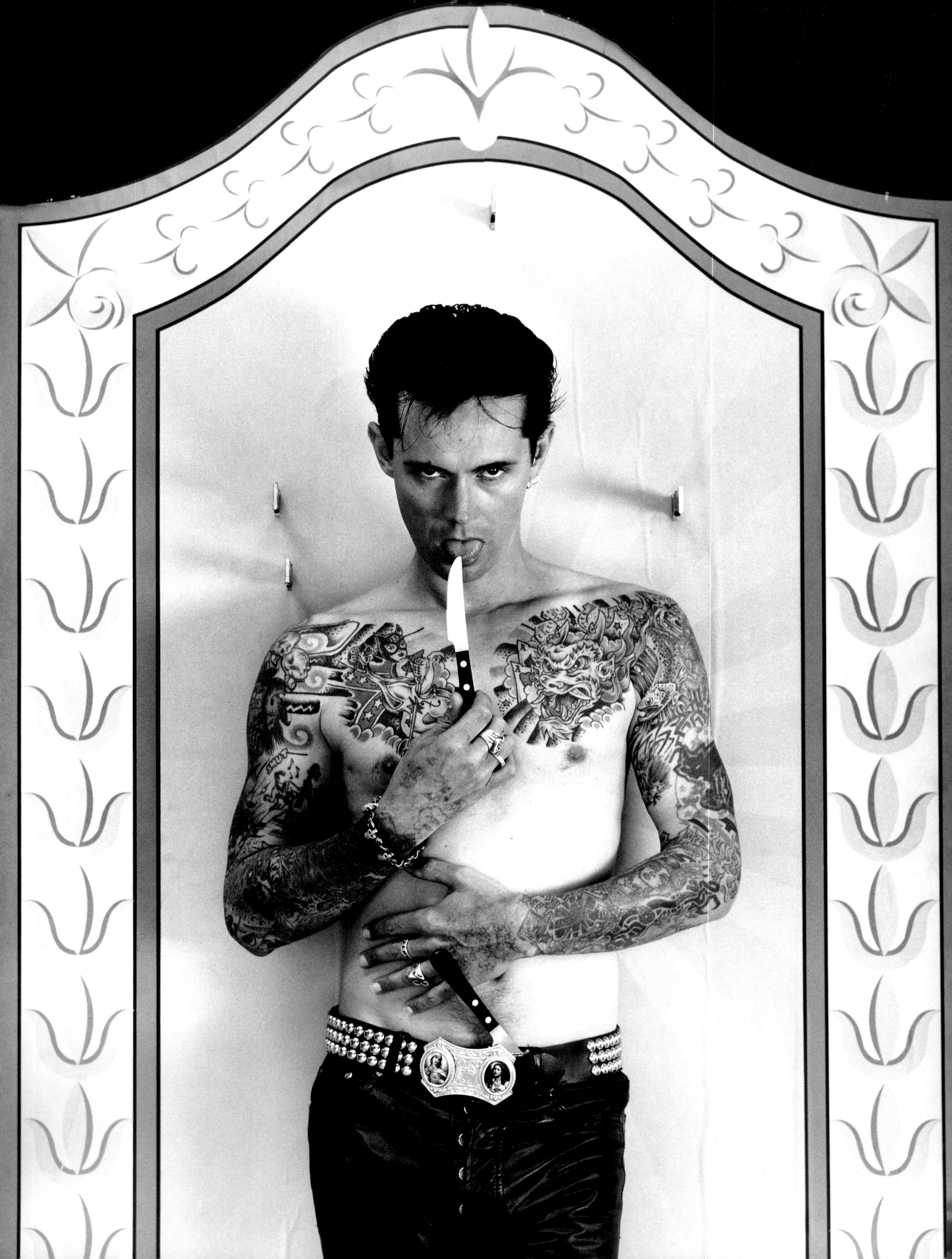

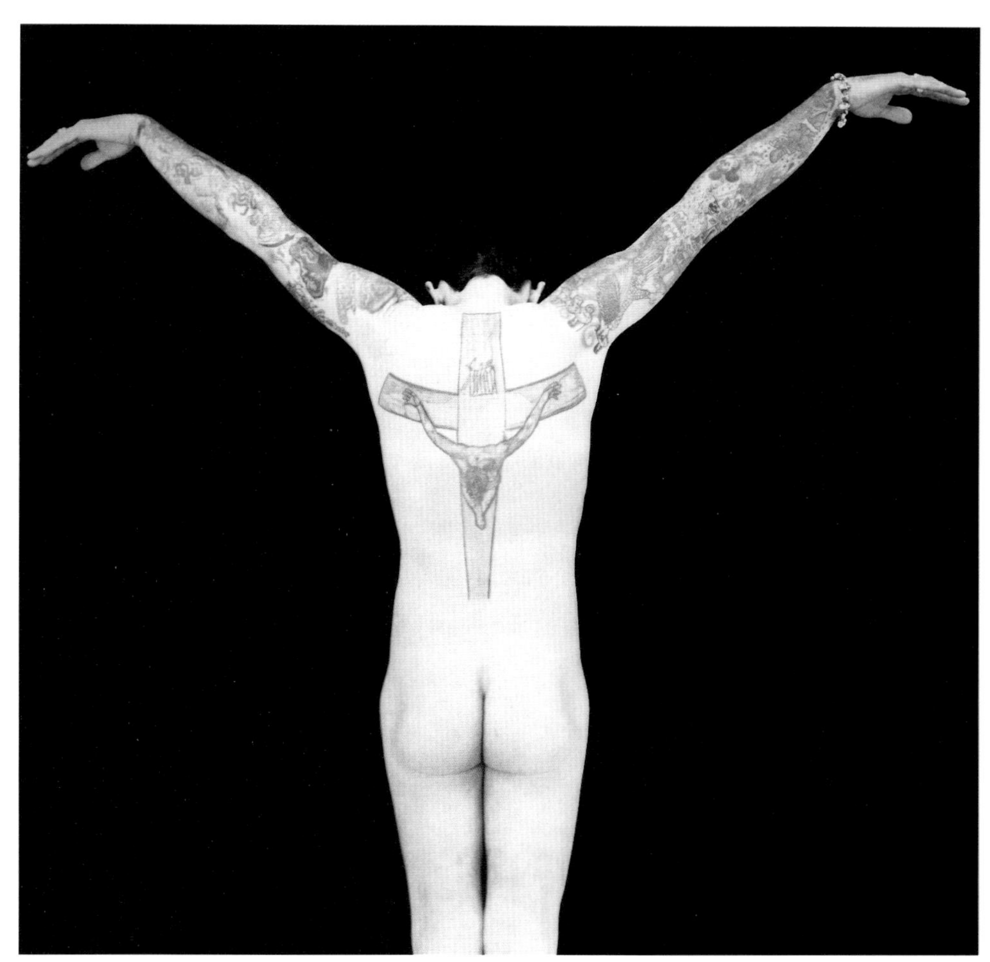

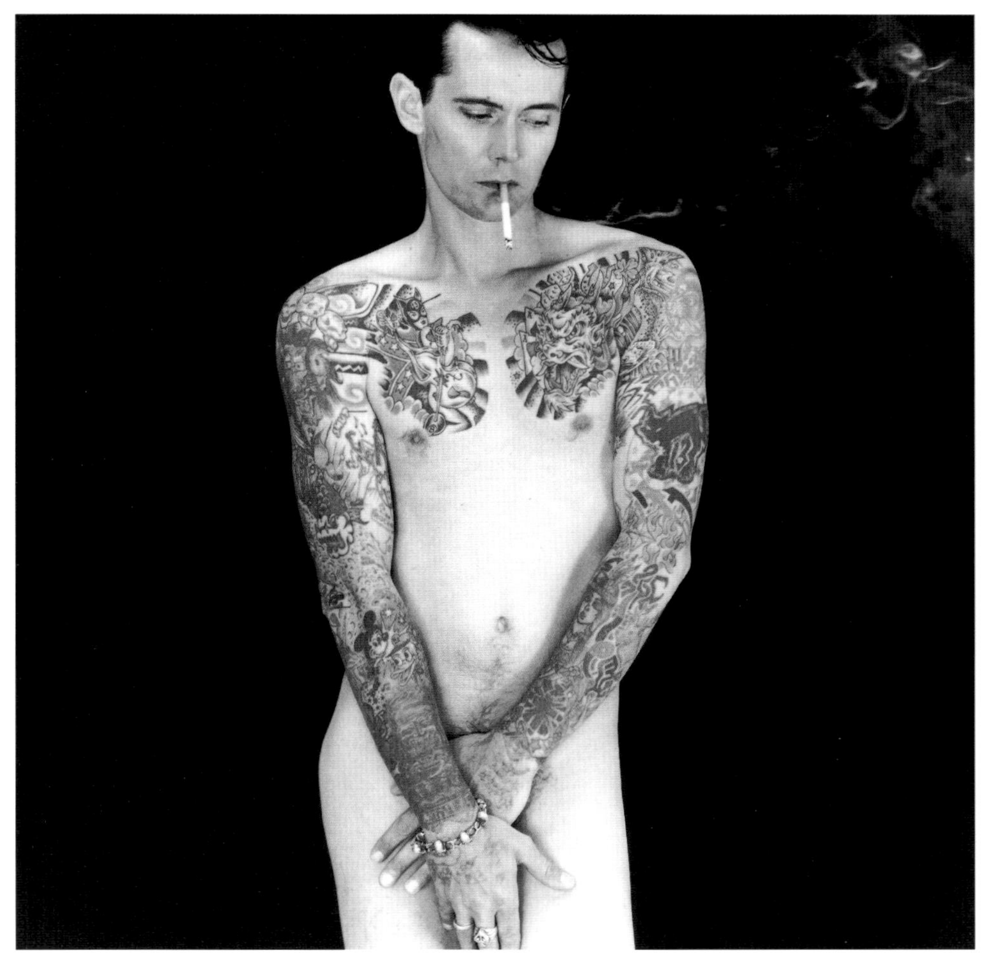

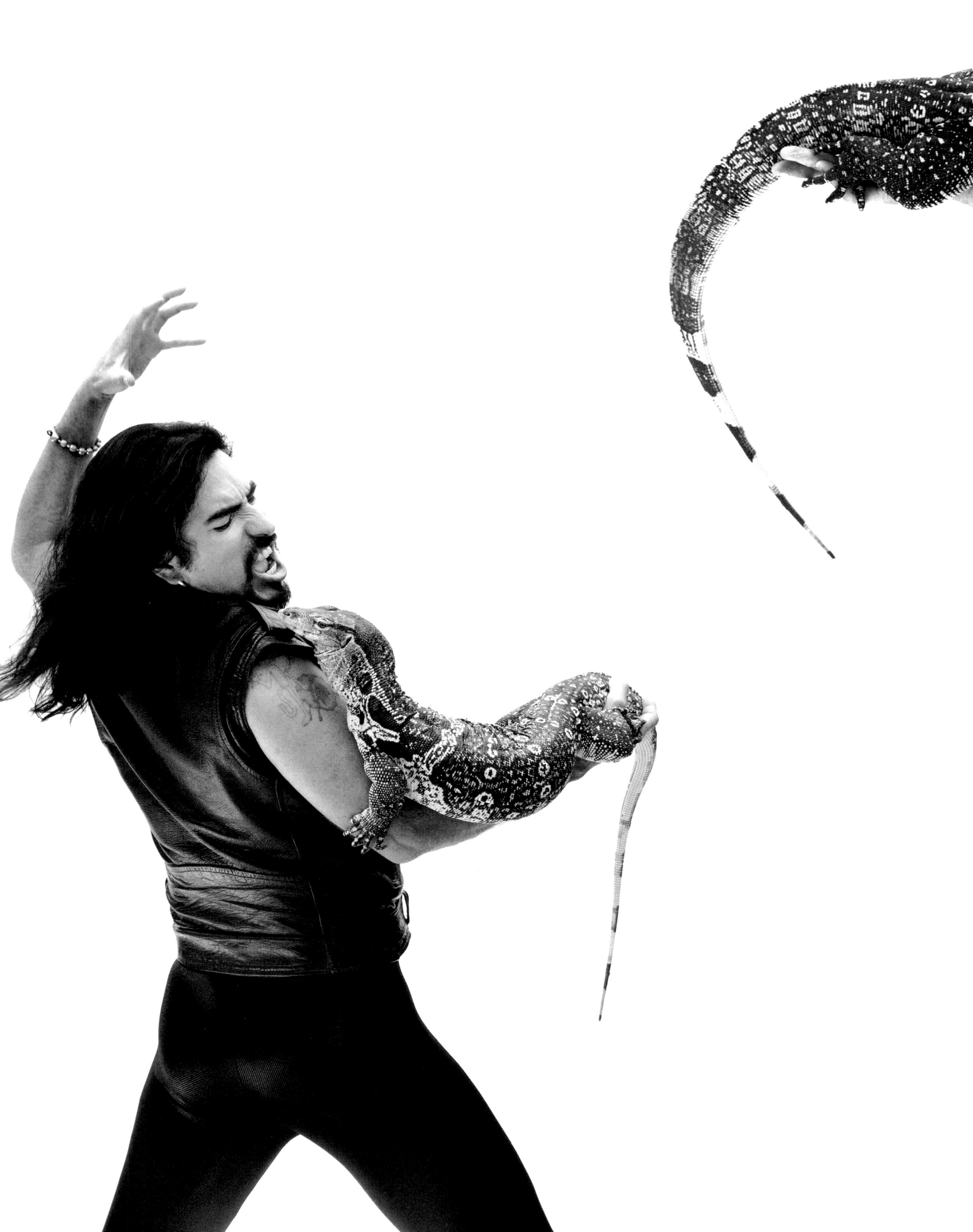

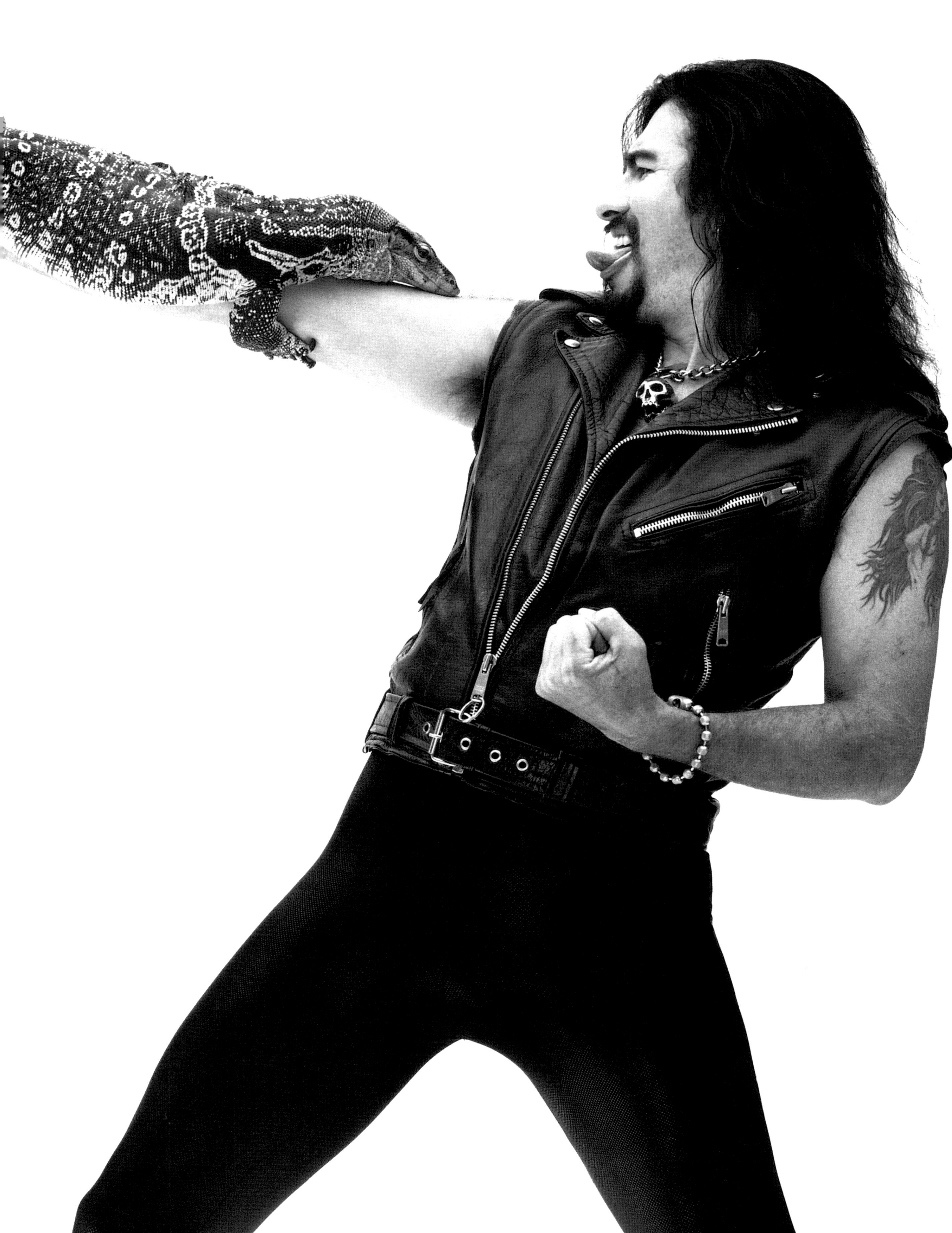

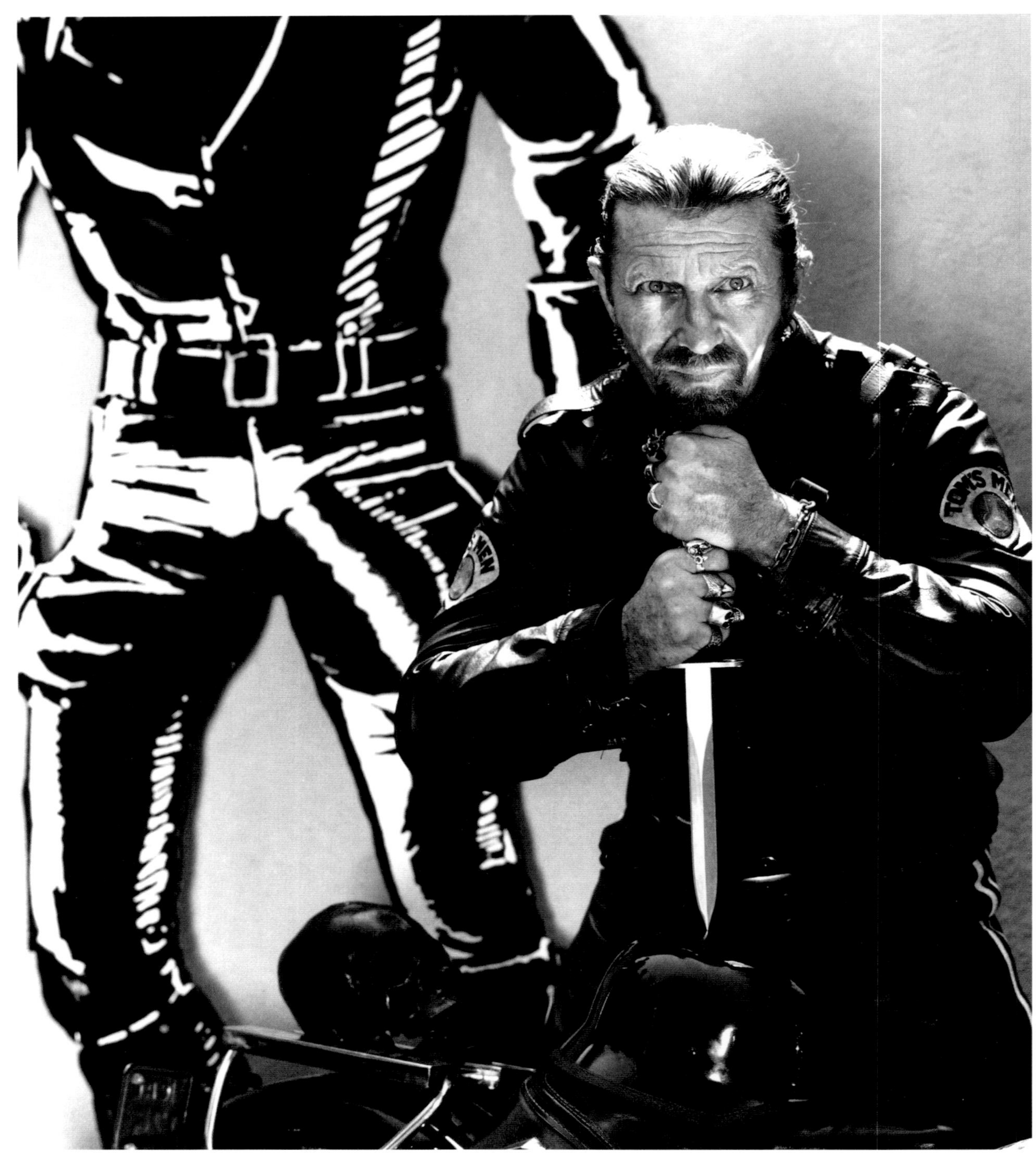

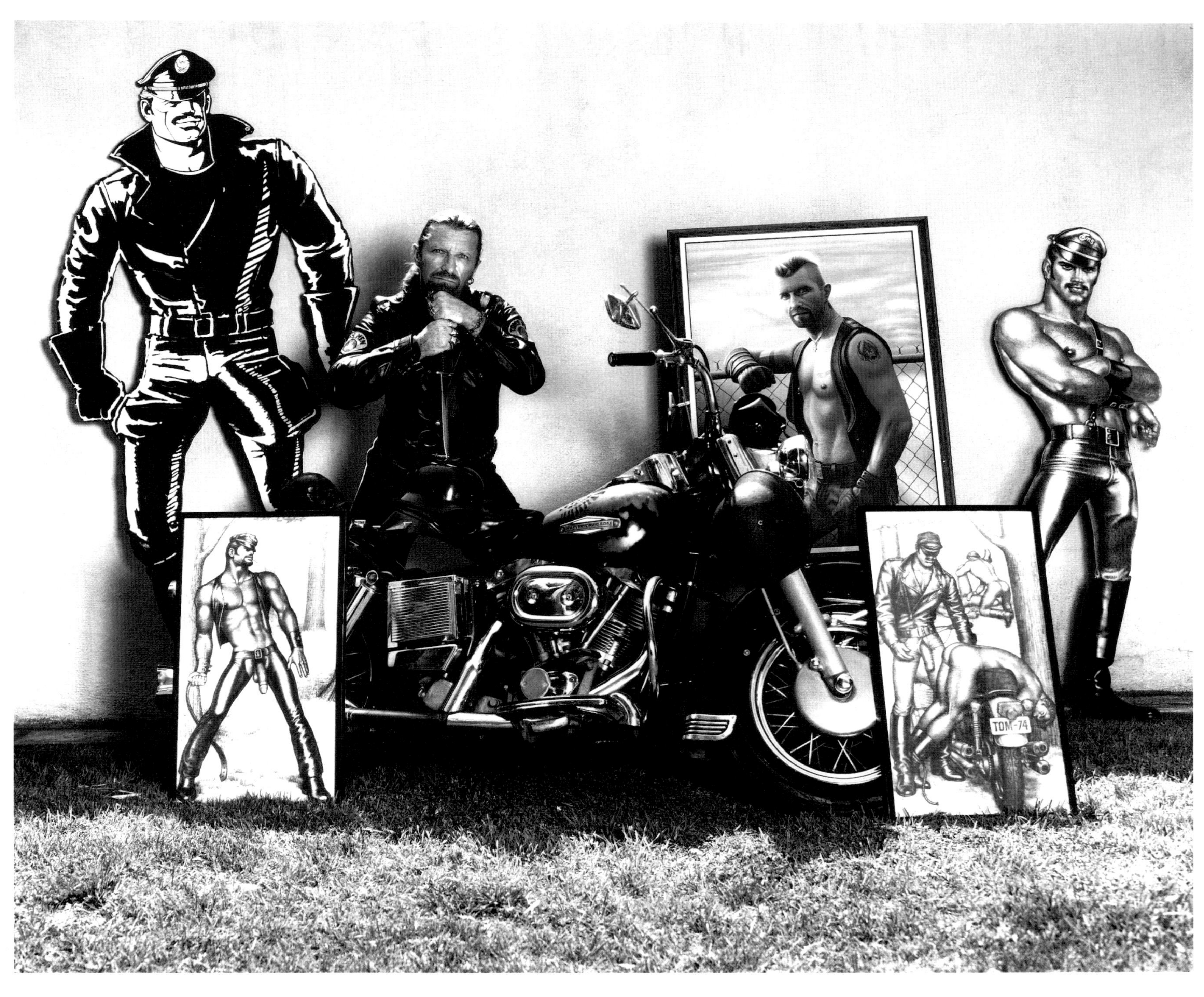

Durk Dehner president of the Tom of Finland Foundation

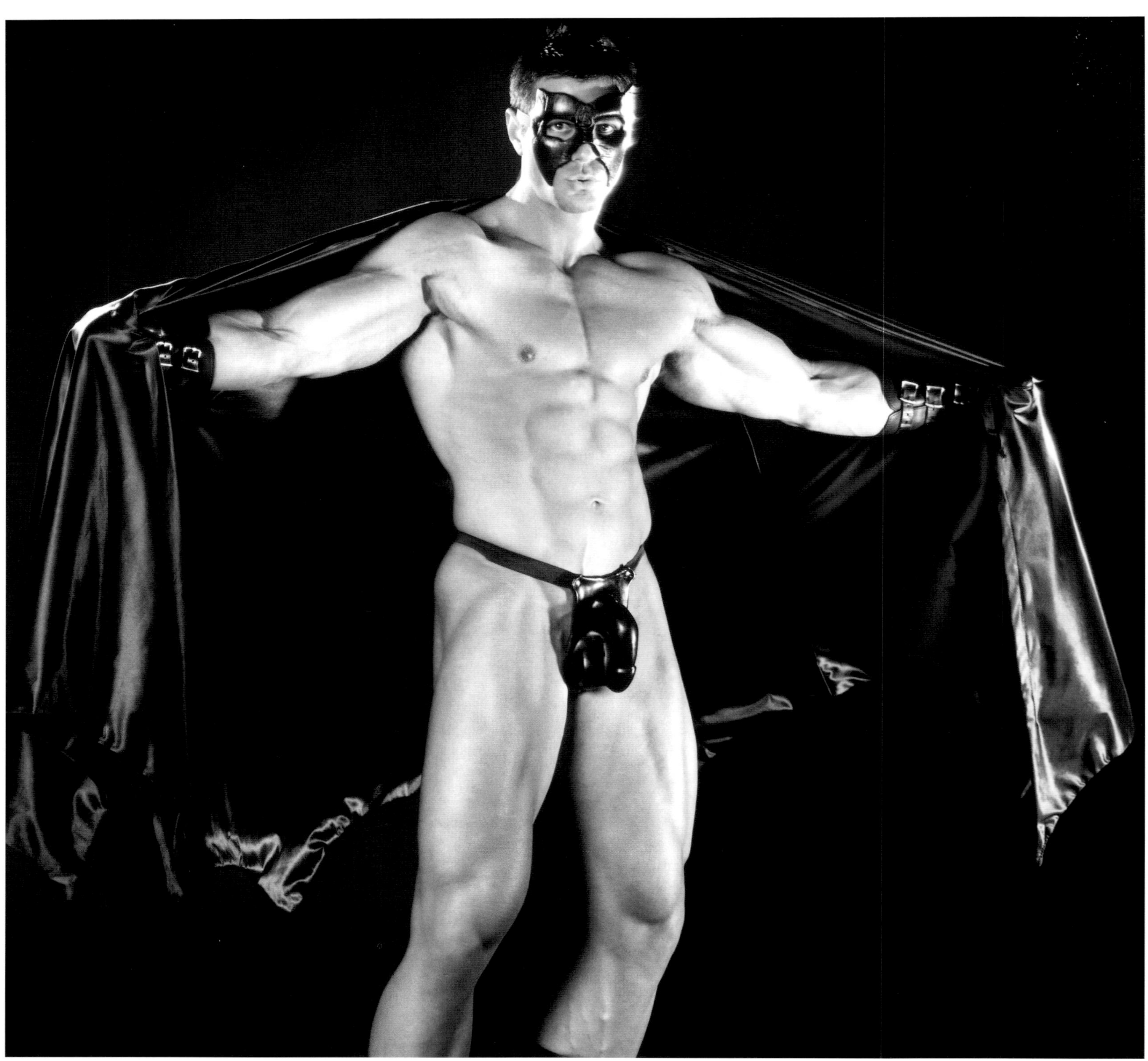

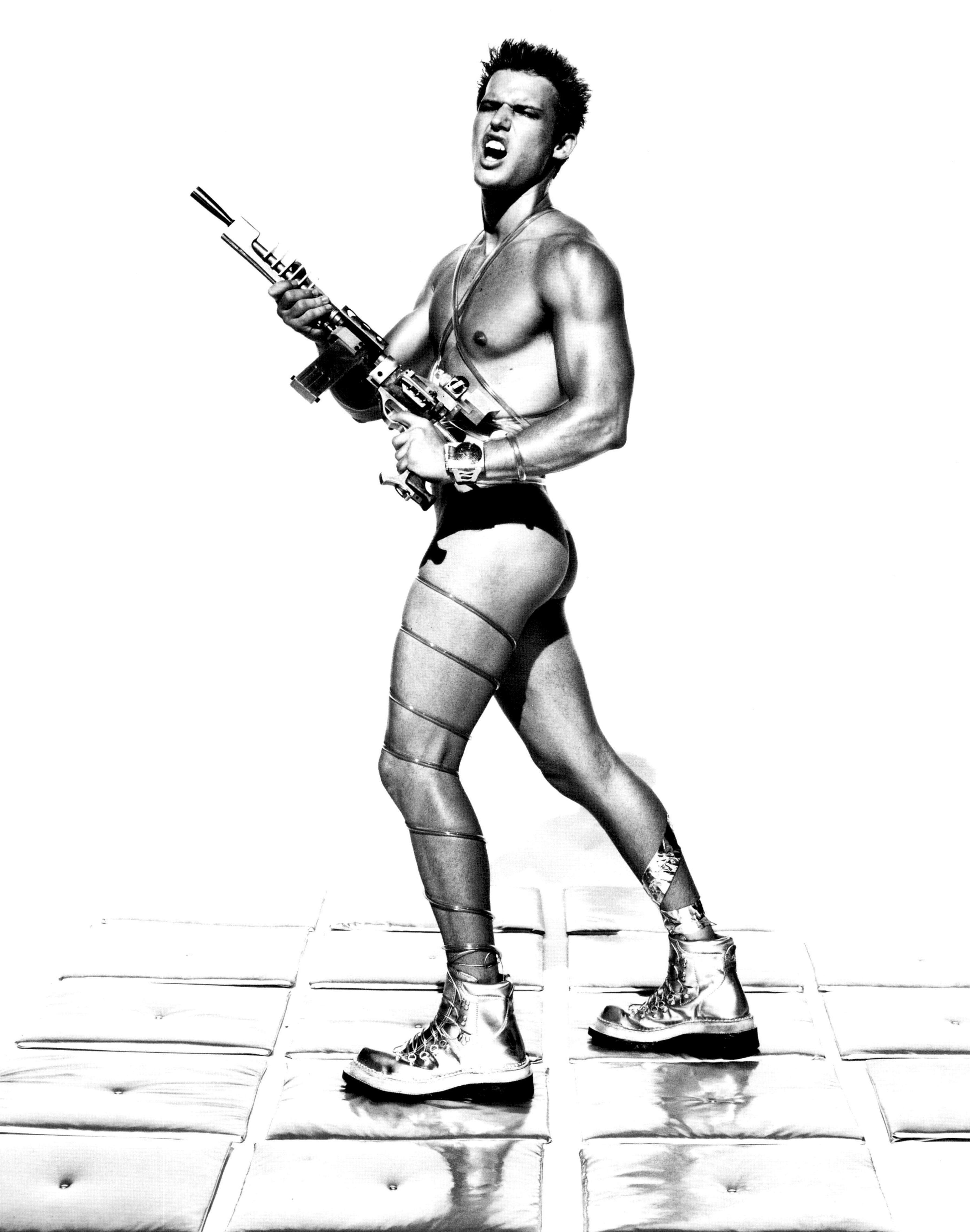

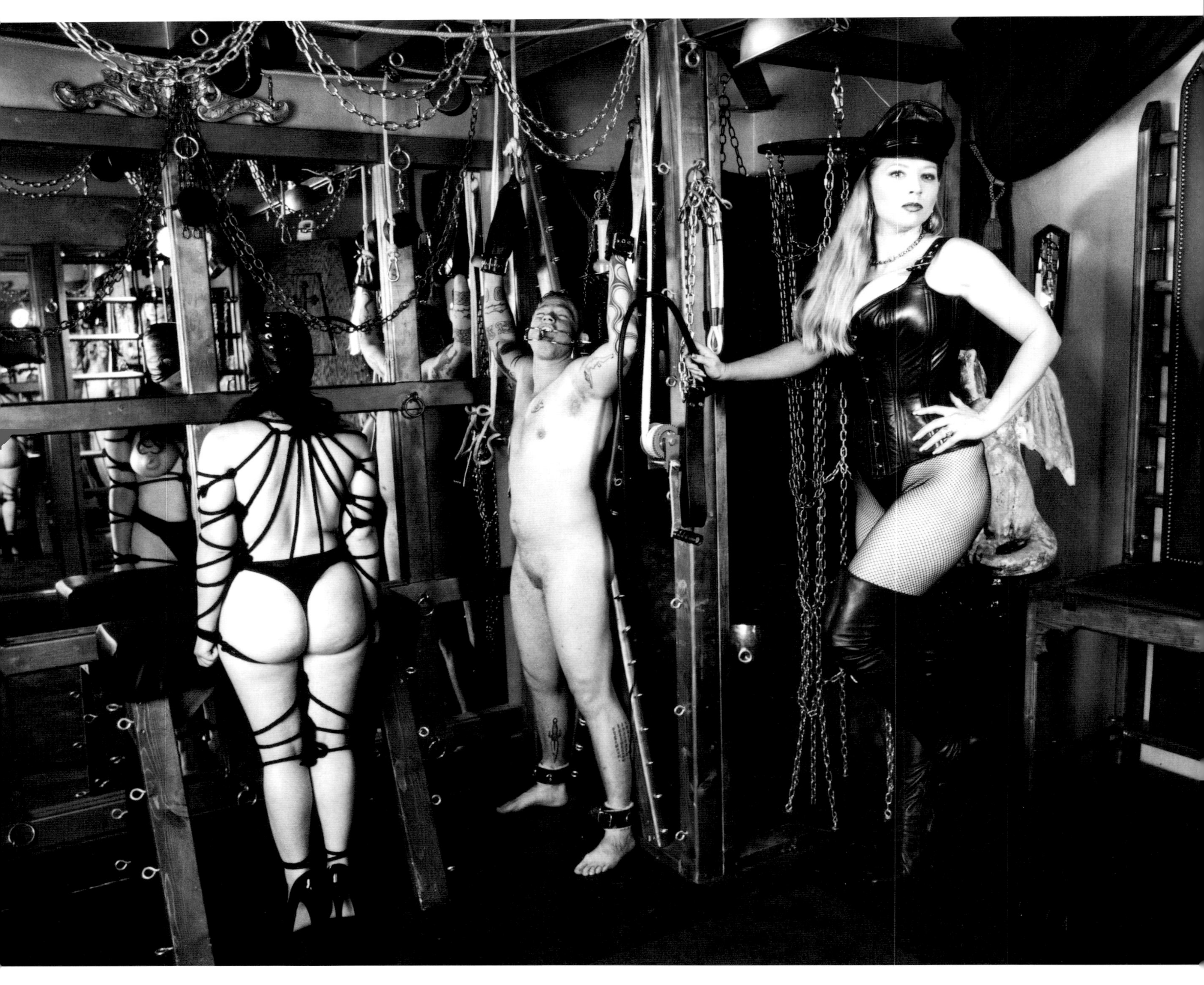

Mistress Ilsa Strix in her Hollywood dungeon

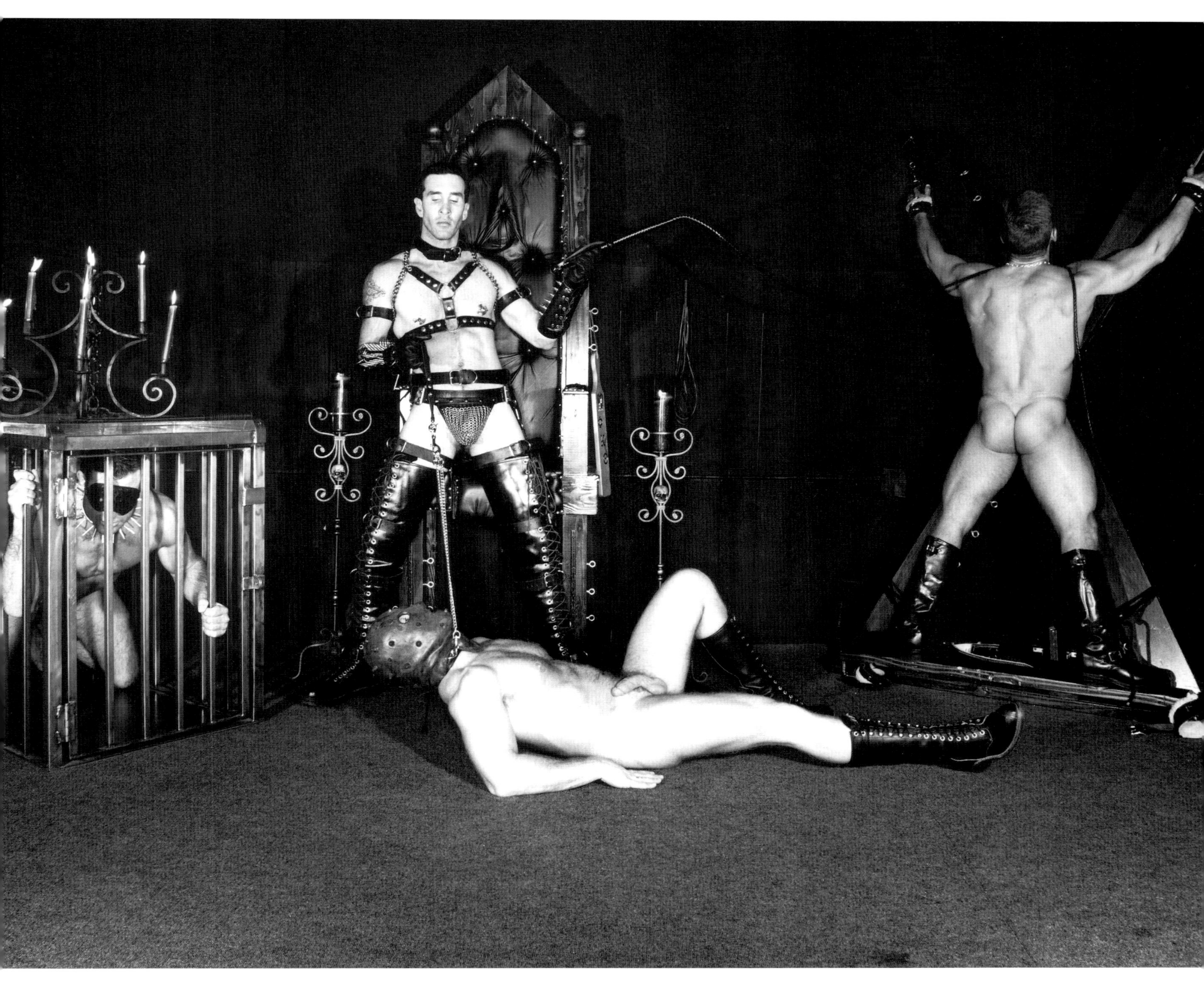

Master Scott and slaves in his Melrose dungeon

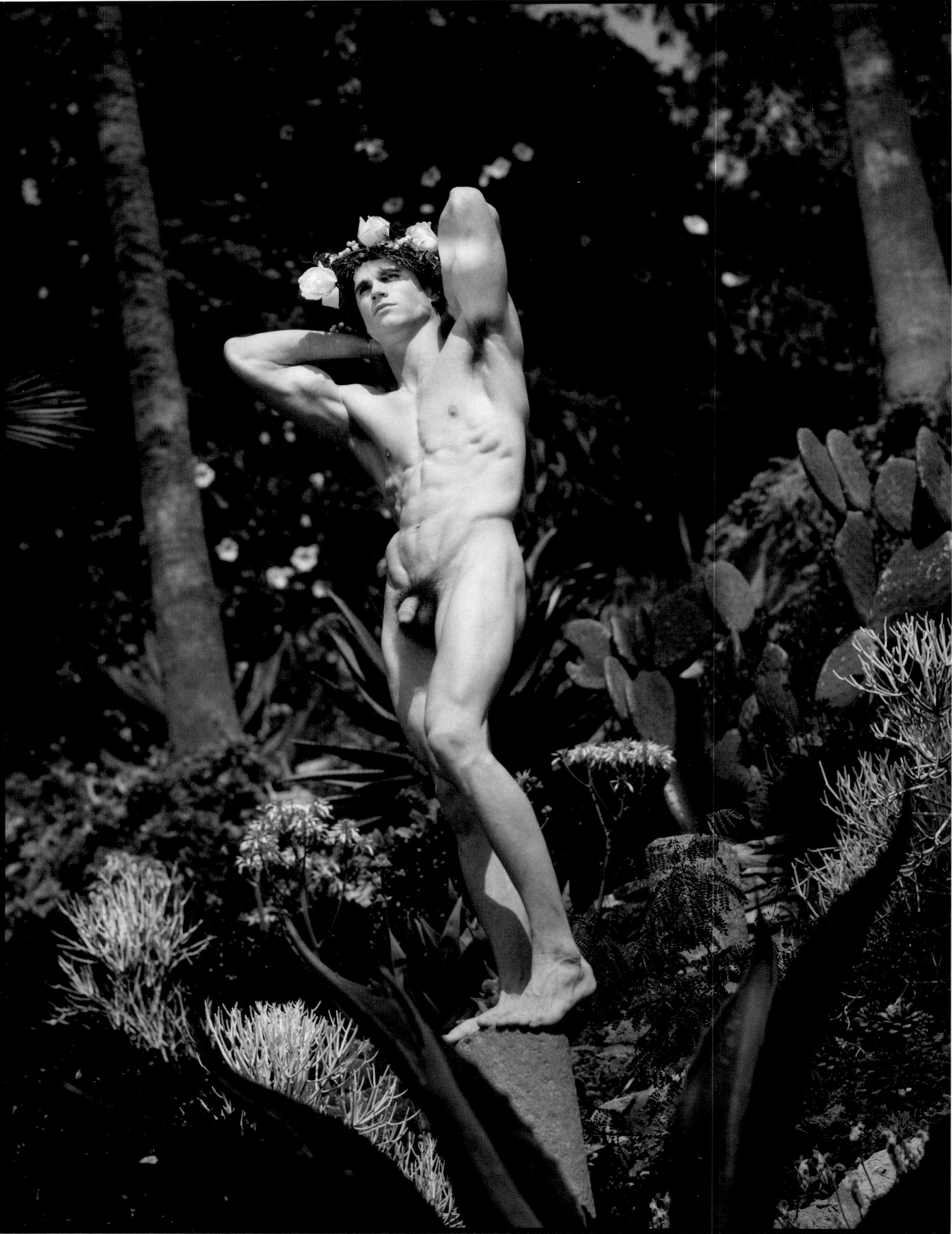

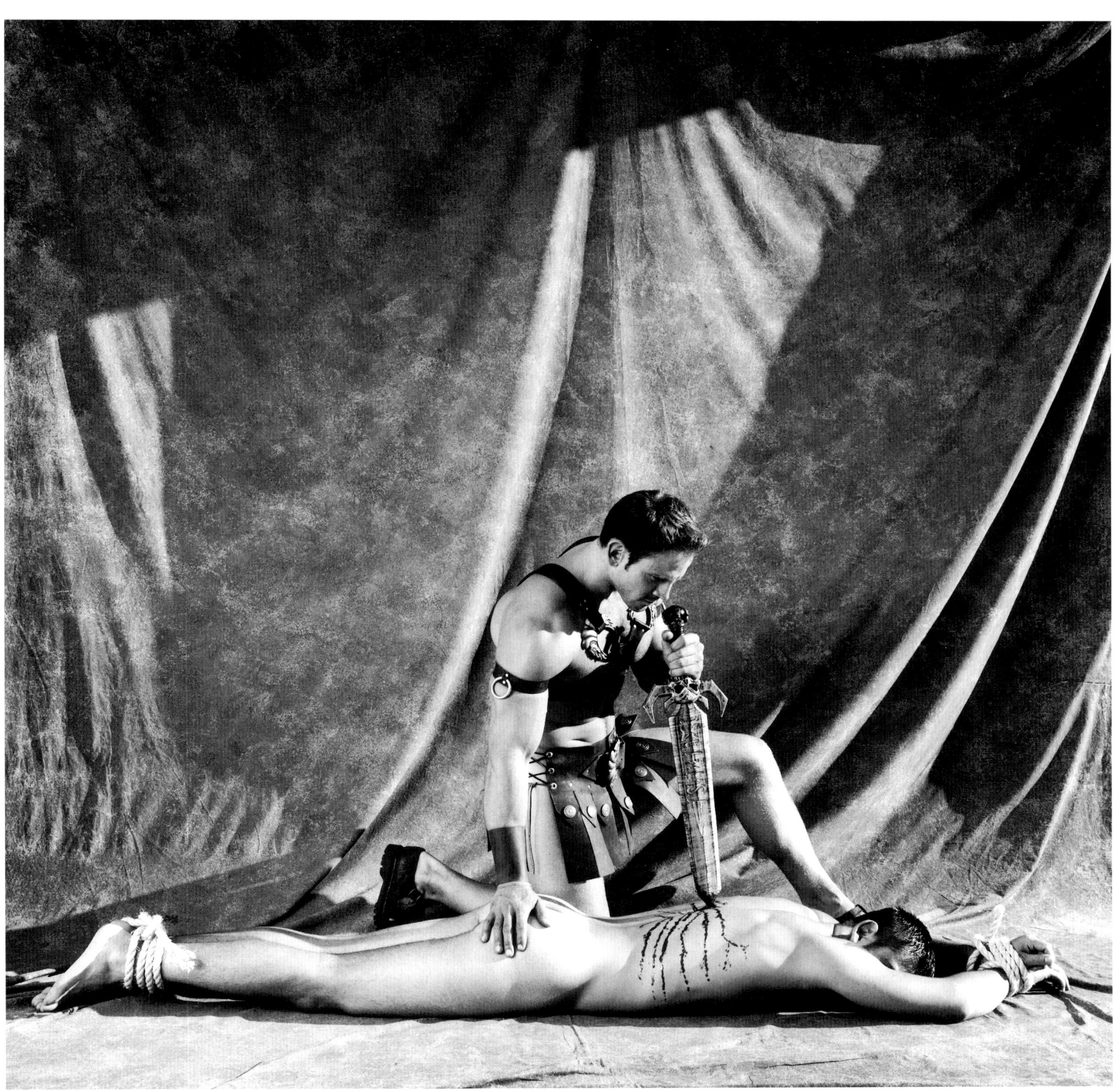

Michael Childers
Biography

Among the entertainment industry's most renowned photographers, Michael Childers began his career in the 70s and greatly influenced other professionals who remain at the top of the field today. Instrumental in creating the early images of such notable stars as Mel Gibson, Demi Moore, Richard Gere, John Travolta, Sissy Spacek and Tom Berenger, he brings a look and style to celebrity photography that is erotic and stylish. Other celebrity subjects have included Al Pacino, Dustin Hoffman, Warren Beatty, Ted Dansen, Brooke Shields, Angelica Huston, Pat Metheny, and Arnold Schwarzenegger, Elton John, and David Bowie.

Born in North Carolina, Childers gratuated from UCLA Film School where he directed student films and began his photography career. Childers created the mixed media work for the record breaking run of the hit off-Broadway musical "Oh Calcutta" for Ken Tynan, who subsequently invited him to work for Sir Laurence Olivier's National Theatre in London where he was the first American to photograph many of their productions. He went on to become a founding photographer for Andy Warhol's *Interview,* and *After Dark* magazine. For *Dance* magazine he produced many covers including the Joffrey Ballet, The Royal Ballet, and The Alvin Ailey Company, and co-authored a book, "Bejart - The World of Dance."

From his Melrose and Venice Beach studios Childers photographed over 200 magazine covers including *GQ, New York, TV Guide, Esquire, Los Angeles, Elle, Paris Match, Life, London Sunday Times Magazine,* and both English and Italian *Vogue*. He created more than 100 film posters for major motion picture studios. In 1988, Michael won Best Poster of the Year Award from New York Art Director's Circle for the film 'Siesta'. He has also worked as a special photographer on many films including 'Grease,' 'Marathon Man,' 'The Year of Living Dangerously,' 'Coal Miners Daughter', 'Pennies From Heaven,' 'Hammett' and 'Endless Love' to name but a few. His work in feature films extends past photography. Starting as a production assistant on the Academy Award winning 'Midnight Cowboy', he worked his way up the production ranks on such films as 'Day of the Locust' and Marathon Man' before going on to co-produce 'The Falcon and the Snowman' and 'The Believers'.

He has expanded his photographic repertoire to include architectural and interior photography published in *Elle Décor,* English *Vogue, House and Garden* and *World of Interiors*. Clients have included Seiko Watches, Swatch Watches, Tova Cosmetics, After 6 Tuxedo's, Head Tennis Rackets, Hasselblad Corporation, Fuji Film, Saks 5th Avenue, Jose Eber Cosmetics, Remi-Men's Fashion Corportion, Tiffany's, Revillion Furs, Van Heusen Shirts, Pendelton Wools, and Coca Cola.

Over the past eight years, Childers has helped raise more than six million dollars for various AIDS foundations and charities. In 1991, he set the standard for creative fundraisers as the creator and producer of Divine Design, benefiting Project Angel Food and Design Industries Foundation for AIDS. Through a unique blending of the work of the world's top interior and fashion designers, Childers created what has become one of the West Coast's most high profile and successful annual fundraising events. For Divine Design, he featured Bette Midler in an impressive public service announcement he produced for Project Angel Food. In Santa Fe, Childers produced "Live at the Lensic" featuring Lauren Bacall, Michael Feinstein, Margaret Cho, Beverly D'Angelo, Tim Curry, Michael York, and Carol Burnett to benefit local AIDS patients. He co-chaired the 1999 Pets Are Wonderful Support/Los Angeles (PAWS/LA) celebrity art auction with Greg Gorman, David Hockney, and Angelica Huston.

Though he has created an impressive body of work throughout his prolific career, his artistic endeavor continues with his book of photographs "Hollywood Voyeur," set for publication in 2000, with forward by Gavin Lambert and an introduction by David Hockney. About his successful exhibit at Couturier Gallery, the *LA Weekly* quoted "Micheael Childers is Helmut Newton dressed as Oscar Wilde in a wildly entertaining and stylized show." The *LA Times* said: "enjoy this theatrical and stylish show."

Childers next book "Now and Then," for Twin Palms Publishing will feature defining images of 1970s life in London, New York, Paris and Hollywood. He is finishing work on a new project "The Passion of Yoga", a photo book of beautifully toned prints of nude couples practicing yoga positions. He has also been selected as one of the 100 most important photographers of erotic art who will be featured in "Masterpieces of Erotic Photography", to be published in London by Carlton Books, fall of 1999.

Recent exhibitions include "The Sensual in Photography", at the BGH Gallery, at Bergamot Station in Santa Monica, "The Lost Warhols", a collection of previously unpublished portraits of Andy Warhol which showed in Los Angeles at the Stephen Cohen Gallery and in Santa Fe at the LewAllen Gallery. He also exhibited in the Stephen Cohen Gallery's "Dogs and Cats", and has been selected as a contributor to Carlton Books' "Femmes", a collection of photos of the most erotic women of the world.

Michael Childers Studio
1627 N. Gower St., Studio 1
Hollywood, CA 90028

Phone: (323) 466-9951
Fax: (323) 466-9952

Marie Chambers
Studio Manager

Jim Roehrig/Outline
Agent

Phone: (323) 954-9422
Fax: (323) 954-9455

Museums

National Portraits Gallery - London, England
Marion Center for Photographic Art - Santa Fe

Private collectores include:

Warren and Annette Beatty - Los Angeles
Kenneth Jay Lane - New York City
Aileen Getty - Los Angeles
Simon Saimsbury - London
Ed Limato - Los Angeles
Alleen Lapides - Santa Fe
Michael and Pat York - Los Angeles
Tim Curry - Los Angeles
Stephen Sondheim - New York
Jerry Herman - Los Angeles
Eli Broad - Los Angeles
Bill and Nancy Rollnick - New York
David Geffen - Los Angeles
Lester Persky - Los Angeles

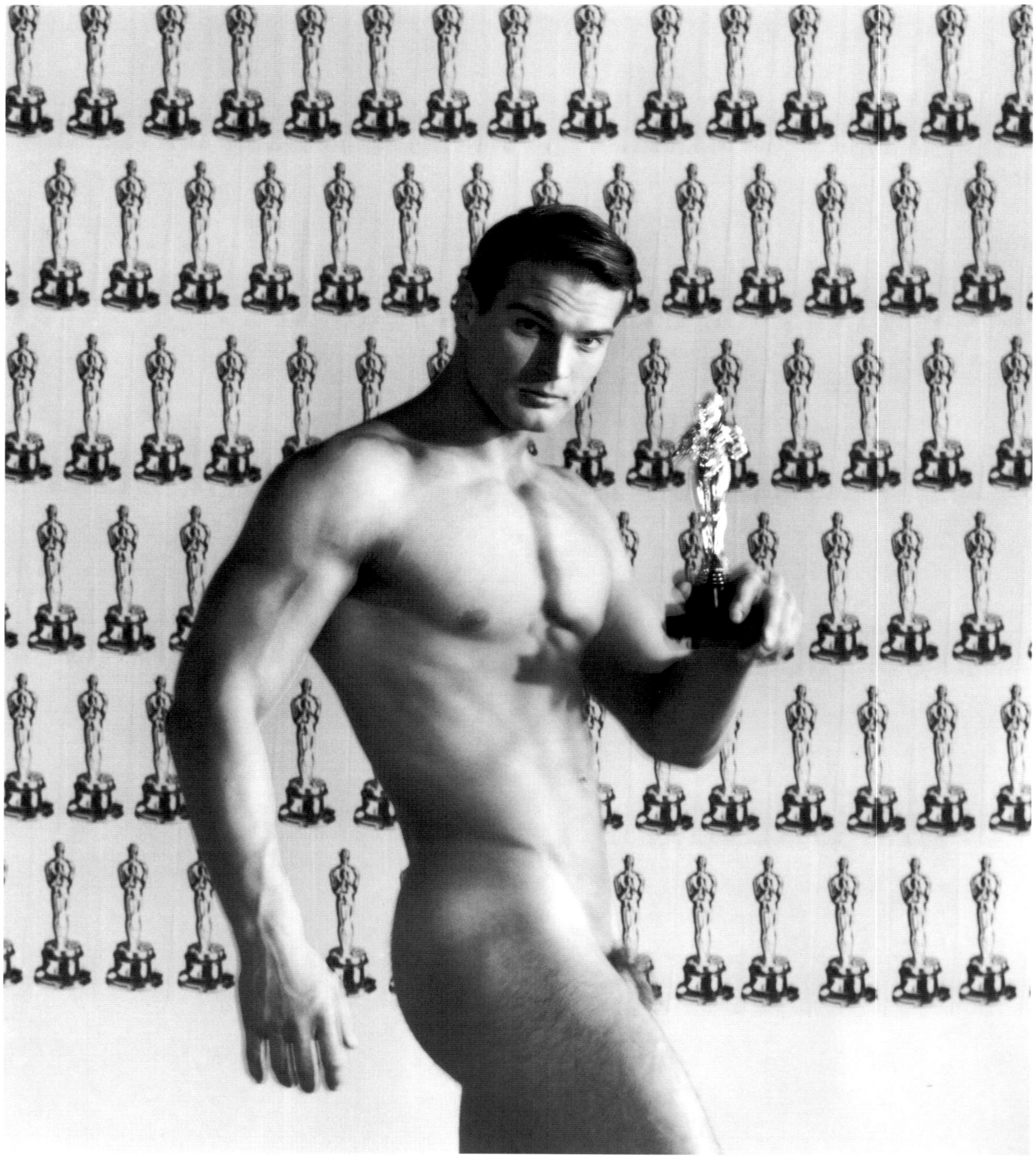

Thanks to all the wonderful models

Ron Athey	Paul Logan
Russell Barslow	Kelly Lynden
Tom Bianchi	Kelly McCool
Brian Bianchini	Tim McElwee
Christian Boeving	Justin Melvey
Marcel Bouchard	Jake Miller
Aaron Brumfield	Robert Musselman
Christian Burnham	Alex Nesic
Brian Buzzini	Sarah Penman
Dennis Christopher	Peter Purtell
Will Clark	Allie Riley
Todd Cunningham	Scott Saunders
Joe Dallesandro	Gary Shaw
Joseph Daube	Ted Shred
Jermyn Daube	John Simmons
Vaginal Davis	Smutty
Durk Dehner	Glenn Soukesian
Benoit Demouy	Ilsa Strix
Bo Garrett	Matt Tanner
Paul Gois	Tegr
Bruce Hall	Brian To
Seth Hall	Mark Tobler
Fred Harris	Spike Trevino
David Hockney	Rob Turner
Mike Hockett	Charles Waldheim
Jimmy James	Daniel Weaver
Jason Jensen	Holly Woodlawn
Patrick Kaiser	Albert Wyss
Dean Keefer	Matt Zarley
John Knight	
Chuck Kreuser	
Chi Chi LaRue	

©JANSSEN PUBLISHERS CC
P.O.Box 404, ZA 7995 Simon's Town, South Africa

Produktion: Druck- und Verlagshaus Erfurt GmbH

Distribution: LKG, Pötschauer Weg, D-04579 Espenhain, Germany

ISBN: 0-9584 4314-1-8

Printed in Germany 2000

Please visit our website under: www.janssenbooks.co.za

E-mail to Publisher: janssenp@iafrica.com